REA's Test Prep Books Are The Best!

(a sample of the <u>hundreds of letters</u> REA receives each year)

" Your Fundamentals of Engineering Exam book was the absolute best preparation I could have had for the exam, and it is one of the major reasons I did so well and passed the FE on my first try. "
Student, Sweetwater, TN

" My students report your chapters of review as the most valuable single resource they used for review and preparation. "
Teacher, American Fork, UT

" Your book was such a better value and was so much more complete than anything your competition has produced (and I have them all!) "
Teacher, Virginia Beach, VA

" Compared to the other books that my fellow students had, your book was the most useful in helping me get a great score. "
Student, North Hollywood, CA

" Your book was responsible for my success on the exam, which helped me get into the college of my choice... I will look for REA the next time I need help. "
Student, Chesterfield, MO

" Just a short note to say thanks for the great support your book gave me in helping me pass the test... I'm on my way to a B.S. degree because of you! "
Student, Orlando, FL

(more on next page)

" I just wanted to thank you for helping me get a great score
on the AP U.S. History exam... Thank you for making great test preps! "
Student, Los Angeles, CA

" I did well because of your wonderful prep books... I just wanted to thank
you for helping me prepare for these tests. "
Student, San Diego, CA

" I used your book to prepare for the test and found that the advice and the
sample tests were highly relevant... Without using any other material, I earned
very high scores and will be going to the graduate school of my choice. "
Student, New Orleans, LA

" What I found in your book was a wealth of information sufficient to shore up
my basic skills in math and verbal... The section on analytical analysis was
excellent. The practice tests were challenging and the answer explanations most
helpful. It certainly is the Best Test Prep for the GRE! "
Student, Pullman, WA

" I really appreciate the help from your excellent book. Please keep up
the great work. "
Student, Albuquerque, NM

" I am writing to thank you for your test preparation... your book helped me
immeasurably and I have nothing but praise for your GRE preparation."
Student, Benton Harbor, MI

(more on back page)

The Best Test Preparation & Review Course

FE/EIT

Fundamentals of Engineering / Engineer-in-Training

PM Exam in
Chemical Engineering

Michael Riordan, P.E.
Senior Systems Engineer
Sverdrup Technology
Dumfries, VA

Bruce A. Williams, M.S.
Research Assistant, Process Monitoring & Control Group
Illinois Institute of Technology
Chicago, IL

Supplemental Text Provided by:

V.L. Tolani, M.S.
and
James Colaizzi, Ph.D.

And the Staff of REA
Dr. M. Fogiel, Director

 **Research & Education Association**
61 Ethel Road West
Piscataway, New Jersey 08854

The Best Test Preparation and Review Course for the FE/EIT
(Fundamentals of Engineering/Engineer-in-Training)
PM Exam in Chemical Engineering

Printed in the United States of America

Library of Congress Catalog Card Number 00-130622

International Standard Book Number 0-87891-263-0

Research & Education Association
61 Ethel Road West
Piscataway, New Jersey 08854

ABOUT RESEARCH & EDUCATION ASSOCIATION

Research & Education Association (REA) is an organization of educators, scientists, and engineers specializing in various academic fields. Founded in 1959 with the purpose of disseminating the most recently developed scientific information to groups in industry, high schools and universities, Research and Education Association has become a successful and highly respected publisher of study aids, test preps, handbooks, and reference works.

REA's Test Preparation series includes study guides for all academic levels in almost all disciplines. Research & Education Association publishes test preps for students who have not yet completed high school, as well as high school students preparing to enter college. Students from countries around the world seeking to attend college in the United States will find the assistance they need in REA's publications. For college students seeking advanced degrees, REA publishes test preps for many major graduate school admission examinations in a wide variety of disciplines, including engineering, law, and medicine. Students at every level, in every field, with every ambition can find what they are looking for among REA's publications.

Unlike most test preparation books—which present only a few practice tests that bear little resemblance to the actual exams—REA's series presents tests that accurately depict the official exams in both degree of difficulty and types of questions. REA's practice tests are always based upon the most recently administered exams, and include every type of question that can be expected on the actual exams.

REA's publications and educational materials are highly regarded and continually receive an unprecedented amount of praise from professionals, instructors, librarians, parents, and students. Our authors are as diverse as the fields represented in the books we publish. They are well-known in their respective disciplines and serve on the faculties of prestigious universities throughout the United States and Canada.

ACKNOWLEDGMENTS

In addition to our authors, we would like to thank the following:

Dr. Max Fogiel, President, for his overall guidance which has brought this publication to its completion.

Nicole Mimnaugh, New Book Development Manager, for directing the editorial staff throughout each phase of the project.

Kelli A. Wilkins, Assistant Editorial Manager, for coordinating the development of the book.

Martin Perzan for typesetting the book, and Gary DaGiau for his editorial contributions.

CONTENTS

FE/EIT

FE: PM Chemical Engineering Exam

CHAPTER 1

You Can Succeed on the FE: PM Chemical Engineering Exam

CHAPTER 1

YOU CAN SUCCEED ON THE FE: PM CHEMICAL ENGINEERING EXAM

By reviewing and studying this book, you can succeed on the Fundamentals of Engineering Examination PM Portion in Chemical Engineering. The FE is an eight-hour exam designed to test knowledge of a wide variety of engineering disciplines. The FE was formerly known as the EIT (Engineer-in-Training) exam. The FE Exam format and title have now replaced the EIT completely.

The purpose of REA's *Best Test Preparation and Review Course for the FE: PM Chemical Engineering Exam* is to prepare you sufficiently for the afternoon portion of the Chemical Engineering FE exam by providing 12 review chapters, including sample problems in each review, and two practice tests. The review chapters and practice tests reflect the scope and difficulty level of the actual FE: PM Exam. The reviews provide examples with thorough solutions throughout the text. The practice tests provide simulated FE exams with detailed explanations of answers. While using just the reviews or the practice tests is helpful, an effective study plan should incorporate both a review of concepts and repeated practice with simulated tests under exam conditions.

ABOUT THE TEST

The Fundamentals of Engineering Exam (FE) is one part in the four-step process toward becoming a professional engineer (PE). Graduating from an approved four-year engineering program and passing the FE qualifies you for your certification as an "Engineer-in-Training" or an "Engineer Intern." The final two steps towards licensing as a PE involve completion of four years of additional engineering experience and passing the Principles and Practices of Engineering Examination administered by the National Council of Examiners for Engineering and Surveying (NCEES). Registration as a professional engineer is deemed both highly rewarding and beneficial in the engineering community.

In order to register for the FE, contact your state's Board of Examiners for Professional Engineers and Land Surveyors. To determine the location for the Board in your state, contact the main NCEES office at the following address:

National Council of Examiners for Engineering and Surveying
PO Box 1686
Clemson, SC 29633-1686
(864) 654-6824
Website: http://www.ncees.org

TEST FORMAT

The FE consists of two distinct sections. One section is given in the morning (FE: AM) while the other is administered in the afternoon (FE: PM). This book will prepare you for the FE: PM exam in Chemical Engineering.

The FE: PM is a *supplied reference exam,* and students are not permitted to bring reference material into the test center. Instead, you will be mailed a reference guide when you register for the exam. This guide will provide all the charts, graphs, tables, and formulae you will need. The same book will be given to you in the test center during the test administration.

You will have four hours to complete the exam. The FE: PM in Chemical Engineering consists of 60 questions covering 12 different engineering subjects. The subjects and their corresponding percentages of questions are shown on the next page.

FE: PM CHEMICAL ENGINEERING SUBJECT DISTRIBUTION

Subject	Percentage of Problems
Chemical Reaction Engineering	10
Chemical Thermodynamics	10
Computer and Numerical Methods	5
Heat Transfer	10
Mass Transfer	10
Material/Energy Balances	15
Pollution Prevention	5
Process Control	5
Process Design and Economics Evaluation	10
Process Equipment Design	5
Process Safety	5
Transport Phenomena	10

Our review book covers all of these topics. Each subject is explained in detail, with example problems, diagrams, charts, and formulae.

You may want to take a practice exam at various studying stages to measure your strengths and weaknesses. This will help you to determine which topics need more study. Take one test when you finish studying so that you may see how much you have improved. For studying suggestions that will help you to make the best use of your time, see the "Study Schedule" presented after this chapter.

SCORING THE EXAM

Your FE: PM score is based upon the number of correct answers you choose. No points are taken off for incorrect answers. A single score of 0 to 100 is given for the entire (both AM and PM sections) test. Both the AM and PM sections have an equal weight. The grade given is on a pass/fail basis. The point between passing and failing varies from state to state, although 70 is a general reference point for passing. Thus, this general reference point for the FE: PM section alone would be 35.

The pass/fail margin is not a percentage of correct answers, nor a percentage of students who scored lower than you. This number fluctuates from year to year and is reestablished with every test administration. It is based on previous exam administrations and relates your score to those of previous FE examinees.

Because this grading system is so variable, there is no real way for you to know exactly what you got on the test. For the purpose of grading the practice tests in this book, however, REA has provided the following formula to calculate your score on the FE: PM practice tests:

$$\left[\frac{\text{No. of questions answered correctly on the FE: PM}}{240} \right] \times 100 = \text{your score}$$

Remember that this formula is meant for the computation of your grade for the practice tests in this book. It does not compute your grade for the actual FE examination. For more specific information on actual test scoring, contact NCEES.

TEST-TAKING STRATEGIES

How to Beat the Clock

Every second counts, and you will want to use the available test time for each section in the most efficient manner. Here's how:

1. Bring a watch! This will allow you to monitor your time.

2. Become familiar with the test directions. You will save valuable time if you already understand the directions on the day of the test.

3. Pace yourself. Work steadily and quickly. Do not spend too much time on any one question. Remember, you can always return to the problems that gave you the most difficulty. Try to answer the easiest questions first, then return to the ones you missed.

Guessing Strategy

1. When all else fails, guess! The score you achieve depends on the number of correct answers. There is no penalty for wrong answers, so it is a good idea to choose an answer for all of the questions.

2. If you guess, try to eliminate choices you know to be wrong. This will allow you to make an educated guess.

3. Begin with the subject areas you know best. This will give you more time and will also build your confidence. If you use this strategy, pay careful attention to your answer sheet; you do not want to mismatch the ovals and answers. It may be a good idea to check the problem number and oval number *each time* you mark down an answer.

4. Break each problem down into its simplest components. Approach each part one step at a time. Use diagrams and drawings whenever possible, and do not wait until you get a final answer to assign units. If you decide to move onto another problem, this method will allow you to resume your work without too much difficulty.

HOW TO STUDY FOR THE FE: PM EXAM

Two groups of people take the FE examination: college seniors in undergraduate programs and graduate engineers who decide that professional registration is necessary for future growth. Both groups begin their Professional Engineer career with a comprehensive exam covering the entirety of their engineering curriculum. How does one prepare for an exam of such magnitude and importance?

Time is the most important factor when preparing for the FE: PM. Time management is necessary to ensure that each section is reviewed prior to the exam. Once the decision to test has been made, determine how much time you have to study. Divide this time amongst your topics, and make up a schedule that outlines the beginning and ending dates for study of each exam topic and include time for a final practice test followed by a brief review. Set aside extra time for the more difficult subjects, and include a buffer for unexpected events such as college exams or business trips. There is never enough time to prepare, so make the most of the time that you have.

You can determine which subject areas require the most time in several ways. Look at your college grades: those courses with the lowest grades probably need the most study. Those subjects outside your major are generally the least used and most easily forgotten. These will require a good deal of review to bring you up to speed. Some of the subjects may not be familiar at all because you were not required to study them in college. These subjects may be impossible to learn before the examination, although some can be self-taught.

Another way to determine your weakest areas is to take one of the practice tests provided in this book. The included simulated exams will help you assess your strengths and weaknesses. By determining which type of questions you answered incorrectly on the practice tests, you find the areas that need the most work. Be careful not to neglect the other subjects in your review; do not rule out any subject area until you have reviewed it to some degree.

You may also find that a negative attitude is your biggest stumbling block. Many students do not realize the volume of material they have covered in four years of college. Some begin to study and are immediately overwhelmed because they do not have a plan. It is important that you get a good start and that you are positive as you review and study the material.

You will need some way to measure your preparedness, either with problems from books or with a review book that has sample test questions similar to the ones on the FE: PM Chemical Engineering Exam. This book contains sample problems in each section which can be used before, during, or after you review the material to measure your understanding of the subject matter. If you are a wizard in heat transfer, for example, and are confident in your ability to solve problems, select a few and see what happens. You may want to perform at least a cursory review of the material before jumping into problem solving, since there is always something to learn. If you do well on these initial problems, then momentum has been established. Being positive is essential as you move through the subject areas.

The question that comes to mind at this point is: "How do I review the material?" Before we get into the material itself, let us establish rules that lead to **good study habits**. Time was previously mentioned as the most important issue. When you decide to study, you will need blocks of uninterrupted time so that you can get something accomplished. Two hours should be the minimum time block allotted, while four hours should be the maximum. Schedule five-minute breaks into your study period and stay with your schedule. Cramming for the FE can give you poor results, including short-term memory and confusion when synthesis is required.

Next, you need to work in a quiet place, on a flat surface that is not cluttered with other papers or work that needs to be completed before the next day. **Eliminate distractions**—they will rob you of time while you pay attention to them. **Do not eat while you study**—few of us can do two things at once and do them both well. Eating does require a lot of attention and disrupts study. Eating a sensible meal before you study resolves the "eating while you work" problem. We encourage you to have a large glass of water available since water quenches your thirst and fills the void which makes you want to get up and find something to eat. In addition, **you should be well rested when you study**. Late nights and early mornings are good for some, especially if you have a family, but the best results are associated with adequate rest.

Lastly, **study on weekend mornings while most people are still asleep**. This allows for a quiet environment and gives you the remainder of the day to do other things. If you must study at night, we suggest two-hour blocks ending before 11 p.m.

Do not spend time memorizing charts, graphs, and formulae; the FE is a supplied reference exam, and you will be provided a booklet of equations and other essential information during the test. This reference material will be sent to you prior to your examination date. You can use the supplied reference book as a guide while studying, since it will give you an indication of the depth of study you will need to pursue. Furthermore, familiarity with the book will alleviate some test anxiety since you will be given the same book to use during the actual exam.

While you review for the test, use the review book supplied by the NCEES, paper, pencil, and a calculator. Texts can be used, but reliance on them should be avoided. The object of the review is to identify what you know, the positive, and that which requires work, the negative. As you review, move past those equations and concepts that you understand and annotate on the paper those concepts that require more work. Using this method you can review a large quantity of material in a short time and reduce the apparent workload to a manageable amount. Now go back to your time schedule and allocate the remaining time according to the needs of the subject under consideration. Return to the material that requires work and review it or study it until you are satisfied that you can solve problems covering this material. When you have finished the review, you are ready to solve problems.

Solving problems requires practice. To use the problems in this book effectively, you should cover the solution and try to solve the problem on your own. If this is not possible, map out a strategy to answer the problem and then check to see if you have the correct procedure. Remember that most problems that are not solved correctly were never started correctly. Merely reviewing the solution will not help you to start the problem when you see it again at a later date. Read the problems carefully and in parts. Many people teach that reading the whole problem gives the best overview of what is to come; however, solutions are developed from small clues that are in parts of a sentence. **Read the problem and break it into**

manageable parts. Next, **try to avoid numbers until the problem is well formulated.** Too often, numbers are substituted into equations early and become show stoppers. You will need numbers, just use them after the algebra has been completed. **Be mechanical**, list the knowns, the requirements of the problem, and check off those bits of knowledge you have as they appear. Checking off the intermediate answers and information you know is a positive attitude builder. Continue to solve problems until you are confident or you exceed the time allowed in your schedule for that subject area.

As soon as you complete one subject, move to the next. Retain all of your notes as you complete each section. You will need these for your final overall review right before the exam. After you have completed the entire review, you may want to take a practice test. Taking practice exams will test your understanding of all the engineering subject areas and will help you identify sections that need additional study. With the test and the notes that you retained from the subject reviews, you can determine weak areas requiring some additional work.

You should be ready for the exam if you follow these guidelines:

- Program your time wisely.

- Maintain a positive attitude.

- Develop good study habits.

- Review the material and maximize the learning process.

- Do practice problems and practice tests.

- Review again to finalize your preparation.

GOOD LUCK!

STUDY SCHEDULE

The following is a suggested eight-week study schedule for the Fundamentals of Engineering: PM Exam in Chemical Engineering. You may want to condense or expand the schedule depending on the amount of time remaining before the test. Set aside some time each week, and work straight through the activity without rushing. By following a structured schedule, you will be able to complete an adequate amount of studying, and be more confident and prepared on the day of the exam.

Week 1	Acquaint yourself with this FE: PM Chemical Engineering Test Preparation Book by reading the first chapter: "You Can Succeed on the FE: PM Chemical Engineering Exam." Take Practice Test 1. When you score the test, be sure to look for areas where you missed many questions. Pay special attention to these areas when you read the review chapters.
Week 2	Begin reviewing Chapters 2 and 3. As you read the chapters, try to solve the examples without aid of the solutions. Use the solutions to guide you through any questions you missed.
Week 3	Study and review Chapters 4 and 5. Take notes as you read the chapters; you may even want to write concepts on index cards and thumb through them during the day. As you read the chapters, try to solve the examples without the aid of the solutions.
Week 4	Review any notes you have taken over the last few weeks. Study Chapters 6 and 7. As you read the chapters, try to solve the examples without the aid of the solutions.
Week 5	Study Chapters 8 and 9 while continuing to review your notes. As you read the chapters, try to solve the examples without the aid of the solutions.
Week 6	Study Chapters 10 and 11. As you read the chapters, try to solve the examples without the aid of the solutions to guide you through any questions you missed.
Week 7	Study Chapters 12 and 13. As you read, try to solve the examples without the aid of the solutions. Use the solutions to guide you through any questions you missed.
Week 8	Take Practice Test 2. When you score the test, be sure to look for any improvement in the areas that you missed in Practice Test 1. If you missed any questions in any particular area, go back and review those areas. Be patient and deliberate as you review; with careful study, you can only improve.

FE/EIT

FE: PM Chemical Engineering Exam

CHAPTER 2

Chemical Reaction Engineering

CHAPTER 2

CHEMICAL REACTION ENGINEERING

CHEMICAL REACTION

Equilibrium conversion depends upon three conditions:

1. **Temperature**

2. **Pressure**—Only for gas reactions where there is a change in the number of moles

3. **Initial composition of reaction mixture**

Rate of Reaction—The rate of a chemical reaction (r) of the components in a mixture is a function of the following:

- concentrations of the components

- temperature

- pressure

- variables associated with the catalyst if one is present

Batch System—Under constant volume conditions, the concentration (moles/unit volume) of a component, A, in the system can change only because of the reaction.

$$r_A = \frac{dC_A}{d\theta}$$

where:

$r \equiv$ rate of reaction

$C_A \equiv$ concentration of component A (moles/volume)

$\theta \equiv$ time (minutes)

In addition, for the conversion of component A into products:

$$A \longrightarrow \text{Products}$$

$$r_A = -k \times C_A$$

where:

$k \equiv$ rate law constant.

PROBLEM 1:

Phenol is produced by hydrolyzing monochlorobenzene in the presence of sodium hydroxide and copper chloride at a pressure of 10.3 MPa and a temperature of 350°C. The reaction is unimolecular. The rate constant is $k = 9.8 \times 10$ minutes^{-3}. What reaction time in minutes is required to produce 400 kilograms of phenol from a 500 kilogram charge of monochlorobenzene?

SOLUTION:

$$C_6H_5Cl + H_2O \xrightarrow{k} C_6H_5OH + HCl$$

$$\text{M.W. } C_6H_5Cl = 112.5 \text{ kg/kg-moles}$$
$$\text{M.W. } C_6H_5OH = 94 \text{ kg/kg-moles}$$

$$\text{initial charge} = \frac{500 \text{ kg}}{112.5 \text{ kg/kg-mole}} = 4.44 \text{ kg-moles}$$

$$\text{final product} = 4.44 \text{ kg-moles} - \frac{400 \text{ kg}}{94 \text{ kg/kg-moles}}$$

$$= 4.44 - 4.26 = 0.18 \text{ kg-mole}$$

$$r = -k \times C_{C_6H_5Cl} = \frac{dC}{d\theta}$$

where:

$$k = 9.8 \times 10^{-3} \text{ min}^{-1}$$

$$\int_{4.44}^{0.18} \frac{dC}{C} = -9.8 \times 10^{-3} \text{ min}^{-1} \times \int_{0}^{\theta} d\theta$$

$$\ln \frac{0.18}{4.44} = -9.8 \times 10^{-3} \text{ min}^{-1} \times \theta \implies \theta = \frac{-3.162}{-9.8 \times 10^{-3} \text{ min}^{-1}}$$

$$\theta = 322 \text{ minutes}$$

Flow System—is defined as the change in the product flow rate per unit volume and is a function of the conversion due to a chemical reaction.

$$r = \frac{dN'}{dV_R} = Fx \frac{dx'}{dV_R}$$

where:

$N' \equiv$ product flow rate

$F \equiv$ total feed rate

$dx' \equiv$ fraction of total feed that reacts in a volume dV_R

Reaction order is defined by:

$$r = k_i \times C_i$$

where:

$k_i \equiv$ specific reaction rate or reaction velocity.

If the reaction is first order, then the rate is proportional to the first power of concentration.

Consider the following reaction:

$$A + B \rightarrow C$$

If the order of the reaction is α with respect to A, β with respect to B, and γ with respect to C, then:

$$r = k_{\alpha,\beta,\gamma} \times C_A^{\alpha} \times C_B^{\beta} \times C_C^{\gamma}$$

When a chemical reaction occurs at equilibrium, the temperature and pressure in the system remain constant and the change in free energy *(F)* of the reaction is zero.

$$\Delta F = 0$$

However, there will be a change in the free energies of the products and reactants at standard state. Thus,

$$\Delta F^\circ = -RT \ln K$$

where:

$F^\circ \equiv$ standard free energy at standard conditions

$K \equiv$ equilibrium constant

KINETICS OF CONSTANT VOLUME GASEOUS REACTIONS

$$p = \frac{N_t \times R \times T}{V} \text{ for an ideal gas}$$

initial pressure $p = p_o$

$$p_o = \frac{N_o \times R \times T}{V}$$

However,

$$C = \frac{N}{V}, \ C_o = \frac{N_o}{V}$$

and

$$C_i = \frac{N_i}{V}$$

Therefore:

$$r_i = \frac{dC_i}{d\theta}$$

Then:

$$r_i = \frac{1}{V} \times \frac{dN_i}{d\theta}$$

and

$$\frac{N_i}{V} = \frac{p_i}{R \times T}$$

$$r_i = \frac{1}{R \times T} \times \frac{dp_i}{d\theta}$$

$$p_i = C_i \times R \times T$$

Reversible reactions are of the form:

$$A + B \Leftrightarrow C + D$$

rate in the $\rightarrow$ direction:

$$r_F = k_F \times C_A \times C_B$$

rate in the $\leftarrow$ direction:

$$r_R = k_R \times C_C \times C_D$$

Net rate of reaction:

$$r = k_F \times C_A \times C_B - k_R \times C_C \times C_D$$

At equilibrium $r = 0$, therefore:

$$k_F \times C_A \times C_B - k_R \times C_C \times C_D = 0$$

$$\frac{k_F}{k_R} = \frac{C_C \times C_D}{C_A \times C_B} = k_C$$

where:

$k_C \equiv$ equilibrium constant.

Rearranging terms and substituting yields:

$$r_{net} = k_F \times C_A \times C_B - \frac{k_F}{k_C} \times C_C \times C_D$$

$$r_{net} = k_F \left(C_A \times C_B - \frac{1}{k_C} \times C_C \times C_D \right)$$

if $k_C \gg C_C \times C_D$, then:

$$r_{net} = k_F \times C_A \times C_B$$

Arrhenius Equation:

$$\frac{d\ln K}{dT} = \frac{\Delta H}{R \times T^2}$$

$$\frac{d\ln k_F}{dT} - \frac{d\ln k_R}{dT} = \frac{\Delta H}{R \times T^2} = \frac{E_F}{R \times T^2} - \frac{E_R}{R \times T^2}$$

$$k_F = A \times e^{-E/RT}$$

$$\ln k_F = \ln A - \frac{E}{R \times T}$$

where $E \equiv$ activation energy or the excess energy over average energy reactants must possess in order for the reaction to occur.

$$E_F - E_R = \Delta H_{r_x n}$$

A plot of $\ln k_F$ versus $1/T$ gives a straight line with a slope of $-E/R$ and the intercept at the value of $\ln A$.

$$E_R > E_F,$$

then the reaction is endothermic and heat is absorbed, and

$$\Delta H_{r_x n} < 0$$

$$E_R < E_F,$$

then the reaction is exothermic and heat is given off, and

$$\Delta H_{r_x n} > 0$$

PROBLEM 2:

For the reaction $CH_3OH + HCl \rightarrow CH_3Cl + H_2O$ calculate the equilibrium constant at 150°C from the following data:

	CH$_3$OH	**HCl**	**CH$_3$Cl**	**H$_2$O**
H° kg-cal/mole	– 48.10	–22.06	–24.00	–59.56
S° cal/moleK	56.80	44.62	70.86	47.38
C_p cal/gm-°C	0.68	0.21	0.26	0.47

SOLUTION:

H° products = −24.0 + (−59.56) = −83.56 kcal/mole

H° reactants = − 48.10 + (−22.06) = −70.16 kcal/mole

$\Delta H° = -83.56 - (-70.16) = -13.4$ kcal/mole

$\Delta S° = (70.86 + 47.83) - (56.8 + 44.62) = +16.82$ cal/mole K

$$\Delta H° - T \times \Delta S° = -R \times T \times \ln(K)$$

$$\ln(K) = \frac{\Delta H° - T \times \Delta S°}{-R \times T} = \frac{-13,400 - (272+150) \times 16.82 \ \text{cal/mole-K}}{-2 \ \text{cal/mole K} \times (273+150) \ \text{K}}$$

$$\ln(K) = 24.25 \Rightarrow K = e^{+24.25} \Rightarrow K = 3.4 \times 10^{10}$$

COLLISION THEORY

Collision Theory—Collision between molecules of reactants provides a means to obtain the activation energy necessary for a reaction to occur. This assumes that molecules behave as hard spheres. We define the rate of reaction as the number of product molecules formed per unit time. If we assume that a reaction occurs every time there is a collision between reactant molecules that possess the required activation energy, then the rate of reaction is proportional to the number of collisions.

$$r = z \times F$$

where:

$F \equiv$ fraction of collisions that involve molecules that possess necessary activation energy to react

$z \equiv$ number of collisions

$$z = C_A \times C_B \times \sigma_{AB}^2 \times \left(8 \times \pi \times R \times T \times \frac{M_A + M_B}{M_A \times M_B} \right)^{0.5}$$

where:

$C_A \ C_B \equiv$ concentration of A and B (molecules/cm³)

$\sigma_{AB}^2 \equiv$ effective diameter of $A + B$ upon collision

$M \equiv$ molecular weight

But,

$$r = z \times F = k \times C_A \times C_B,$$

therefore:

$$k \times C_A \times C_B = C_A \times C_B \times \sigma_{AB}^2 \times \left(8 \times \pi \times R \times T \times \frac{M_A + M_B}{M_A \times M_B} \right)^{0.5} \times F$$

since $F = e^{-E/RT}$

$$k = \sigma_{AB}^2 \times \left(8 \times \pi \times R \times T \times \frac{M_A + M_B}{M_A \times M_B} \right)^{0.5} \times e^{-E/RT}$$

Batch Reactor—Reactants are added to equipment at one time and entire contents withdrawn at a subsequent time.

Continuous (Flow) Reactor—Reactants are added continuously and products are removed continuously.

Steady-State Flow—No change in any of the properties of the reaction system with respect to time.

Semi-Batch Reactor—Combination of Batch and Continuous Reactor usually with a step-wise sequence.

Design Equation for Batch Reactor

$$-r \times V_B = -m_T \times \frac{dx'}{d\theta}$$

$m_T \equiv$ total mass change

$x' \equiv$ conversion at time θ (mass of reactant $\div$ total mass)

$r \equiv$ rate of reaction (mass of reactant converted/unit volume $\times$ unit time)

$V_B \equiv$ effective volume (volume occupied by the reaction mixture).

$$-m_T = \rho \times V_B$$

$$\theta = m_T \times \int_0^{x'} \frac{dx'}{V_B \times r} = \int_0^{x'} \rho \times \frac{dx'}{r}$$

$$x = \text{conversion} = \frac{\text{mass of reactant converted}}{\text{mass of reactant available}}$$

$$x' = x \times \left(\frac{m}{m_T}\right)$$

$$dx' = \left(\frac{m}{m_T}\right) \times dx$$

For liquid phase reactions,

$$\rho = \text{constant}$$

$$V_B = \text{constant}$$

therefore:

$$\theta = \frac{m}{mT} \times \int_0^x \rho \times \left(\frac{dx}{r}\right) = C_0 \times \int_0^x \frac{dx}{r}$$

where $C_0 \equiv$ original concentration of reactants:

$$C_0 = \frac{m}{V_B}$$

Design Equation for Continuous Reactors

Tubular reactor:

$z_0 \equiv$ weight fraction of reactant in feed

$x' \equiv$ conversion

$F \equiv$ mass feed rate (gms/hr)

$r \equiv$ rate of reaction:

$$r = \frac{mT}{V_R} \times \frac{dx'}{d\theta}$$

$V_R \equiv$ volume of tubular reactor and is derived from:

$$F \times (z_o - x') - F \times (z_o - x' - dx') \times r \times dV_R F \times dx' = r \times dV_R$$

$$\frac{V_R}{F} = \int_0^{x'} \frac{dx'}{r}$$

When a chemical reaction takes place at the surface of a catalyst, then:

$$\frac{W}{F} = \int_0^{x'} \frac{dx'}{r_c}$$

where:

$W \equiv$ mass of catalyst

$r_c \equiv$ rate

$$r_c = \frac{\text{mass of product produced}}{\text{unit mass of catalyst} \times \text{unit time}} = \frac{\text{grams}}{\text{grams} \times \text{sec}} = \text{sec}^{-1}$$

Tank Flow Reactor—Mass rate of feed and exit streams are equal.

$$F \times \left(z_o - x'_{\text{feed}}\right) - F \times \left(z_o - x'_{\text{exit}}\right) - r \times V_R = 0$$

Rearranging terms:

$$\frac{V_R}{F} = \frac{\left(x'_{\text{feed}} - x'_{\text{exit}}\right)}{r}$$

Space Velocity (*SV*) is a measure of the *ease* of reaction

$$SV = \frac{F \times V_F}{V_R} = \frac{\text{gms/sec} \times \text{cm}^3/\text{gm-mole}}{\text{cm}^3} = \text{gms/gm-mole-sec}$$

where:

$V_F \equiv$ volume per mole of feed (cm^3/gm-mole)

$\theta_F \equiv$ hypothetical residence time:

$$\theta_F = \frac{1}{V_F} \times \int_0^{x'} \frac{dx'}{r}$$

Actual residence time for an element of gas to pass through a volume (dV_R) of a reactor:

$$d\theta_F = \frac{\text{distance}}{\text{velocity}} = \frac{dV_R}{N_T \times V}$$

where:

$N_T \equiv$ molal flow rate (gm-mole/sec)

$V \equiv$ volume of reaction mixture (cm^3)

$$d\theta_F = \frac{F'dx'}{N_T \times V \times r} \Rightarrow \theta_F = F' \times \int_0^{x'} \frac{dx'}{N_T \times V \times r}$$

Chemical Reaction Rate Equations:

Reaction	Rate	Type
$A \rightarrow B$	$r = -\dfrac{dC_A}{dt} = kC_A$	First Order
$A + B \rightarrow P$	$r = -\dfrac{dC_A}{dt} = kC_A^2$ for $C_A = C_B$	Second Order

PROBLEM 3:

A 10-liter reactor is reacting a gas in a reaction that has a space velocity of 10 grams/gram-mole-sec. The volume per mole of feed is 2,000 cm^3/gm-mole. What is the feed rate of that gas?

SOLUTION:

$SV = 10$ gm/gm-mol-sec

$V_R = 10$ liters

$V_F = 2,000$ cm^3/sec

$$SV = \frac{F \times V_F}{V_R} \Rightarrow F = \frac{SV \times V_R}{V_F} = \frac{10 \text{ gm/gm-mol-sec} \times 10 \text{ liter} \times 10^3 \text{cm}^3/\text{liter}}{2000 \text{cm}^3/\text{gm-mol}}$$

$$F = 50 \text{ gm/sec}$$

FE/EIT

FE: PM Chemical Engineering Exam

CHAPTER 3

Chemical Engineering Thermodynamics

CHAPTER 3

CHEMICAL ENGINEERING THERMODYNAMICS

CHEMICAL THERMODYNAMICS

Conservation of Energy—In any system, the sum of the changes in the kinetic energy and the potential energy are zero.

Kinetic Energy:

$$\text{K.E.} = \frac{m \times u^2}{2 \times g_c}$$

Potential energy:

$$\text{P.E.} = \frac{m \times h \times g}{g_c}$$

where:

$g \equiv$ acceleration due to gravity = 980 cm/sec^2

$g_c \equiv$ gravitational constant = 980 gm-cm/gm$_f$-sec^2

$h \equiv$ height (cm)

$m \equiv$ mass (gram)

$u \equiv$ velocity (cm/sec)

$$\Delta K.E. + \Delta P.E. = 0$$

FIRST LAW OF THERMODYNAMICS

First Law of Thermodynamics—States the change in internal energy of a system is equal to the heat added to the system minus the work done by the system.

$$\Delta E + \Delta K.E. + \Delta P.E. = Q - W$$

or, since $\Delta K.E. + \Delta P.E. = 0$,

$$dE = dQ - dW$$

where:

$E \equiv$ internal energy

$Q \equiv$ heat added to system

$W \equiv$ work done by the system

$$dE = C_v \times dT$$

where:

$C_v =$ heat capacity at constant volume

Enthalpy—Is a property of the system as are internal energy (E), pressure (p), and volume (V). Enthalpy is defined by:

$$H = E + pV$$

$$dH = dE + d(pV)$$

For the special case where both the pressure (p) and volume (V) are constant:

$$dH = dE = dQ - dW$$

For the special case of a reversible process where $dW = 0$:

$$dH = dQ = C_p \times dT$$

where $C_p \equiv$ heat capacity at constant pressure.

For liquids and solids, $C_p = C_v$.

Ideal Gas Law

Ideal Gas Law:

$$p \times V = n \times R \times T$$

where:

$p \equiv$ pressure of ideal gas

$n \equiv$ number of moles

$R \equiv$ Ideal Gas Constant

$T \equiv$ absolute temperature

There are several values of R depending on the dimensions used for the other parameters.

Values of the Ideal Gas Constant

$R = 1.987$ calories/gram-mole-K

$R = 1.987$ kcal/kg-mole-K

$R = 8.305$ Joules/gram-mole-K

$R = 8.306$ Pascals-m^3/gram-mole-K

$R = 82.06$ atmospheres-cm^3/gram-mole-K

$R = 83.14$ bars-cm^3/gram-mole-K

In many situations that occur in thermodynamics, a gas or mixture of gases can be considered to behave as ideal gases and are subject to the Ideal Gas Law.

For an ideal gas, the internal energy (dE) is a function of the temperature *only*.

$$d(pV) = n \times R \times dT$$
$$dH = dE + d(pV)$$
$$C_p \times dT = C_v \times dT + n \times R \times dT$$

Rearranging terms and letting $n = 1$ mole gives:

$$C_p = C_v + R$$

For an isothermal process, the temperature is constant and $dT = 0$ as well as $dE = 0$, thus:

$$dE = dQ - dW = 0$$
$$dQ = dW$$

$$dW = \int p \; dV = R \times T \times \int \frac{dV}{V}$$

$$Q = W = R \times T \times \ln \frac{V_2}{V_1} = R \times T \times \ln \frac{p_2}{p_1}$$

For an adiabatic process ($dQ = 0$) and no heat is lost to or gained from the surroundings:

$$dE = -dW = -p \times dV$$

$$C_v \times dT = -p \times dV = -R \times T \frac{dV}{V}$$

Rearranging terms:

$$C_v \times \frac{dT}{T} = -R \times \frac{dV}{V}$$

Define an adiabatic exponent (γ):

$$\gamma = \frac{C_v + R}{C_v} = 1 + \frac{R}{C_v} = \frac{C_p}{C_v}$$

$$\int \frac{dT}{T} = \frac{-R}{C_v} \times \int \frac{dV}{V}$$

$$\frac{T_2}{T_1} = \left(\frac{V_1}{V_2} \right)^{(\gamma-1)}$$

$$p_1 \times (V_1)^{\gamma} = p_2 \times (V_2)^{\gamma}$$

$$W = \frac{p_1 \times V_1 - p_2 \times V_2}{(\gamma - 1)}$$

Gas	γ
Air	1.399
CO	1.399
CO_2	1.288
Methane	1.304
Nitrogen	1.400
Oxygen	1.396
Steam	1.329

Table 1. Values for γ for Certain Gases

PROBLEM 1:

An air compressor compresses an initial volume of 1 m³ of air adiabatically from 100 kPa to 500 kPa at a constant rate. What is the work done in kg$_f$-m during compression in assuming the entrance and exit velocities are the same?

SOLUTION:

The value of $\gamma = 1.4$ for air, and $p_1 \times (V_1)^\gamma = p_2 \times (V_2)^\gamma$

$$V_2 = V_1 \times \left(\frac{p_1}{p_2}\right)^{1/\gamma} = 1\ \text{m}^3 \times \left(\frac{100}{500}\right)^{1/1.4} = (0.2)^{0.714} = 0.32\ \text{m}^3$$

$$W = \frac{p_1 \times V_1 - p_2 \times V_2}{(\gamma - 1)} = \frac{[(100 \times 1) - (500 \times 0.32)]\text{kPa-m}^3}{(1.4 - 1)}$$

$$= -145.95\ \text{kPa-m}^3$$

$$W = -145.95\ \text{kPa-m}^3 \times 1.0197 \times 10^{-2}\ \text{kg}_f/\text{cm}^2\text{-kPa} \times 10^4 \text{cm}^2/\text{m}^2$$

$$W = -14{,}883\ \text{kg}_f\text{-m}$$

Partial pressures can be defined by the Ideal Gas Law.

$$p_i = \frac{n_i \times R \times T}{V},\ p = \Sigma p_i,\ \text{and}\ \ p_i = \frac{n_i}{n}$$

Latent Heat of Fusion (ΔH_{fus})—Heat associated with liquefying a solid at constant temperature and pressure.

Latent Heat of Vaporization (ΔH_{vap})—Heat associated with vaporizing a liquid at constant temperature and pressure.

Clausius-Clapeyron Equation—Relates the latent heat of a system changing phase (solid-to-liquid or liquid-to-vapor) to pressure-volume-temperature (pVT) data.

$$\frac{dp'}{dT} = \frac{\Delta H}{T \times \Delta V}$$

where:

$\Delta H \equiv$ latent heat

$\Delta V \equiv$ volume change

$$\frac{dp'}{dT} \equiv \text{rate of change of phase equilibrium (or vapor) pressure with}$$

temperature

At low pressures $\Delta V = V_{gas} - V_{liq} \approx V_{gas}$, and the Ideal Gas Law may be applied where:

$$V_{gas} = \frac{R \times T}{p} \Rightarrow \frac{dp'}{dT} = \frac{\Delta H \times p}{R \times T^2}$$

$$\frac{d(\ln p')}{dT} = \frac{\Delta H}{RT^2} \Rightarrow \int d(\ln p') = \frac{\Delta H}{R} \times \int \frac{dT}{T^2}$$

$$\ln \frac{p'_2}{p'_1} = -\frac{\Delta H}{R} \times \left(\frac{1}{T_2} - \frac{1}{T_1} \right)$$

Trouton's Rule—The ratio of the molal heat of vaporization (H_{vap}) to the absolute boiling point is a constant for all liquids.

$$\frac{\Delta H_{vap}}{T_{b.p.}} = 8.75 + 1.987 \times \ln T_{b.p.}$$

where $T_{b.p.}$ is in K

Standard Heat of Reaction—The difference between the enthalpies of the products in their standard states and the enthalpies of the reactants in their standard states all at the same temperature.

$$\Delta H^{\circ}_{r_x n} = \Sigma H^{\circ}_{prod} - \Sigma H^{\circ}_{react}$$

where $H^{\circ} \equiv$ indicates enthalpies at standard states.

Combustion Reaction—Reaction between an element or compound and oxygen to form specified combustion products, usually CO_2 and H_2O.

ΔH_{comb} = **HHV** (*higher heating value*) if H_2O formed as a liquid.

ΔH_{comb} = **LHV** (*lower heating value*) or net heating value if H_2O formed as a vapor.

PROBLEM 2:

Find the heat of combustion for benzene (C_6H_6).

SOLUTION:

$$C_6H_6 + 7\tfrac{1}{2}O_2 \rightarrow 6CO_2 + 3H_2O \text{ (liquid)}$$

$$H^\circ_{CO_2} = -94.052$$

$$H^\circ_{H_2O(L)} = -68.3174$$

$$H^\circ_{C_6H_6} = +19.820$$

$$H^\circ_{O_2} = 0 \text{ all in kcal/mole}^2$$

(Ref: *Perry's Chemical Engineers Handbook*, 4th Edition, Section 3, McGraw-Hill.)

$$\Delta H_{comb} = \Sigma H^\circ \text{ for } CO_2 \text{ and } H_2O - \Sigma H^\circ \text{ for } C_6H_6 \text{ and } O_2$$

$$\Delta H_{comb} = 6\times(-94.052) + 3\times(-68.3174) - (19.82) = -769.264 - 19.82$$

$$\Delta H_{comb} = -789.08 \text{ kcal/mole}$$

Heat Engine

Heat Engine—A machine or system for producing work from heat. For a heat engine the internal energy change of the cycle is zero.

$$\Delta E_{cycle} = 0 = Q_1 - Q_2 - W$$

Efficiency of a heat engine:

$$\eta = \frac{W}{Q_1} = 1 - \frac{Q_2}{Q_1} = \frac{T_1 - T_2}{T_1}$$

The absorption and rejection of heat by the fluid of a reversible heat engine is zero for the entire cycle.

$$\frac{Q_1}{T_1} + \frac{Q_2}{T_2} = 0 \Rightarrow \frac{dQ_{rev}}{T} = 0$$

Entropy—The total increase in entropy accompanying an actual process is the measure of the loss in capacity of the system and surroundings to do work. No process is possible for which the *total entropy* decreases.

$$dS = \frac{dQ_{rev}}{T} \Rightarrow dQ = T \times dS, \text{ and } dS \geq 0$$

Compressors (gas pumps): $\qquad W_{loss} = T_o \times dS$

Isothermal Process:
$$W_s = R \times T \times \ln \frac{p_2}{p_1}$$

Reversible Isothermal Process: $W_s = T \times \Delta S - \Delta H$

Adiabatic Compression:
$$W_s = -\frac{\gamma \times p_1 \times V_1}{(\gamma - 1)} \times \left(\left(\frac{p_2}{p_2} \right)^{(\gamma-1)/\gamma} - 1 \right)$$

$$-W_s = \Delta H = H_2 - H_1$$

If a thermodynamic chart, such as a Molliere Diagram, is available, then follow the constant entropy line from initial conditions to final conditions and read H_2 and H_1 accordingly. The path followed by steam in reversible adiabatic turbines is simply a vertical line from the initial pressure down to the final pressure on either a *T-S* or *H-S* (Molliere) Diagram.

PROBLEM 3:

An ideal gas undergoes an isothermal expansion in which its volume doubles. For one mole of this gas calculate the change in entropy for the surroundings if the process is assumed to be reversible.

SOLUTION:

For a reversible isothermal process, the surrounding temperature and the system temperature are the same; therefore:

$$\Delta S_{sur} = \frac{(Q_{rev})_{sur}}{T} = -\frac{(Q_{rev})_{sys}}{T} = -\Delta S_{sys}$$
$$(Q_{rev})_{sys} = T \times \Delta S_{sys}$$

$$\Delta S_{sys} = R \times \ln \frac{V_2}{V_1} = 1.987 \text{ calories/gram-mole-K} \times \ln(2)$$

$$\Delta S_{sur} = -\Delta S_{sys} = 1.987 \times 0.6931 = -1.377 \text{ calories/gram-mole-K}$$

STEAM POWER PLANT CYCLE

Steam Power Plant Cycle

- Heat absorbed by water is equal to increase in enthalpy,

  $Q = \Delta H_{water}$

- Work obtained is entirely at the expense of the change in enthalpy of the expanding steam through the turbine, $W_s = -\Delta H_{\text{steam}}$.

- Loss in work accompanying an irreversible process is equal to the product of total change in entropy accompanying that process and the lowest temperature at which heat can be discarded, $W_{\text{loss}} = T \, dS$.

Refrigeration—Maintenance of a temperature below that of surroundings.

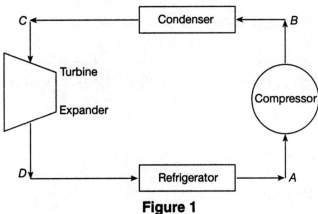

Figure 1

$Q_R \equiv$ heat absorbed in refrigerator

$Q_R = m \times C_p \times (T_A - T_D)$

$Q_C \equiv$ heat rejected in cooler

$Q_C = m \times C_p \times (T_B - T_C)$

p_R and p_C are constant.

$$\frac{T_c}{T_D} = \left(\frac{p_R}{p_c}\right)^{(\gamma-1)/\gamma} = \frac{T_B}{T_A}$$

Work:

$$W = m \times C_p \times [(T_B - T_C) - (T_A - T_D)]$$

Efficiency:

$$\eta = \frac{W}{Q_R}$$

Coefficient of Performance (C.O.P.):

$$C.O.P. = \frac{1}{\eta} = \frac{T_A}{T_B - T_A}$$

Vapor Compression Cycle—Evaporation of a liquid at constant pressure provides a means of absorbing heat at constant temperature.

$Q_R = H_A - H_D$ (heat absorbed in the refrigerator per pound of fluid)

$Q_C = H_B - H_C$ (heat rejected in the condenser per pound of fluid)

$$W = (H_B - H_C) - (H_A - H_D)$$

$$C.O.P. = \frac{1}{\eta} = \frac{H_A - H_D}{(H_B - H_C) - (H_A - H_D)}$$

FE/EIT

FE: PM Chemical Engineering Exam

CHAPTER 4

Computers and Numerical Methods

CHAPTER 4

COMPUTERS AND NUMERICAL METHODS

INTRODUCTION

When preparing for computers and numerical methods questions, one is not required to learn a specific computer language or computer system type. Successful candidates will have a practical knowledge of computers, some basic numerical applications in the engineering discipline, and general programming structure. The test participants are foreseen to be familiar with flowcharts, spreadsheets, e.g., Lotus, Quattro-Pro, Excel, etc., and "pseudo code." A candidate who has an aptitude with any structured programming language, e.g., Fortran, C, etc., will have little difficulty understanding and interpreting "pseudo code" as encountered in the exam. In the area of numerical methods, a basic understanding is required of solving simultaneous linear equations, numerical integration and numerically solving differential equations.

FLOWCHARTS

By definition a flowchart is "a method of diagramming the logic of an algorithm using a standardized set of symbols to indicate the various elements of the program." A flowchart is a tool programmers use to organize the major functions and subroutines required within a program. Flowcharts are commonly used as a first step in writing a program because the symbolic representations free the user from the constraints of writing the specific code that will be implemented. As a consequence of different programming styles, many programs performing the same set of operations can be written from the same flowchart.

When constructing a flowchart, messages are written within each symbol to explain that symbol's function. Programming etiquette prefers one start and one stop in the flowchart, and the sequence of functions should be arranged (or "flow") from top to bottom. Arrowheads indicate the direction of the sequence of calculations. Connector symbols allow the merging of two or more computational paths. Table 1 shows the most common symbols utilized in a flowchart:

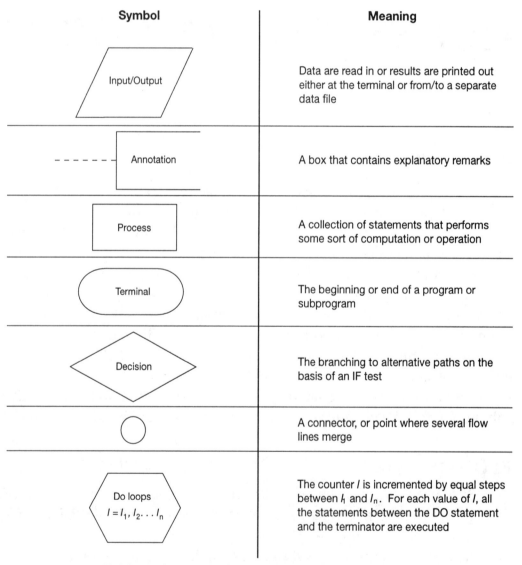

Symbol	Meaning
Input/Output	Data are read in or results are printed out either at the terminal or from/to a separate data file
Annotation	A box that contains explanatory remarks
Process	A collection of statements that performs some sort of computation or operation
Terminal	The beginning or end of a program or subprogram
Decision	The branching to alternative paths on the basis of an IF test
(connector)	A connector, or point where several flow lines merge
Do loops $I = I_1, I_2 \ldots I_n$	The counter I is incremented by equal steps between I_1 and I_n. For each value of I, all the statements between the DO statement and the terminator are executed

Table 1. Common Symbols Used in Flowcharts

PROBLEM 1:

Suppose you are required to write a computer program to calculate the wage $WAGE_i$ for an employee *I*, working H_i hours per week in a company having *n* employees. Each employee *i* is paid at a certain rate $PAYRAT_i$ in dollars per hour for the first 40 hours and then at a higher rate $OVTRAT_i$ for the time worked over 40 hours. Create a flowchart for such a program.

SOLUTION:

Step #1

Define some key variable quantities.

$WAGE_i$ = wages for employee *i*

n = number of employees

H_i = number of hours employee *i* worked in a week

$PAYRAT_i$ = rate of pay for the first 40 hours worked by employee *i*

$OVTRAT_i$ = rate of pay for the hours over 40 worked by employee *i*

Step #2

List the various tasks required.

Some tasks in a program aid in the execution of the program, but usually are specific to the language to be used. In this problem, such tasks would be:

1. Start and stop of program
2. Declaration of variables
3. Output of the results

Other tasks in a program are directly involved in the computation of results. These actions must be included in order for the program to output the desired results. In this problem, such tasks would be:

1. Decide if the number of hours for employee *i* is greater than 40 hours.
2. Compute $WAGE_i$ at $PAYRAT_i$ when H_i is less than 40 hours for employee *i.*
3. Compute $WAGE_i$ at $OVTRAT_i$ when H_i is greater than 40 hours for employee *i.*
4. Input the variable quantities.

Realize that in the task "Input the variable quantities," one may need to make sure that for *n* employees there are *n* H_i, *n* $PAYRAT_i$, and *n* $OVTRAT_i$.

Step #3

Create the flowchart for the defined tasks:

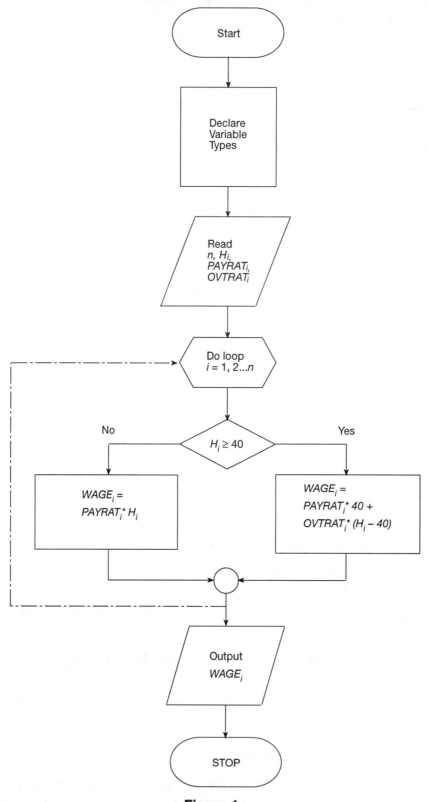

Figure 1

PROBLEM 2:

In a given test, a person *i* unconditionally passes if he/she has a score S_i above 60, conditionally passes if the score is between 40 and 60, and fails with a score below 40. For a class of *n* students, create the flowchart of a program that will calculate the percentage of the class that passes *%P*, conditionally passes *%CP* and fails *%F*. Also, calculate the average score of the students that pass *AVEP*, conditionally pass *AVECP*, and fail *AVEF*.

SOLUTION:

Step #1

Define some key variable quantities:

n = number of students

S_i = score of student *i*

%P = percentage of students that unconditionally pass

%CP = percentage of students that conditionally pass

%F = percentage of students that fail

AVEP = average score of students that unconditionally pass

AVECP = average score of students that conditionally pass

AVEF = average score of students that fail

Step #2

Apart from the Start, Stop Variable Declaration and Result Output, the other important tasks involved are:

1. Determine if each student passes or fails.

2. Determine if each passing student unconditionally passes or not.

3. Find the average score of each of the three groups.

4. Input score of student *i*.

Step #3

Create the flowchart for the defined tasks:

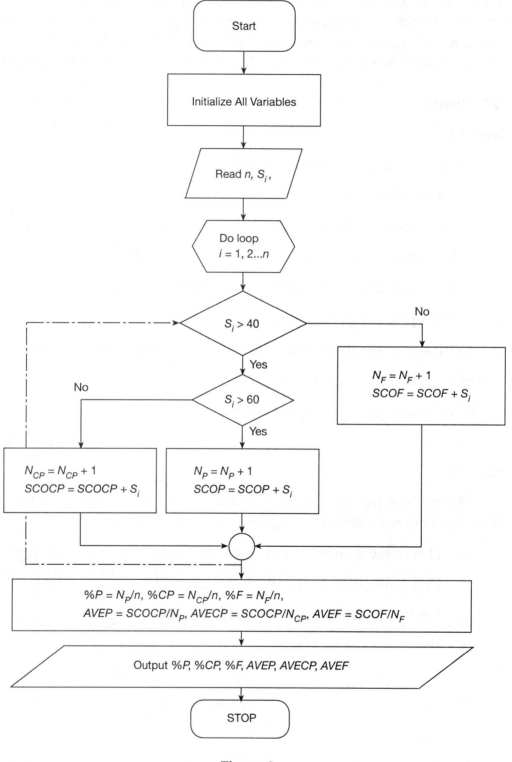

Figure 2

Note that the desired output values, %P, %CP, %F, AVEP, AVECP, and *AVEF* were not calculated until *after* the do-loop was completed. The program flowchart was structured with the intermediate calculations of N_P, N_{CP}, N_F, SCOP, SCOCP, and SCOF instead of the desired output values because one had not grouped the students (and their corresponding scores) into one of the three groups until *after* the do-loop had been completed. The benefit of using a flowchart before actual programming is evident here; though the primary goal was to calculate the percentages and averages in each of the three groups, the flowchart made clear the premise that sorting the data needed to be complete before the desired calculations could be made.

PSEUDO CODE

In addition to the flowchart, pseudo code is another method used in drafting computer programs. The main idea behind pseudo code is to characterize the main operations of the program in a simplified mix of English and simple computer jargon. In an effort to make pseudo code an amorphous, fluid language, there are few standard rules one follows in pseudo code structure. The primary idea is to express operations performed by the program in English and computer commands, which are capitalized.

In the context of the exam, the predefined functions to consider usually include arithmetic operators, e.g., addition, subtraction, multiplication, and division, trigonometric function, such as sine, cosine, and tangent, and a few commonly used constants, e.g., pi (3.14159...) and *e* (2.71828....). If a function other than those mentioned above is utilized during a segment of pseudo code, its execution will probably be explained and an example of its application would be given within the confines of the problem.

Other than predefined mathematical functions, the commands generally seen in pseudo code are do-loops and logical expressions. Do-loops have a basic structure as follows:

DO i = (start index), (index end), (index increment) Set of executables

ENDDO

The purpose of a do-loop is primarily to execute the same operations a number of times. For example, in the pseudo code below,

DO i = 1,5

ENDDO

i takes on the values 1, 2, 3, 4, and 5 successively. If the index increment is not included, it is usually +1. Usually the index start, the index end, and the index increment are integers, but that does not have to be the case. Note that when *i* exceeds the index end, then no more iterations are performed and the program continues to execute commands given after the ENDDO line of code. For example, in the pseudo code

DO *i* = 1, 9, 3

ENDDO

i takes on the values 1, 4, and 7 *only*.

The basic structure of any logical expression can be seen in the following form:

IF ("logical expression #1") THEN

    Set of executable statements #1

ELSEIF ("logical expression #2") THEN

    Set of executable statements #2

ELSEIF ("logical expression #3") THEN

    Set of executable statements #3

....

ELSEIF ("logical expression #[*N*–1]") THEN

    Set of executable statements #[*N*–1]

ELSE

    Set of executable statements #*N*

ENDIF

Note that within the "IF-THEN" structure, the set of executables associated with each IF-THEN clause is only executed if the logical expression is found to be true. Also observe that each IF-THEN is called in a program sequentially *until a statement is found to be true.* When a logical statement is found to be true, the associated set of executables are performed and the program continues to perform operations *after* the ENDIF statement. Therefore, even if more than one IF-THEN statement can be true for a set of variable values, *only the first true logical expression will have its commands executed.*

PROBLEM 3:

A program has the following segment:

1. $VAR = 1$

2. IF $VAR < 4$ THEN

3. $VAR = VAR + 2$

4. ENDIF

What is the value of VAR at the termination of this program segment?

SOLUTION:

The solution procedure to solving pseudo code problems is not rigorous, as the language intends. Therefore, one steps through the program, line by line, until all do-loops and true logical expressions have been executed.

Line of Code	Analysis	Result
1	Initialization of VAR	$VAR = 1$
2	True logical statement	$VAR = 1$
3	Value of VAR changed	$VAR = 3$
4	End of executables associated with logical statement	$VAR = 3$

Table 2

Note that though it is tempting to repeat executing the logical statement after VAR has changed value, that would only be correct if the logical statement was preceded in a do-loop that iterated more than once. Therefore, $VAR = 3$.

PROBLEM 4:

The production of six batches is recorded into the plant computer system. The batch production values are (kg) 16.0, 14.2, 13.7, 15.0, 16.5, and 15.4. The values are read into an array P and the following pseudo code segment is executed:

1. Set $X = 100$; $Y = 0$; $Z = 0$

2. DO $N = 1, 6$

3. IF $P(N) < X$ THEN

4. $X = P(N)$

5. ENDIF

6. IF $P(N) > Y$ THEN

7. $Y = P(N)$

8. ENDIF

9. $Z = Z + P(N)$

10. ENDDO

11. $Z = Z/6$

12. OUTPUT X, Y, Z

SOLUTION:

Line of Code	Analysis	Result
1	Initialization of variables	$X = 100; Y = 0$ $Z = 0$
2	Start of do-loop. Will iterate six times.	
3	True logical statement #1	$P(1) = 16.0$ $X = 100$
4	Executable of logical statement #1	$X = 16.0$
5	End of executables of logical statement #1	
6	True logical statement #2	$P(1) = 16.0$ $Y = 0$
7	Executable of logical statement #2	$Y = 16.0$
8	End of executables of logical statement #2	
9	Z changes value	$Z = 16.0$
2	Second Iteration	
3	True logical statement #1	$P(2) = 14.2$ $X = 16.0$
4	Executable of logical statement #1	$X = 14.2$
5	End of executables of logical statement #1	
6	False logical statement #2	$P(2) = 14.2$ $Y = 16$

7	Executable of logical statement #2	
8	End of executables of logical statement #2	
9	Z changes value	$Z = 30.2$
2	Third Iteration	
3	True logical statement #1	$P(3) = 13.7$ $X = 14.2$
4	Executable of logical statement #1	$X = 13.7$
5	End of executables of logical statement #1	
6	False logical statement #2	$P(3) = 13.7$ $Y = 16$
7	Executable of logical statement #2	
8	End of executables of logical statement #2	
9	Z changes value	$Z = 43.9$
2	Fourth Iteration	
3	False logical statement #1	$P(4) = 15.0$ $X = 13.7$
4	Executable of logical statement #1	
5	End of executables of logical statement #1	
6	False logical statement #2	$P(4) = 15.0$ $Y = 16$
7	Executable of logical statement #2	
8	End of executables of logical statement #2	
9	Z changes value	$Z = 58.9$
2	Fifth Iteration	
3	False logical statement #1	$P(5) = 16.5$ $X = 13.7$
4	Executable of logical statement #1	
5	End of executables of logical statement #1	
6	True logical statement #2	$P(5) = 16.5$ $Y = 16$
7	Executable of logical statement #2	$Y = 16.5$
8	End of executables of logical statement #2	
9	Z changes value	$Z = 75.4$
2	Sixth Iteration	
3	False logical statement #1	$P(6) = 15.4$ $X = 13.7$

4	Executable of logical statement #1	
5	End of executables of logical statement #1	
6	False logical statement #2	$P(6) = 15.4$ $Y = 16.5$
7	Executable of logical statement #2	
8	End of executables of logical statement #2	
9	Z changes value	$Z = 90.8$
10	End of do-loop	
11	Z changes value	$Z = 15.1$
12	Output X, Y, Z	$X = 13.7$ $Y = 16.5$ $Z = 15.1$

Table 3

Note that even though the task of analyzing and transcribing the results to each line of code separately is cumbersomely exhaustive, it ensures no errors due to memory lapses.

PROBLEM 5:

The numbers –3, 5, 2, –7, and 6, respectively, are read into a computer data file called *P*. Then the ensuing pseudo code is executed.

1. Set $Y = 0$
2. DO $I = 1, 5$
3. IF $I \leq 3$,
4. $X = P(I)$
5. ENDIF
6. IF $X < 0$ THEN
7. ELSE
8. $Y = Y + X*X$
9. ENDIF
10. ENDDO
11. $Z = Y/I$

Find the value of Z.

SOLUTION:

Line of Code	Analysis	Result
1	Initialization of Variable	$Y = 0$
2	Start of do-loop. Will iterate five times.	
3	True logical statement #1	$I = 1$
4	Executable associated with logical statement #1	$X = -3$
5	End of executables associated with logical statement #1	
6	True logical statement #2	$X = -3$
7	False *branch* of logical statement #2	
8	Executable associated with *branch* of logical statement #2	
9	End of executables associated with logical statement #2	
2	Second iteration	
3	True logical statement #1	$I = 2$
4	Executable associated with logical statement #1	$X = 5$
5	End of executables associated with logical statement #1	
6	False logical statement #2	$X = 5$
7	True *branch* of logical statement #2	
8	Executable associated with *branch* of logical statement #2	$Y = 25$
9	End of executables associated with logical statement #2	
2	Third iteration	
3	True logical statement #1	$I = 3$
4	Executable associated with logical statement #1	$X = 2$
5	End of executables associated with logical statement #1	
6	False logical statement #2	$X = 2$
7	True *branch* of logical statement #2	
8	Executable associated with *branch* of logical statement #2	$Y = 29$
9	End of executables associated with logical statement #2	
2	Fourth iteration	
3	False logical statement #1	$I = 4$
4	Executable associated with logical statement #1	
5	End of executables associated with logical statement #1	
6	False logical statement #2	$X = 2$
7	True *branch* of logical statement #2	
8	Executable associated with *branch* of logical statement #2	$Y = 33$
9	End of executables associated with logical statement #2	
2	Fifth iteration	
3	False logical statement #1	$I = 5$
4	Executable associated with logical statement #1	
5	End of executables associated with logical statement #1	
6	False logical statement #2	

7	True *branch* of logical statement #2	
8	Executable associated with *branch* of logical statement #2	$Y = 37$
9	End of executables associated with logical statement #2	
10	End of do-loop	
11	Z changes value	$Z = 7.4$

Table 4

Note how the ELSE branch is always activated when the second logical statement is found to be false.

PROBLEM 6:

Calculate the sum S found by the segment of the pseudo code.

1. Set $S = 1$; $T = 1$

2. DO $K = 1, N$

3. $T = T*Z/K$

4. $S = S + T$

5. ENDDO

SOLUTION:

Note that since the values of N and Z are not explicitly stated, then the value of S sought must be in the form of a patterned series.

Line of Code	Analysis	Result
1	Initialization of variables	$S = 1$ $T = 1$
2	Start of do-loop. Will iterates N times.	
3	T value updated	$T = Z/1$
4	S value updated	$S = 1 + Z/1$
2	Second iteration	
3	T value updated	$T = Z^2/(2\times1)$
4	S value updated	$S = 1 + Z/1 + Z^2/(2\times1)$
2	Third iteration	
3	T value updated	$T = Z^3/(3\times2\times1)$

4	S value updated	$S = 1 + Z/1 + Z^2/(2\times1) + Z^3/(3\times2\times1)$
2	Fourth iteration	
3	T value updated	$T = Z^4/(4\times3\times2\times1)$
4	S value updated	$S = 1 + Z/1 + Z^2/(2\times1) +$ $Z^3/(3\times2\times1) + Z^4/(4\times3\times2\times1)$
	Now one can see the pattern	
2	Nth iteration	
3	T value updated	$T = Z^N/N!$
4	S value updated	$S = 1 + Z/1 + Z^2/(2\times1) + Z^3/(3\times2\times1)$ $+ Z^4/(4\times3\times2\times1) + ... + Z^N/N!$
5	End of do-loop	

Table 5

PROBLEM 7:

A segment of pseudo code has been written to calculate the translation of different numbers to their corresponding values under a binary basis. Use the segment below to find the output for the given number *NUM* translated into the binary basis.

1. Set $NUM = 101$; $X = []$

2. $DUM = log(NUM)/log(2)$

3. $START$ = ROUND (DUM)

4. $REM = NUM$

5. DO $I = START, 0, -1$

6. IF $REM \geq 2^I$

7. $X = [X\ 1]$; $REM = REM - 2^I$

8. ELSE

9. $X = [X\ 0]$

10. ENDIF

11. ENDDO

12. Output X

Note: The function ROUND(*X*) for a real number *X*, returns the integer value of the number. For example, if *X* = 12.78, ROUND(*X*) returns the value of 12.

SOLUTION:

Line of Code	Analysis	Result
1	Initialization of variable	$NUM = 101$ $X = []$ (Empty matrix)
2	Calculation	$DUM = 6.6582$
3	Specialized Function	$START = 6$
4	Calculation	$REM = 101$
5	Start of do-loop. Will iterates 7 times.	
6	True logical statement #1	REM 64
7	Executables associated with statement #1	$X = [1]$; $REM = 37$
8	False branch of logical statement #1	
9	Executables associated with false branch of statement #1	
10	End of executables associated with false branch of statement #1	
5	Second iteration	
6	True logical statement #1	REM 32
7	Executables associated with statement #1	$X = [1 \ 1]$; $REM = 5$
8	False branch of logical statement #1	
9	Executables associated with false branch of statement #1	
10	End of executables associated with false branch of statement #1	
5	Third iteration	
6	False logical statement #1	
7	Executables associated with statement #1	

8	True branch of logical statement #1	
9	Executables associated with true branch of statement #1	$X = [1\ 1\ 0]$
10	End of executables associated with true branch of statement #1	
5	Fourth iteration	
6	False logical statement #1	
7	Executables associated with statement #1	
8	True branch of logical statement #1	
9	Executables associated with true branch of statement #1	$X = [1\ 1\ 0\ 0]$
10	End of executables associated with true branch of statement #1	
5	Fifth iteration	
6	True logical statement #1	$REM \geq 4$
7	Executables associated with statement #1	$X = [1\ 1\ 0\ 0\ 1];$ $REM = 1$
8	True branch of logical statement #1	
9	Executables associated with true branch of statement #1	
10	End of executables associated with true branch of statement #1	
5	Sixth iteration	
6	False logical statement #1	
7	Executables associated with statement #1	
8	True branch of logical statement #1	
9	Executables associated with true branch of statement #1	$X = [1\ 1\ 0\ 0\ 1\ 0]$
10	End of executables associated with true branch of statement #1	
5	Seventh iteration	
6	True logical statement #1	$REM \geq 1$
7	Executables associated with statement #1	$X = [1\ 1\ 0\ 0\ 1\ 0\ 1];$ $REM = 0$

8	False branch of logical statement #1	
9	Executables associated with false branch of statement #1	
10	End of executables associated with false branch of statement #1	
11	End of do-loop	
12	Output of solution X	$X = [1\ 1\ 0\ 0\ 1\ 0\ 1]$

Table 6

SPREADSHEETS

Spreadsheets are a familiar tool in all disciplines of chemical engineering. The ability to access data and perform various calculations with relative ease is at the heart of numerical analysis and interpretation. One needs to be familiar with data entry, formula entry, and formula filling guidelines. The vast majority of problems involving spreadsheets will involve applying basic rules that are not specific to Excel, Quattro Pro, Lotus, or any other particular spreadsheet.

The crux of data entry lies within the spreadsheet setup. Each cell is assigned a specific address, which is composed of a letter or letters (indicating the column) and a number (indicating the row). For example, in Table 7

| AS | | ■ | 4.5 | |
A	B	C	D	E
1 Data	Result			
2	5.6			
3	6.3			
4	6.5			
5	4.5			
6	5.4			
7	2.4			
8				

Table 7

the highlighted cell has the address of "A5" (Column A, Row 5) and has a data value of 4.5. Cells can also have text entries. Referring to the same table, cell B1 has the text entry of "Result."

A3		= =A2+0.1*PI()		
	A	**B**	**C**	**D**
1	Input	Output		
2	0	0		
3	0.314159	0.309017		
4	0.628319	0.587785		
5	0.942478	0.809017		
6	1.256637	0.951057		
7	1.570796	1		
8	1.884956	0.951057		
9	2.199115	0.809017		
10	2.513274	0.587785		
11	2.827433	0.309017		
12	3.141593	1.23E-16		
13				

Table 8

Cells can also be assigned to a formula entry. For example, in Table 8 cell A3 has the value "0.314159," but that value refers to a formula entered into that cell, "=A2+0.1*PI()." Note that the formula "=A2+0.1*PI()" contains the reference to another cell, A2. Therefore, when a formula refers to another cell, the numerical evaluation of the cell that is referenced, e.g., A2, will be used in the formula. Note also that the formula refers to a predefined function, "PI()." (For clarity, PI() outputs the constant pi to a number of decimal places.) In the context of the exam, the predefined functions to consider will *only* include arithmetic operators, trigonometric functions, and a few commonly used constants.

Formula filling is the common, timesaving task that allows a user to copy cell expressions into a number of other cells. To illustrate the properties associated with expression filling, let us use Table 9 as a working example:

A3		= =A2+0.1*PI()				B3		= =SIN(A3)	
	A	**B**	**C**	**D**			**A**	**B**	**C**
1	Input	Output				1	Input	Output	
2	0	0				2	0	0	
3	0.314159	0.309017				3	0.314159	0.309017	
4						4			
5						5			
6						6			
7						7			
8						8			
9						9			
10						10			
11						11			
12						12			
13									

Table 9

One sees that both cells A3 and B3 are highlighted. A3 contains the formula "=A2+0.1*PI()" and B3 contains the formula "SIN(A3)." ("SIN()" refers to the trigonometric sine function.) Theoretically, one can copy the formulae contained in these cells in any directional combination (up, down, left, or right). However, when copying the expressions of a group of *M* by *N* cells, the cells that are designated to be filled with the formulae must have a dimensionality of *aM* by *bN*, where *a* and *b* are positive integers. If we copy cells A3 and B3 "down" into the next nine rows (cell A3 copied into A4, A5, A6, etc., cell B3 copied into B4, B5, B6, etc.), the result is shown in Table 10.

The formula in A12, "=A11+0.1*PI()," essentially takes the value of the previous cell (A11) and adds 0.1*PI(). The formula ascribed to B12 evaluates the value of sine at the value calculated in A12.

A special feature of spreadsheets is the nature of the cell address. In a formula, placing a symbol, usually a dollar sign "$" in front a component in a cell address, makes that component "absolute." When a cell component is absolute, it will not change if the formula is copied into another cell. In order to make an entire cell address constant, a dollar sign must be placed in front of *both* the column letter(s) and the row number.

A12 ▼	= =A11+0.1*PI()				B12 ▼	= =SIN(A12)			
A	**B**	**C**	**D**	**E**	**A**	**B**	**C**	**D**	**E**
1 Input	Output				1 Input	Output			
2 0	0				2 0	0			
3 0.314159	0.309017				3 0.314159	0.309017			
4 0.628319	0.587785				4 0.628319	0.587785			
5 0.942478	0.809017				5 0.942478	0.809017			
6 1.256637	0.951057				6 1.256637	0.951057			
7 1.570796	1				7 1.570796	1			
8 1.884956	0.951057				8 1.884956	0.951057			
9 2.199115	0.809017				9 2.199115	0.809017			
10 2.513274	0.587785				10 2.513274	0.587785			
11 2.827433	0.309017				11 2.827433	0.309017			
12 3.141593	1.23E-16				12 3.141593	1.23E-16			
13					13				

Table 10

PROBLEM 8:

In a spreadsheet, the number in cell A4 is set to 6. The A5 is set to A4+A4, where $ indicates an absolute cell address. This formula is copied into cells A6 and A7. What is the value of the cell A7?

SOLUTION:

Using the concept of absolute cell address, the simplest method of solution is to approach the cell value as the solution to an algebraic expression. Therefore:

Step #1

Implement the "copying" of the formula into cells A6 and A7:

$$A5 = A4 + \$A\$4 \Rightarrow A6 = A5 + \$A\$4 \Rightarrow A7 = A6 + \$A\$4$$

Step #2

Solve numerically for A7:

$$A5 = 6 + 6 = 12 \Rightarrow A6 = 12 + 6 = 18 \Rightarrow A7 = 18 + 6 = 24$$

PROBLEM 9:

In a spreadsheet, you have 5, 12, 8, 10, and 0 in column B, rows 2 through 6, respectively. In column C, row 1, there is the number 5, and in column C, row 2, one has the formula "=C1+B$2*B3" (within the quotes). The formula is copied down the column. What is the value in column C, row 3?

SOLUTION:

Step #1

Implement the "copying" of the formula into cell C3. Realize that since the formula is copied "down," only the row (numbered) indexes will be changed by the copy command:

$$C2 = C1 + B\$2 \times B3 \Rightarrow C3 = C2 + B42 \times B4$$

Step #2

Solve numerically for C3:

$$C2 = 5 + 5 \times 12 = 65 \Rightarrow C3 = 65 + 5 \times 8 = 105$$

PROBLEM 10:

The following values appear in a spreadsheet that has been created to document the solubility of a material in a solution. Column A contains the solution temperature (degrees Celsius), and Column B contains the mass of solid recovered (grams).

	A	B	C	D
1	40	426.43		
2	45	425.89		
3	50	425.29		
4	55	425.09		
5	60	425.29		
6	65	425.89		
7	70	426.89		
8	75	428.29		
9	80	430.09		

The formula "=B3–B2" (without the quotes) is input into cell C3 and the formula "=C4–C3" (without the quotes) is input into cell D4. These two formulae are copied down from C3 and D3 into all the cells up to and including C9 and D9, respectively. What pattern emerges in the values of column D?

SOLUTION:

Step #1

Implement the "copying" of the formula into cells:

	A	B	C	D
1	40	426.43		
2	45	425.89		
3	50	425.29	=B3–B2	
4	55	425.09	=B4–B3	=C4–C3
5	60	425.29	=B5–B4	=C5–C4
6	65	425.89	=B6–B5	=C6–C5
7	70	426.89	=B7–B6	=C7–C6
8	75	428.29	=B8–B7	=C8–C7
9	80	430.09	=B9–B8	=C9–C8

Step #2

Solve numerically for the cells, and look for a pattern to emerge within column D:

	A	B	C	D
1	40	426.43		
2	45	425.89		
3	50	425.29	–0.6	
4	55	425.09	–0.2	0.4
5	60	425.29	0.2	0.4
6	65	425.89	0.6	0.4
7	70	426.89	1	0.4
8	75	428.29	1.4	0.4
9	80	430.09	1.8	0.4

Therefore, column D has a pattern of "constant values."

SOLVING SIMULTANEOUS LINEAR EQUATIONS (GAUSS-JORDAN METHOD)

The use of algebraic substitution as a means of solving many linear equations can be a very daunting task, especially when time is of the essence. Therefore, the use of the Gauss-Jordan method may be applied to any system of equations to yield the accurate solution.

To illustrate the Gauss-Jordan method, let us consider the simple system of linear equations below:

$$3x_1 - 1x_2 = 7$$
$$2x_1 - 4x_2 = -2$$

For convenience, let us rewrite our system of equations in matrix form, where the coefficients for the variable appear in the left-half of the matrix, and the constant values appear in the right-half of the matrix:

$$\begin{bmatrix} 3 & -1 & | & 7 \\ 2 & -4 & | & -2 \end{bmatrix}$$

Since column one represents x_1 and the second column represents x_2, solving for each variable amounts to creating variable columns that contain one "1" along the diagonal elements and the rest of the cells containing zeros. This task will be accomplished using the basic rules of matrix algebra. To give the method an order, we will work from left to right (producing an identity matrix in the left-half of the full matrix).

Therefore, our first objective is to create a column one, which looks like this:

$$\begin{bmatrix} 1 \\ 0 \end{bmatrix}$$

This is accomplished by multiplying the first row by 1/3:

$$\begin{bmatrix} 3 & -1 & 7 \\ 2 & -4 & -2 \end{bmatrix} \Rightarrow \begin{bmatrix} 1 & -1/3 & 7/3 \\ 2 & -4 & -2 \end{bmatrix}$$

and then subtracting two times the first row from the second row:

$$\begin{bmatrix} 1 & -1/3 & 7/3 \\ 2 & -4 & -2 \end{bmatrix} \Rightarrow \begin{bmatrix} 1 & -1/3 & 7/3 \\ 0 & -10/3 & -20/3 \end{bmatrix}$$

Our next objective is to create a column two, which looks like this:

$$\begin{bmatrix} 0 \\ 1 \end{bmatrix}$$

This task can be accomplished by multiplying the second row by –3/10:

$$\begin{bmatrix} 1 & -1/3 & 7/3 \\ 0 & -10/3 & -20/3 \end{bmatrix} \Rightarrow \begin{bmatrix} 1 & -1/3 & 7/3 \\ 0 & -1 & 2 \end{bmatrix}$$

and then adding one-third of the second row to the first row:

$$\begin{bmatrix} 1 & -1/3 & 7/3 \\ 0 & 1 & 2 \end{bmatrix} \Rightarrow \begin{bmatrix} 1 & 0 & 3 \\ 0 & 1 & 2 \end{bmatrix}$$

Therefore, we have found the solution to be:

$$x_1 = 3 \quad x_2 = 2$$

Though the method appears to be computatively exhaustive, for a large number of equations, the Gauss-Jordan method is the optimal way to obtain a numeric solution by hand.

PROBLEM 11:

Solve the set of linear equations given below:

$$2x_1 - 1x_2 + 3x_3 = 9$$
$$1x_1 - 2x_2 + 2x_3 = 3$$
$$3x_1 + 2x_2 - 3x_3 = -2$$

SOLUTION:

With a system representation as follows:

$$\begin{bmatrix} 2 & -1 & 3 & | & 9 \\ 1 & -2 & 2 & | & 3 \\ 3 & 2 & -3 & | & -2 \end{bmatrix}$$

using the Gauss-Jordan method, one obtains:

$$\begin{bmatrix} 2 & -1 & 3 & | & 9 \\ 1 & -2 & 2 & | & 3 \\ 3 & 2 & -3 & | & -2 \end{bmatrix} \Rightarrow \begin{bmatrix} 1 & -1/2 & 3/2 & | & 9/2 \\ 1 & -2 & 2 & | & 3 \\ 3 & 2 & -3 & | & 2 \end{bmatrix} \Rightarrow$$

$$\begin{bmatrix} 1 & -1/2 & 3/2 & | & 9/2 \\ 0 & -3/2 & 1/2 & | & -3/2 \\ 0 & 7/2 & -15/2 & | & -31/2 \end{bmatrix}$$

$$\begin{bmatrix} 1 & -1/2 & 3/2 & | & 9/2 \\ 0 & 1 & -1/3 & | & 1 \\ 0 & 7/2 & -15/2 & | & -31/2 \end{bmatrix} \Rightarrow \begin{bmatrix} 1 & 0 & 4/3 & | & 5 \\ 0 & 1 & -1/3 & | & 1 \\ 0 & 7/2 & -15/2 & | & -31/2 \end{bmatrix} \Rightarrow$$

$$\begin{bmatrix} 1 & 0 & 4/3 & | & 5 \\ 0 & 1 & -1/3 & | & 1 \\ 0 & 0 & -19/3 & | & -19 \end{bmatrix}$$

$$\begin{bmatrix} 1 & 0 & 4/3 & | & 5 \\ 0 & 1 & -1/3 & | & 1 \\ 0 & 0 & 1 & | & 3 \end{bmatrix} \Rightarrow \begin{bmatrix} 1 & 0 & 0 & | & 1 \\ 0 & 1 & 0 & | & 2 \\ 0 & 0 & 1 & | & 3 \end{bmatrix} \Rightarrow \begin{matrix} x_1 = 1 \\ x_2 = 2 \\ x_3 = 3 \end{matrix}$$

Take care to realize that the final solution to the system of linear equations could contain variables whose values are independent of the solution. For example, if the solution to a set of linear equations is known to be:

$$x_1 = 3$$
$$x_2 = 2$$
$$x_3 = (\text{anything})$$

If one uses the Gauss-Jordan method (and designates the coefficients associated with x_3 as the third column on the left side of the matrix), the third column will be filled with zeros, as illustrated below:

$$\begin{bmatrix} 1 & 0 & 0 & | & 3 \\ 0 & 1 & 0 & | & 2 \\ 0 & 0 & 0 & | & 0 \end{bmatrix}$$

Therefore, in the case where independent variables are found to have values that are unbounded within the set of linear equations, one must switch the independent row with an adjacent row until the independent row becomes "grouped" with the other independent rows (at the bottom of the matrix, for clarity).

NUMERICAL INTEGRATION

The use of numerical integration is based upon the assumption that a complicated function can be replaced by a simpler function over a limited range. A straight line is the simplest approximation to a function, and leads to what is called the trapezoidal rule. If we assume we have a function $f(x)$, the integral I of $f(x)$ from $x = a$ to $x = b$ can be linearly approximated as:

$$I = \frac{1}{2}(f_a + f_b)(b - a) \equiv T_0$$

where T_0 is the result of application of the trapezoidal rule using one panel. By using more panels, one obtains a better approximation for the integral. The formula that describes the integral I for n panels is:

$$T_n \cong \frac{1}{2}T_{n-1} + \Delta x_n \left(\sum_{\substack{i=1 \\ odd}}^{n-1} f(a + i\Delta x_n) \right)$$

where:

$$\Delta x_n = \frac{(b-a)}{2^k}$$

The procedure for using the trapezoidal rule to approximate an integral is as follows:

1. Compute T_0.

2. Repeatedly apply trapezoidal rule for $k = 1, 2, \ldots$ until sufficient accuracy is obtained.

If one approximates a function by using parabolic segments in place of straight lines, then one is applying Simpson's rule. The integration S of a complex function from $x = a$ to $x = b$ for n panels using Simpson's rule is:

$$S_n = \frac{1}{3}\Delta x_k \left[f_a + 4\sum_{\substack{i=1 \\ odd}}^{n-1} f(a + i\Delta x_k) + 2\sum_{\substack{i=2 \\ even}}^{n-2} f(a + i\Delta x_k) + f_b \right]$$

where:

$$\Delta x_n = \frac{(b-a)}{2^k}$$

Higher-level integration algorithms are obtained by approximating $f(x)$ using higher-order polynomial segments. However, knowledge and application of these integration techniques are not required for engineers to successfully answer most of the numerical integration problems.

PROBLEM 12:

Using both the trapezoidal rule and Simpson's rule, find the value of the following integral I using three panels:

$$I = \int_1^2 \left(\frac{1}{x}\right) dx$$

SOLUTION:

Step #1

Identifying $b = 2$ and $a = 1$, one solves for T_0 using the trapezoidal rule:

$$T_0 = \frac{1}{2}\left(\frac{1}{1} + \frac{1}{2}\right)(2 - 1) = 0.75$$

Step #2

Reiterate to solve for T_2:

$$T_1 = \frac{T_0}{2} + \frac{1}{2}\left[f\left(\frac{1}{1} + \frac{1}{2}\right)\right] = \frac{0.75}{2} + \frac{1}{2}\left(\frac{1}{1.5}\right)$$

$$\cong 0.7083$$

$$T_2 = \frac{T_1}{2} + \frac{1}{4}\left[f\left(1 + \frac{1}{4}\right) + f\left(1 + \frac{3}{4}\right)\right] = \frac{0.7083}{2} + \frac{1}{4}\left(\frac{1}{1.25} + \frac{1}{1.75}\right)$$

$$\cong 0.6941$$

Step #3

Solve for S_2 using Simpson's rule:

$$S_1 = \frac{1}{3}\left(\frac{1}{2}\right)\left[1 + 4\left(\frac{1}{1.5}\right) + \frac{1}{2}\right]$$

$$\cong 0.6944$$

$$S_2 = \frac{1}{3}\left(\frac{1}{4}\right)\left[1 + 4\left(\frac{1}{1.25} + \frac{1}{1.75}\right) + 2\left(\frac{1}{1.5}\right) + \frac{1}{2}\right]$$

$$\cong 0.6933$$

Noting that the exact value to the integral is 0.6931 (rounding at the fourth decimal place), we can see that both methods give reasonable approximations using a small number of panels.

NUMERICAL SOLUTIONS TO DIFFERENTIAL EQUATIONS

Numerical methods for solving the differential equation $y' = f(x, y)$ are classified as either one-step or multistep algorithms. In a one-step algorithm, the most recently used value for y at the place x_x and the values for the function $f(x, y)$ evaluated at x_x are used to estimate the next value of y. The Euler method is one such one-step method that is based upon the definition of a derivative:

$$\frac{dy}{dx} \cong \frac{y(x + \Delta x) - y(x)}{\Delta x}$$

Let us suppose that we will approximate the solution to the differential equation at N points. In the Euler equation, each point is sequentially solved for, and the equation for each y_{i+1} is derived to be:

$$y_{i+1} = y_i + f_i \Delta x$$

where:

$f_i =$ The function $f(x, y)$ evaluated at the point (x_i, y_i)

$y_i =$ The previously iterated value of y

Multistep algorithms are more numerically accurate, but are computatively too intensive to apply by hand during the exam.

PROBLEM 13:

Using Euler's method, numerically solve for the following differential equation:

$$y' = y(x) \quad y(x = 0) = 1.0$$

for the range of $x = 0$ to $x = 1$.

SOLUTION:

Applying Euler's formula in an iterative manner yields the following results:

X	Y_i
0.0	1.0
0.1	1.0 + 1.0 x (0.1) = 1.1
0.2	1.1 + 1.1 x (0.1) = 1.21
0.3	1.21 + 1.21 x (0.1) = 1.331
0.4	1.331 + 1.331 x (0.1) = 1.464
0.5	1.464 + 1.464 x (0.1) = 1.611
0.6	1.611 + 1.611 x (0.1) = 1.772
0.7	1.772 + 1.772 x (0.1) = 1.949
0.8	1.949 + 1.949 x (0.1) = 2.144
0.9	2.144 + 2.144 x (0.1) = 2.358
1.0	2.358 + 2.358 x (0.1) = 2.594

Table 11

The exact solution is the very familiar constant *e,* which is approximately 2.71828.

PROBLEM 14:

It is desired to solve the differential equation:

$$\frac{dx}{dt} = x^3 + 1$$

With an initial condition of $x(0) = -2$ using Euler's method, if one uses the time interval of $h = 0.15$, what is the value of the approximate solution at $t = 0.15$?

SOLUTION:

Applying Euler's formula yields the result:

$$y_{i+1} = y_i + fx_i \Delta t$$
$$= (-2) + (-7) \times 0.15$$
$$= -3.05$$

FE/EIT

FE: PM Chemical Engineering Exam

CHAPTER 5

Heat Transfer

CHAPTER 5

HEAT TRANSFER

HEAT TRANSFER

Heat transfer occurs whenever there is a temperature difference between two objects or two systems. There are three ways in which heat can be transferred:

1. **Conduction**—Is a property of matter that permits heat to be transferred even if the physical body of one of the systems is impermeable to radiation and neither system or bodies are in motion.

2. **Convection**—This occurs when heat is transferred as a result of the motion of one of the systems.

3. **Radiation**—Is a property of matter that allows heat to be transferred even through empty space.

Thermal Conductivity—Heat flow by conduction independent of time. This can be expressed by:

$$q = -k \times A \times \frac{dT}{dx}$$

where:

$k \equiv$ thermal conductivity (kcal/hr-m-°C)

$A \equiv$ area (m^2)

$\Delta T \equiv$ temperature difference (°C)

and $\Delta x \equiv$ distance across which heat is transferred (m).

The (–) sign indicates that temperature decreases as the distance from the reference point in the direction of the heat flow increases.

The value of *k, thermal conductivity*, is dependent upon its chemical composition, temperature, pressure, and physical state (gas, liquid, or solid).

Steady State Heat Conduction—Occurs when the temperature and transfer of heat within a material remain independent of time. Therefore:

$$q = k \times A \times \frac{\Delta T}{\Delta x}$$

Often heat is transferred through several layers of dissimilar material with different widths. Then:

$$q = \frac{A \times \Sigma\ (\Delta T)}{\dfrac{\Delta x}{k}}$$

The expression $\dfrac{\Delta x}{k}$ is often replaced by ΣR

where:

$$\Sigma R = \frac{\Delta x_1}{k_1} + \frac{\Delta x_2}{k_2} + ... + \frac{\Delta x_n}{k_n}$$

Heat Conduction through a Homogenous Cylinder Wall—For the cross-section of the cylinder wall, the differential volume is given by $2 \times \pi \times r \times dr \times L$. Heat is transferred radially through this wall; therefore:

$$q = -k \times 2 \times \pi \times r \times L \times \frac{dT}{dr}$$

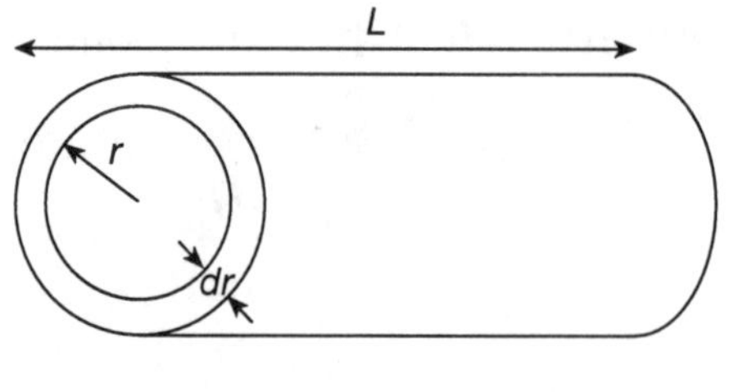

Figure 1. Cylinder Wall

Rearranging terms:

$$dT = \frac{-q}{2 \times \pi \times k \times L} \times \frac{dr}{r} \Rightarrow dT = \frac{-q}{2 \times \pi \times k \times L} \times \int \frac{dr}{r}$$

The inner diameter of the cylinder is r_1, the outer diameter is r_2, and the temperatures at each are T_1 and T_2, respectively.

$$T_2 - T_1 = \frac{-q}{2 \times \pi \times k \times L} \times \ln \frac{r_2}{r_1}$$

$$q = \frac{2 \times \pi \times k \times L \times (T_1 - T_2)}{\ln \frac{r_2}{r_1}}$$

For a composite cylinder with several *walls*, such as a layer of insulation surrounding a pipe wall, the above expression becomes:

$$q = \frac{2 \times \pi \times L \times (T_1 - T_n)}{\frac{\ln r_n / r_{n-1}}{k}}$$

For several layers of insulation, the following equation can be used:

$$q = \frac{\Sigma \Delta T}{\Sigma R}$$

where:

$$\Sigma \Delta T = T_1 - T_n, \text{ and } \Sigma R = \frac{1}{2 \times \pi \times L} \times \left(\frac{1}{k_1} \times \ln \frac{r_2}{r_1} + ... + \frac{1}{k_n} \times \ln \frac{r_n}{r_{n-1}} \right)$$

PROBLEM 1:

Determine the heat flow rate in kcal/hr from a 10-meter length of circular pipe with a 5 cm outside diameter and 0.25 cm thickness carrying hot water at 70°C to a room with an ambient temperature of 20°C. Assume the thermal conductivity of the pipe is 750 cal/hr-cm-°C.

SOLUTION:

This is a straightforward problem to which the equation:

$$q = \frac{2 \times \pi \times k \times L \times (T_1 - T_2)}{\ln \frac{r_2}{r_1}}$$

can be applied, with

$L = 10 \text{ m} = 1,000 \text{ cm}$

$k = 750 \text{ cal/hr-cm-°C}$

$$r_1 = (5 - 0.25) \text{ cm}$$

$$r_2 = 5 \text{ cm}$$

$$T_1 = 70°C$$

$$T_2 = 20°C$$

$$q = \frac{2 \times 3.14 \times 750 \times 1,000 \times (70 - 20)}{\ln(5 / 4.75)}$$

$$= \frac{235.6 \times 10^6 \text{ cal/hr}}{0.0513} \times \frac{1 \text{ kcal}}{1,000 \text{ cal}}$$

$$q = 4.59 \times 10^6 \text{ kcal/hr}$$

Unsteady State Heat Conduction—Occurs when the temperature and heat flow at any point in the system change with time.

Heat Transfer by Free Convection—The motion of the fluid particles in free or natural convection causes heat transfer, due to the difference in densities of the particles.

Newton's Law of Cooling—

$$q = h \times A \times (T_s - T_\infty)$$

The heat transferred to or from the surface of an exposed area *(A)* is dependent upon the difference in temperature of the surface *(T_s)* and the temperature of the surroundings *(T_∞)*, where $h \equiv$ surface coefficient of heat transfer (kcal/m²-hr-°C).

Heat Transfer by Forced Convection—Heat is transferred from a solid surface into a fluid that is already flowing. The temperature difference is between the surface temperature *(T_s)*, and the temperature of the fluid *(T_f)*. For this phenomena the dimensionless Nusselt number is introduced *(N_Nu)*.

$$N_{Nu} = \frac{h \times L}{k}$$

where:

$h \equiv$ surface coefficient of heat transfer (kcal/m²-hr-°C)

$L \equiv$ length (m)

$k \equiv$ thermal conductivity (kcal/hr-m-°C).

Two other dimensionless numbers are important in convective heat transfer. These are the *Reynolds Number* (N_{Re}) and the *Prandtl Number* (N_{Pr}). These are expressed as follows:

$$N_{Re} = \frac{D \times u \times \rho}{\mu}$$

and

$$N_{Pr} = \frac{\mu \times C_p}{k}$$

where:

$D \equiv$ diameter

$u \equiv$ velocity of fluid

$\rho \equiv$ density

$\mu \equiv$ viscosity

$C_p \equiv$ heat capacity

$k \equiv$ thermal conductivity

These dimensionless numbers figure in the calculations for heat transfer for various situations as noted below.

Condition	**Relationship**

Laminar flow in pipes: $\quad N_{Nu} = 1.86 \times N_{Re}^{1/3} \times N_{Pr}^{1/3} \times \left(\dfrac{D}{L}\right)^{1/3} \times \left(\dfrac{\mu}{\mu_w}\right)^{0.14}$

Turbulent flow in pipes: $\quad N_{Nu} = 0.023 \times N_{Re}^{0.8} \times N_{Pr}^{m}$

where $m = 0.4$ for heating and $m = 0.3$ for cooling

Laminar flow over flat plates: $\quad N_{Nu} = 0.664 \times N_{Pr}^{1/2} \times N_{Re}^{1/2}$

Turbulent flow over flat plates: $\quad N_{Nu} = 0.037 \times N_{Pr}^{1/3} \times (N_{Re}^{0.8} - 23,100)$

Heat Transfer between Two Fluids Separated by a Plane Wall—
This is a situation when the effects of conduction and convection are in effect. In the figure on the next page, two fluids flow in opposite directions separated by a wall of thickness (Δx). There is convective heat transfer from each of the fluids that transfer heat by conduction through the wall.

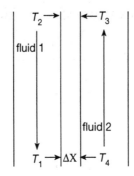

Figure 2

$T_1 \equiv$ temperature of fluid on the left of the wall

$h_1 \equiv$ heat transfer coefficient of fluid on the left of the wall

$T_2 \equiv$ temperature of the left face of the wall

$k \equiv$ thermal conductivity of the wall

$T_3 \equiv$ temperature of the right face of the wall

$T_4 \equiv$ temperature of the fluid on the right of the wall

$h_2 \equiv$ heat transfer coefficient of fluid on the right of the wall

The same quantity of heat is transferred, therefore:

$$Q = h_1 \times A \times (T_1 - T_2)$$
$$= k \times A \times \frac{(T_2 - T_3)}{\Delta x}$$
$$= h_2 \times A \times (T_3 - T_4)$$

$$(T_1 - T_2) = \frac{Q}{h_1 \times A}$$

$$(T_2 - T_3) = \frac{Q \times \Delta x}{k \times A}$$

$$(T_3 - T_4) = \frac{Q}{h_2 \times A}$$

Adding the temperatures together yields:

$$(T_1 - T_4) = \frac{Q}{A} \times \left(\frac{1}{h_1} + \frac{\Delta x}{k} + \frac{1}{h_2} \right)$$

For this situation an overall heat transfer coefficient (U) is defined.

$$U = \cfrac{1}{\cfrac{1}{h_1} + \cfrac{\Delta x}{k} + \cfrac{1}{h_2}}$$

The heat transferred is:

$$q = U \times A \times \Delta T$$

PROBLEM 2:

The inside temperature of a furnace is 1,200°C and the outside wall temperature is 60°C. The furnace wall is made up of 20 cm of chrome brick and 20 cm of fire brick whose thermal conductivities are 15 and 2.7 cal/hr-cm-°C, respectively. The convective heat transfer coefficients at the inside and outside walls of the furnace are 5 and 0.5 cal/hr-cm²-°C, respectively. What is the overall heat transfer coefficient? What is the rate of heat transferred per unit area of the furnace wall?

SOLUTION:

$$k_{cb} = 15, \Delta x_{cb} = 20, k_{fb} = 2.7, \Delta x_{fb} = 20, h_i = 5, h_o = 0.5$$

$$U = \cfrac{1}{\cfrac{1}{5} + \cfrac{20}{15} + \cfrac{20}{2.7} + \cfrac{1}{0.5}} = \cfrac{1}{0.2 + 1.33 + 7.41 + 2} = \cfrac{1}{10.94}$$

$$U = 0.0914 \text{cal/hr-cm}^2\text{-}°C$$

The heat transferred is:

$$\frac{q}{A} = U \times \Delta T = 0.0914 \text{ cal/hr-cm}^2\text{-}°C \times (1,200 - 60)°C$$

$$\frac{q}{A} = 104.23 \text{ cal/hr-cm}^2$$

Condensation

Condensation—There are two methods of condensation, **dropwise** and **film**. *Dropwise condensation* occurs when vapor condenses as drops on a cold surface. *Film condensation* involves the formation of a liquid film as vapor condenses. In both situations the heat of condensation (ΔH_{vap}) is transferred from the vapor to the cooling surface. In film condensation there is a heat transfer film coefficient (h_f) which is much lower than the heat transfer coefficient for dropwise condensation. For film condensation:

$$\frac{h_f \times L}{k} = C \times \left(\frac{g \times \rho^2 \times (\Delta H_{vap})^3}{\mu \times k \times \Delta T} \right)^{1/4}$$

where:

$C = 0.943$ for vertical walls and $C = 0.725$ for horizontal tubes.

Boiling—There are two types of boiling, *film boiling* and *nuclear boiling*. *Film boiling* occurs when a vapor layer is formed on the heating surface. With *nuclear boiling*, heat is transferred by convection to the liquid in contact with the surface which then begins to form bubbles. At the surface of the bubble, liquid is vaporized by the heat flow and the bubbles rise to the surface of the liquid.

Heat Transfer by Radiation—In this mode, heat is transferred in such a way that the medium through which heat flows is not heated. Heat energy is transferred in three steps:

1. conversion of thermal energy into electromagnetic waves

2. transfer of the electromagnetic waves through space

3. reconversion of the electromagnetic waves into thermal energy by adsorption on the cold body

Radiation energy falling onto a cold body can be absorbed, transmitted, or reflected. The total radiation energy is split into these fractions:

$$\alpha + \rho + \tau = 1$$

where:

$\alpha \equiv$ *absorptivity* (fraction of total energy absorbed)

$\rho \equiv$ *reflectivity* (fraction of total energy reflected)

$\tau \equiv$ *transmissivity* (fraction of total energy transmitted)

For most solid opaque materials, the fraction of energy transmitted is almost zero; therefore, $\tau = 0$, and

$$\alpha + \rho = 1$$

Planck's Law—All sources emit radiation depending upon their absolute temperature. The radiant flux density *(W)* is the total radiation emitted by a plane surface per unit area per unit time.

$$W = W \, d\lambda$$

where $\lambda \equiv$ wavelength of radiation.

Kirchoff's Law of Radiation—For a small range of wavelengths, the rate at which radiant energy is emitted by a surface at any temperature is a fraction of the known rate of energy which would be emitted from a black surface or black body (W_b) under the same circumstances. That fraction is the absorptivity (α) and thus:

$$W = \alpha \times W_b$$

Stefan-Boltzmann's Law of Total Radiation—This is defined as:

$$W_b = \sigma \times T^4$$

where $\sigma \equiv$ Boltzmann's constant = 9.8745×10^{-12} kW/hr-m²-K

The heat transferred between two radiating surfaces is dependent upon their absolute temperatures and their shape factors. If the warmer surface area (A_1) is at the absolute temperature (T_1), the net heat radiated between it and the surface at the colder temperature (T_2) is:

$$Q_{1,2} = A_1 \times F_{1,2} \times \sigma \times (T_1^4 - T_2^4)$$

where $F_{1,2} \equiv$ shape factor based on the geometric arrangement of the two surfaces based upon A_1.

PROBLEM 3:

What is the net radiant heat transferred between two flat plates one of which is at 1,000°C and the other at 500°C. Assume the shape factor is 1.

SOLUTION:

Basis:

$A_1 = 1$ m²

$Q_{1,2} = A_1 \times F_{1,2} \times \sigma \times (T_1^4 - T_2^4)$

$Q_{1,2} = 1 \text{ m}^2 \times 1 \times 9.8745 \times 10^{-12} \text{ kW/hr-m}^2\text{- K} \times ((1,000)^4 - (500)^4)$

$Q_{1,2} = 9.8745 \times 10^{-12} \text{ kW/hr-K} \times (10^{12} - 6.25 \times 10^{10})$

$Q_{1,2} = 9.8745 \times 10^{-12} \text{ kW/hr-K} \times 9.375 \times 10^{11} = 9.26 \text{ kW-hr}$

FE/EIT

FE: PM Chemical Engineering Exam

CHAPTER 6

Mass Transfer

CHAPTER 6

MASS TRANSFER

MASS TRANSFER

Fick's Law—In any material substance where there exists one or more components whose concentrations vary throughout, there is a driving force that will cause the concentration differences to equalize. The steady-state rate of diffusion of a material from a region of high concentration to a region of low concentration is proportional to the concentration gradient at the boundary of the region provided no other mechanisms of mass transfer occur. The rate of mass transfer per unit area is:

$$N_A = -D_{AB} \times \frac{dC_A}{dx}$$

where:

$D_{AB} \equiv$ diffusivity (cm²/hr)

$C_A \equiv$ concentration of component A (gm-moles/cm³)

$\frac{dC_A}{dx} \equiv$ concentration gradient in the x direction.

This holds for gases, liquids and solids.

Note: Diffusion takes place in the direction opposite to that of increasing concentration; therefore, the negative (–) sign appears in the expression.

Gilliand Equation —Is defined as:

$$D = D_{AB} = D_{BA} = \frac{4.3 \times 10^{-3} T^{3/2}}{p \times (V_A^{1/3} + V_B^{1/3})^2} \times \sqrt{\frac{1}{M_A} + \frac{1}{M_B}}$$

where:

$p \equiv$ pressure (atmospheres)

M_A, M_B, V_A, and V_B, are the molecular weights (gm/gr-mole) and the molecular volumes at their boiling points (cm³/gm mole) of A and B, respectively. Diffusion coefficients and molecular volumes are given below for several components.

Gas or Vapor	Diffusion Coefficient cm²/sec	Molecular Volume cm³/gm-mole
Hydrogen	0.410	14.3
Oxygen	0.206	25.6
Nitrogen	0.148	31.2
Carbon Dioxide	0.164	34.0
Carbon Monoxide	0.321	30.7
Water	0.256	18.9

Table 1

Diffusion of one ideal gas component through a second ideal gas stagnant layer where $u_B \equiv$ velocity of the diffusing gas:

$$u_B = \frac{D_{BA}}{p_B} \times \frac{dp_B}{dx}$$

$$p = p_A + p_B \Rightarrow u_B = \frac{-D_{BA}}{(p - p_A)} \times \frac{dp_A}{dx}$$

Total mass transfer for diffusion of gas B through stagnant gas A is:

$$N_{AT} = -\frac{D}{R \times T} \times \frac{p}{(p - p_A)} \times \frac{dp_A}{dx}$$

$$N_{AT} = \frac{D \times p}{R \times T \times \Delta x} \times \ln\frac{p_B}{p_A}$$

where $\Delta x \equiv$ thickness of layer through which diffusion occurs.

PROBLEM 1:

Carbon monoxide is diffusing through a 10-meter layer of stagnant air at a velocity of 10 cm/sec and a pressure of 2 atmospheres. The air is at a pressure of 1 atmosphere, and the gas mixture is at 20°C. What is the mass flowrate of carbon monoxide transferred in grams per hour?

SOLUTION:

$$D_{CO} = 0.321 \text{ cm}^2/\text{sec}$$

$$\Delta x = 10 \text{ m} = 1{,}000 \text{ cm}$$

$$T = (273 + 20)\text{K}$$

$$p_{CO} = 2 \text{ atm}$$

$$p_{AIR} = 1 \text{ atm}$$

$$p_T = 3 \text{ atm}$$

M.W.

$$CO = 28 \text{ gm/gm-mole}$$

$$N_{CO} = \frac{D \times p}{R \times T \times \Delta x} \times \ln \frac{p_B}{p_A} = \frac{0.321 \text{cm}^2/\text{sec} \times 1 \text{ atm}}{82.06 \text{ atm-cm}^3/\text{gm-mole-K} \times 293\text{K} \times 1{,}000\text{cm}} \times \ln 2$$

$$N_{CO} = 9.25 \times 10^{-9} \text{gm-mole/sec} \times 28 \text{gm/gm-mole} \times 3{,}600 \text{ sec/hr}$$

$$N_{CO} = 0.0009 \text{ gm / hr}$$

Liquid Diffusion—In liquid diffusion the driving force is the concentration difference of the component which is diffusing. Steady-state equimolar counter diffusion of a solute through a flat film of solvent with thickness (Δx) is defined by:

$$N = \frac{D \times (C_{A1} - C_{A2})}{\Delta x}$$

where $D \equiv$ constant.

Diffusion in Solids—The rate of diffusion is constant, the concentration gradient is independent of time, and the diffusion coefficient is independent of concentration. The rate of diffusion of component A per unit cross-sectional area of solid B is given by:

$$N_A = \frac{D_{AB} \times (C_{A1} - C_{A2})}{\Delta x}$$

where C_{A1} and $C_{A2} \equiv$ concentrations in different faces of Δx.

Radial diffusion through a solid cylinder of length L is given by:

$$N'_A = D_{AB} \times (C_{A1} - C_{A2}) \times \frac{2 \times \pi \times L}{\ln(r_o/r_i)}$$

here $N'_A \equiv$ total mass transfer of A through the solid cylinder.

HUMIDITY AND SATURATION

When a gas or gaseous mixture remains in contact with a liquid surface, this gas or gaseous mixture will acquire vapor from the liquid until the partial pressure of the vapor in the gas mixture equals the vapor pressure of the liquid at its existing temperature.

$$V_{vap} = V_T \times \frac{p_{vap}}{p_T}$$

where:

V_{vap} and $V_T \equiv$ volume of vapor and total volume, respectively

p_{vap} and $p_T \equiv$ vapor pressure and total pressure, respectively

Humidity and Saturation Definitions:

Relative saturation $\equiv$ percent ratio of partial pressure of vapor (p_i) to vapor pressure of the liquid (p_v) at temperature.

Percentage saturation $\equiv$ percent ratio of existing weight of vapor to weight of vapor that would exist if mixture were saturated at temperature and pressure.

Humidity $\equiv$ weight of water per unit weight of moisture-free gas.

Dew point $\equiv$ temperature at which equilibrium vapor pressure of liquid is equal to existing partial pressure of vapor $p_i = p_v$ at $T_{d.p.}$.

Wet-bulb temperature (T_{wb}) $\equiv$ equilibrium temperature attained by a liquid that is vaporizing into a gas.

Dry-bulb temperature (T_{db}) $\equiv$ actual temperature of gas into which water is vaporizing.

For water evaporating into unsaturated air under adiabatic conditions and at constant temperature and pressure, the wet-bulb temperature remains constant throughout the period of evaporation.

Solubility and Crystallization Definitions:

Solute ≡ dispersed solid in a solution (solvent); component to be removed from solution during solvent extraction.

Solubility ≡ concentration of solute in saturated solution.

Eutectic ≡ a solution of eutectic composition solidifies completely at one definite temperature.

Extract ≡ phase that is rich in the extraction solvent.

Raffinate ≡ initial solvent used in solvent extraction.

Crystallization occurs by three different means:

1. *evaporate* some of the pure solvent until the solution becomes super saturated,

2. *lower temperature* of the solution until conditions of super saturation due to lower solubility occur, and

3. change nature of system by *salting* (e.g.:—introduce alcohol to cause crystallization of inorganic salts).

When a solute is added to a system of two immiscible liquids, the solute is distributed between the liquids in such proportion that a definite equilibrium exists between its concentration in the two phases. In dilute solutions the equilibrium distribution is:

$$K_{eq} = \frac{C_e}{C_r}$$

where C_e, C_r ≡ concentrations of solutes in extract and raffinate phases, respectively.

Henry's Law—The equilibrium value of the mole fraction of gas dissolved in a liquid is directly proportional to the partial pressure of that gas above the liquid.

$$y_i = \frac{1}{H} \times p_i$$

where:

$y_i \equiv$ mole fraction of gas

$p_i \equiv$ partial pressure of gas

$H \equiv$ Henry's Law constant

Henry's Law Constant is dependent upon the temperature and gas composition and is in units of atmospheres per mole fraction. Some values of Henry's Law Constants at 25°C are given in the table below.

Gas	Constant atm/mole fraction
Hydrogen	6.7×10^4
Oxygen	4.9×10^4
Nitrogen	9.1×10^4
Carbon Monoxide	5.5×10^2
Carbon Dioxide	1.7×10^2
Methane	4.7×10^4
Ammonia	3.2

Table 2. Henry's Law Constants

Gas Absorption—When material is transferred from one phase to another across an interface that separates the two, the rate of transfer is proportional to the difference between the bulk concentration and the concentration at the interface.

$$N_A = k_l \times (x - x_i) = k_g \times (y_i - y)$$

Rearranging terms:

$$\frac{y_i - y}{x - x_i} = \frac{k_l}{k_g} = \frac{L_M \times H_G}{G_M \times H_L}$$

where:

$N_A \equiv$ mass transfer rate

$k_l, k_g \equiv$ liquid and gas mass transfer coefficients, respectively

x, x_i ≡ bulk and interface liquid mole fractions

y, y_i ≡ bulk and interface gas mole fractions

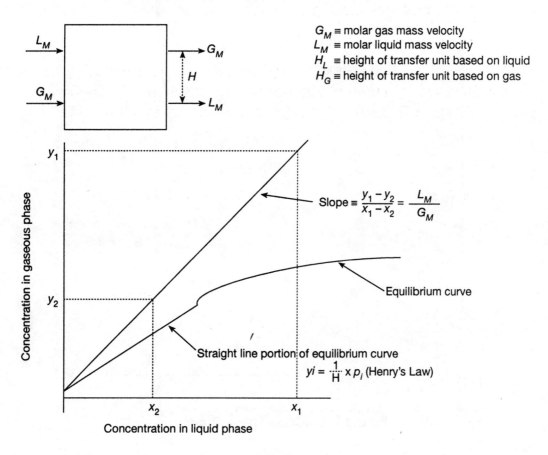

G_M ≡ molar gas mass velocity
L_M ≡ molar liquid mass velocity
H_L ≡ height of transfer unit based on liquid
H_G ≡ height of transfer unit based on gas

Slope ≡ $\dfrac{y_1 - y_2}{x_1 - x_2} = \dfrac{L_M}{G_M}$

Equilibrium curve

Straight line portion of equilibrium curve
$yi = \dfrac{1}{H} \times p_i$ (Henry's Law)

Figure 1

McCabe-Thiele Diagram—Given the operating line for the solution to be distilled, draw an operating line whose slope is:

$$m = \frac{y_{n+1} - y_1}{x_n - x_1}$$

From y_1, step off line parallel to x-axis to point on equilibrium line, then from this point, step off line parallel to y-axis to point on operating line. Repeat until you reach or pass point (x_n, y_{n+1}) on operating line. The number of steps equals the number of stages. This is illustrated in Figure 2.

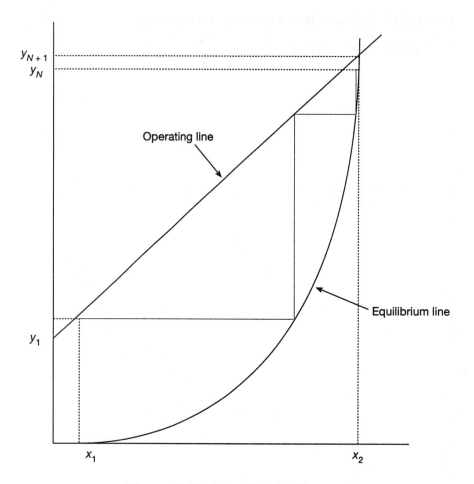

Figure 2. McCabe-Thiele Diagram

DISTILLATION

Raoult's Law—For ideal liquids, the partial pressure (p_i) in the vapor phase is equal to the mole fraction of that component in the liquid phase (x_i) times the vapor pressure of the pure component (p_{vi}) at the same temperature.

$$p_i = x_i \times p_{vi}$$

Dalton's Law—For ideal gases, the partial pressure (p_i) in the vapor phase is equal to the mole fraction of the component (y_i) in the vapor times the total pressure of the system (p_T).

$$p_i = y_i \times p_T$$

Steam Distillation—Vaporization of charge is achieved by injecting live superheated steam directly through it. So long as steam remains superheated:

$$\frac{p_s}{p_T} = \frac{L_s}{L_T}$$

where:

p_s, $p_T \equiv$ are the partial pressure of the superheated steam, and total pressure, respectively

L_s, $L_T \equiv$ moles of steam and total moles, respectively.

PROBLEM 2:

A soap plant purifies its by-product, glycerine, by steam distillation at reduced pressure. The operation is conducted at a temperature of 180°C and 15 kPa pressure. The vapor pressure of glycerine is 2.8 kPa. Data show that a ratio of 1.1 to 1 for weight of steam consumed over the weight of glycerine distilled. What is the percentage of excess actual steam consumption to the theoretical steam requirement?

SOLUTION:

$$p_v = x_i \times p_T = 2.8 \text{ kPa} = x_i \times 15 \text{ kPa} \Rightarrow x_i = \frac{2.8}{15} = 0.187$$

$$p_T = p_s + p_v = 15 \Rightarrow p_s = 15 - 2.8 = 12.2 \text{ kPa}$$

$$x_s = \frac{p_s}{p_T} = \frac{12.2}{15} = 0.813 \text{kg - moles}$$

Thus, for one kg-mole basis:

Steam = 0.813kg-moles $\times$ 18 kg/kg-mole = 14.64 kg

Glycerine = 92 gm/gm-mole $\times$ 0.187 = 17.20 kg

$$\text{kg steam/kg glycerine} = \frac{14.64}{17.2} = 0.85$$

actual steam = 1.1 kg/kg glycerine

$$\text{excess} = \frac{1.1 - 0.85}{0.85} \times 100\% = 29.4\%$$

Simple Continuous Distillation—The feed stream is partially vaporized, and the vapor and liquid portions are continuously withdrawn at such a rate that the level in the still pot remains constant. The vapor-liquid mixture may go to a flash chamber where vapor and liquid portions are continuously removed (Flash Vaporization).

$$F = V + L$$

$$z_F \times F = y \times V + x \times L$$

where:

F, L, and $V \equiv$ moles of feed, liquid, and vapor per unit time, respectively

x, y, and $z_F \equiv$ mole fractions of feed, liquid, and vapor per unit time, respectively

Define equilibrium constant (K_i):

$$K_i = \frac{y_i}{x_i}$$

since

$$x_i = \frac{y_i}{K_i}$$

then

$$y_i = \frac{(1 + L/V) \times z_F}{1 + L/(K_i \times V)}$$

and

$$x_i = \frac{(1 + L/V)}{K_i + L/V}$$

FE/EIT

FE: PM Chemical Engineering Exam

CHAPTER 7

Material and Energy Balances

CHAPTER 7

MATERIAL AND ENERGY BALANCES

MATERIAL AND ENERGY BALANCES

Conversion of Units—In many engineering calculations different units are given for the various numerical values. Usually there is a mix of engineering or British units (e.g., Btus, feet, pounds, °F) and metric units (e.g., calories, meters, kilograms, °C) given. Therefore, these values must be converted to common units. The table below gives some common values for converting engineering units into their metric equivalent.

Engineering Unit	×	Factor	=	Metric Unit
atmosphere (atm)	×	1.0132	=	bar
barrels (bbl)	×	0.159	=	cubic meter (m^3)
Btu	×	0.252	=	kilocalorie (kcal)
cubic feet (ft^3)	×	2.832×10^{-2}	=	cubic meter (m^3)
feet (ft)	×	0.3048	=	meter (m)
foot-pounds (ft-lb)	×	1.3558	=	Joules (J)
gallons (gal)	×	3.7854	=	liters (L)
horsepower (hp)	×	0.7457	=	kilowatts (kW)
pounds (lb)	×	0.454	=	kilogram (kg)
pounds per sq in (lb/in^2)	×	6.895	=	kilopascal (kPa)
pounds per sq in (lb/in^2)	×	6.895×10^{-2}	=	bars
square feet (ft^2)	×	9.29×10^{-2}	=	square meter (m^2)
tons (T)	×	1,106	=	kilograms (kg)

Table 1. Conversion Factors for Engineering to Metric Units

The equation for converting degrees Fahrenheit (°F) to degrees Celsius (°C) is:

$$°C = (°F - 32) \times 0.556$$

and its reciprocal converting degrees Celsius (°C) to degrees Fahrenheit (°F):

$$°F = (1.8 \times °C) + 32$$

Conservation of Mass—In any closed system the quantity of mass remains constant. For problems involving the conservation of mass, it is critical to correctly define the boundaries of the system. Once this is done, a **mass balance** can be developed for that system. In many mass balance problems, the various streams contain more than one component. Thus, to solve these problems it is often necessary to perform mass balances for one of the components in addition to performing an overall mass balance.

PROBLEM 1:

A distillation column is fed 3,000 kg/hr of a mixture containing equal mass fractions of components *A* and *B*. The distillate contains a mixture of 75% component *A*, and the waste stream is a mixture containing 35% of component *A*. What is the flow rate of the distillate in kg/hr?

SOLUTION:

Basis:

3,000 kg/hr feed; let $D \equiv$ distillate stream flow rate and $W \equiv$ waste stream flow rate.

Overall Mass Balance:

$$3,000 = D + W$$
$$W = 3,000 - D$$

Mass Balance for Component *A*:

$$3,000 \times 0.5 = 0.75 \times D + 0.35 \times W$$

Substituting for *W*:

$$1{,}500 = 0.75 \times D + 0.35 \times (3{,}000 - D)$$

$$975 = 0.4 \times D$$

$$D = 2{,}437.5 \text{ kg/hr}$$

Conservation of Energy—In any closed system the total energy will be conserved. That energy may be changed from one form to another such as heat to work, potential to mechanical energy, etc. However, the total energy of the system will remain constant.

PROBLEM 2:

One hundred kilograms of saturated steam at atmospheric pressure is condensed to 50°C and atmospheric pressure. (a) How much heat in kcal can be recovered by the condenser assuming 100% efficiency? (b) If the enthalpy of the steam at the original conditions was $H = 639.1$ cal/gm, what is the enthalpy of the condensed water?

SOLUTION:

(a) For water:

$$\Delta H_{vap} = 538.6 \text{ cal/gm}$$

$$C_p = 1.0 \text{ cal/gm-°C}$$

$$Q = 100 \text{ kg} \times 1{,}000 \text{ gm/kg} \times [538.6 \text{ cal/gm} + (100 - 50)°C \times 1.0 \text{ cal/gm–°C}]$$

$$Q = 58.86 \times 10^6 \text{ cal}$$

$$Q = 58{,}860 \text{ kcal}$$

(b) For conservation of energy, the enthalpy of the steam less the enthalpy of the condensed water will equal the heat recovered in the condenser.

Therefore:

$$58.86 \times 10^6 \text{ cal} = 100 \text{ kg} \times 1{,}000 \text{ gm/kg} \times [639.1 \text{ cal/gm-}H_{cond}]$$

$$H_{cond} = \frac{63.9 \text{ cal/gm} - 58.86 \times 10^6 \text{ cal}}{100 \text{kg} \times 1{,}000 \text{gm/kg}} = 50.5 \text{ cal/gm}$$

$$H_{cond} = 50.5 \text{ cal/gm}$$

Atomic Mass—The atomic mass of an element is a relative measure. It is based on the relative mass of an element with respect to oxygen, which is defined as having 16.000 atomic mass units. The table below lists *atomic weights* for some common elements.

Element	Symbol	Atomic Weight
Aluminum	Al	26.98
Calcium	Ca	40.08
Carbon	C	12.01
Chlorine	Cl	35.45
Copper	Cu	63.55
Hydrogen	H	1.008
Iron	Fe	55.85
Lead	Pb	207.20
Mercury	Hg	200.59
Nitrogen	N	14.01
Oxygen	O	16.000
Phosphorous	P	30.97
Potassium	K	39.10
Sodium	Na	22.99
Silicon	Si	28.09
Sulfur	S	32.06

Table 2. Atomic Weights for Several Elements

Elements combine with one another to form compounds. The atomic weight of these compounds is the sum of the atomic weights of all the atoms that make up those compounds. This weight is called the *molecular weight*.

PROBLEM 3:

Phosphoric acid has the formula H_3PO_4. Therefore, its molecular weight would be:

SOLUTION:

Element	No. of Atoms	×	Atomic Weight	=	Total Atomic Weight
H	3	×	1.008	=	3.008
P	1	×	30.970	=	30.970
O	4	×	16.000	=	64.000
			Molecular Weight	=	97.978

This can be rounded off to 98.

Elemental gases such as hydrogen and oxygen, when not combined with other elements in a compound are represented as double atoms and their atomic, or molecular, weight is twice the atomic weight. Thus, oxygen would be represented as O_2, and therefore has a molecular weight of $2 \times 16 = 32$.

However, compounds made up of elemental gases such as ammonia (NH_3) and hydrogen chloride (HCl) follow the rule for compounds.

$$NH_3 = 1 \times N \times 14.01 + 3 \times H \times 1.008 = 17.034$$
$$HCl = 1 \times H \times 1.008 + 1 \times Cl \times 35.45 = 36.458$$

In many problems, gases can be considered to follow the *Ideal Gas Law*. For this situation at standard conditions of temperature and pressure (1 atmosphere and 0°C), the molecular weight in grams of a gas or mixture of gases will occupy a volume of 22.4 liters. Using this phenomena, one can calculate the density of a gas at standard conditions of temperature and pressure.

PROBLEM 4:

Air is a mixture of 79% nitrogen and 21% oxygen. Assuming air behaves as an ideal gas, what is its density at 1 atmosphere pressure and 0°C?

SOLUTION:

Gas Element	Symbol	Molecular Weight	Volume Percent	Weight
Nitrogen	N_2	28.02	0.79	22.14
Oxygen	O_2	32.00	0.21	6.72
			Molecular Weight	28.86

Thus, a gram molecular weight of air has a mass of 28.86 grams.

$$\text{Density } (\rho) = \frac{28.86 \text{ gm/gm-mole}}{22.4 \text{ liters/gm-mole}} = 1.28 \text{ grams/liter}$$

$$\rho = \frac{1.28 \text{ grams/liter}}{1,000 \text{ cm}^3\text{/liter}} = 0.00128 \text{ grams/cm}^3$$

This value is very close to the published value for the density of air as 1.2929 gm/liter.

Chemical Stoichiometry—This is a method for determining the amount of one component in a reaction from a known amount of another. Solutions obtained by this process consist of the following:

1. The amount of the initial component is converted from the given units to moles,

2. The moles of this component are converted to the required component, and

3. The moles of the required component are converted to the amount in the desired units.

PROBLEM 5:

(a) How many grams of carbon dioxide (CO_2) will be produced by the complete combustion of 100 liters of propane (C_3H_8) assuming ideal gas conditions? (b) For stoichiometric combustion, how many liters of air are required?

SOLUTION:

(a) Basis: 100 liters of propane and the reaction

$$C_3H_8 + 5O_2 \rightarrow 3CO_2 + 4H_2O$$

For an ideal gas, 1 gram mole occupies 22.4 liters; therefore:

$$\frac{100 \text{ liters } C_3H_8}{22.4 \text{ liter/gm-mole}} = 4.646 \text{ gm-mole } C_3H_8$$

In the reaction for each mole of C_3H_8 burned, three moles of CO_2 are produced.

Thus:

$$3 \times 4.646 \text{ gm-moles} = 13.393 \text{ gm-moles of } CO_2 \text{ are produced, and}$$

$$13.393 \text{ gm-mole } CO_2 \times 44 \text{ grams/gram-mole } CO_2 = 589.3 \text{ grams}$$

$$CO_2 \text{ produced} = 589.3 \text{ grams}$$

(b) From the reaction equation we know that 5 moles of oxygen (O_2) are required for each mole of propane (C_3H_8). We calculated that there were 4.646 gm-moles of C_3H_8 in 100 liters.

Thus,

$$5 \times 4.646 \text{ gm-moles} = 23.23 \text{ gm-moles } O_2$$

Air is 21% O_2, so

$$air = \frac{23.23 \text{ gm-moles } O_2}{0.21 \text{ } O_2/air} = 110.62 \text{ gm-moles air}$$

$$22.4 \text{ liters/gm-mole} \times 110.62 \text{ gm-moles air} = 2,478 \text{ liters of air}$$

Recycle Processes—In many processes a portion of one of the streams is recycled to the process. When this occurs the recycle stream does not effect the overall material and energy balance calculations. However, it may be necessary to determine some parameter of that recycle stream as illustrated in the example below.

PROBLEM 6:

In the block flow diagram below, new material (N) is supplied to a process along with recycled material (R) to give a total feed stream (F) to the process. The R stream is from the bottom stream (B) and is 10% of that quantity while the waste stream (W) is 90% of the quantity. Product (P) leaves the process overhead. The N stream has a composition of 60% A and 40% B, the product stream (P) has a composition of 95% A and the waste stream has a composition of 20% A. What is the percent composition of A in the feed (F) stream?

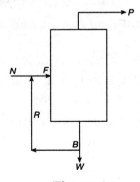

Figure 1

SOLUTION:

The key point is that the composition of R is the same as W.

Basis: 1 gm-mole of N

Overall Balance: $N = P + W$

Balance for A: $0.6 \times N = 0.95 \times P + (1 - P) \times 0.2$

$$P = \frac{0.6 \times N - 0.2}{0.75} = 0.8 \times N - 0.2667$$

For $N = 1$ gm-mole: $P = 0.5333$

Therefore:

$$W = 1 - 0.5333 = 0.4667$$
$$R = 0.1 \times B = B - W = B - 0.4667$$
$$0.9 \times B = 0.4667$$
$$B = \frac{0.4667}{0.9} = 0.5186$$
$$R = 0.1 \times B = 0.1 \times 0.5186 = 0.05186$$
$$F = N + R = 1 + 0.05186$$
$$F = 1.05186$$

Percent of A in $R = 0.2 \times R$

$$0.2 \times 0.05186 = 0.0104$$

A in $N = 0.6$

$$\text{percent } A \text{ in } F = \frac{0.6 + 0.0104}{1.05186} = \frac{0.6104}{1.05186} = 0.5803$$
$$\text{percent } A \text{ in } F = 58 \text{ percent}$$

Orsat Analysis—An Orsat Analyzer determines the volumetric analyses of flue gases formed by combustion in a boiler furnace. The gases measured are carbon dioxide (CO_2), carbon monoxide (CO), and oxygen (O_2). Nitrogen in the flue gas is determined by difference in the total mass and mass of the other three flue gases. From an Orsat analysis, the mass of excess air can be calculated by the following:

$$\text{percent air}_{\text{xsr}} = \frac{O_2 - 0.5CO}{0.264 \times N_2 - (O_2 - 0.5 \times CO)} \times 100 \text{ percent}$$

PROBLEM 7:

(a) From the following Orsat analysis of a flue gas: $CO_2 = 11.1\%$, $CO = 0.6\%$, $N_2 = 80.5\%$, and $O_2 = 7.8\%$, calculate the percent excess air. (b) Assuming 100 gm-mole of dry flue gas and complete combustion, how many gram-moles of carbon are in the fuel?

SOLUTION:

(a) This is a straightforward application of the formula given.

$$\text{percent air}_{\text{xs}} = \frac{0.078 - (0.5 \times .006)}{(0.264 \times .805) - [0.078 - (0.5 \times .006)]} \times 100 \text{ percent}$$

$$= \frac{0.075}{0.2125 - 0.075} \times 100 \text{ percent}$$

$$\text{percent air}_{\text{xs}} = 54.55 \text{ percent}$$

(b)

$$C + O_2 \rightarrow CO_2 \text{ and } C + \frac{1}{2}O_2 \rightarrow CO$$

are the governing reactions. For every mole of CO_2 and CO, one mole each of C is burned; therefore, based on 100 gm-moles of flue gas:

$$C \text{ from } CO_2 = 11.1 \text{ gm-mole}$$
$$C \text{ from } CO = 0.6 \text{ gm-mole}$$
$$Total \ C = 11.7 \text{ gm-mole}$$

Another type of problem gives the wet flue gas composition and asks for the composition of the fuel. This is done by using the mole basis of the flue gas and the fact that volumetric percent is equivalent to mole percent assuming ideal gas behavior.

PROBLEM 8:

Analysis of a wet flue gas gives the following: $CO_2 = 10.16\%$, $CO =$

0.78%, N_2 = 74.06%, H_2O = 12.5%, and O_2 = 2.5%. What is the carbon-to-hydrogen ratio of the fuel?

SOLUTION:

Basis: 100 gm-mole of flue gas

Flue gas	Vol. percent	Gm-mole
N_2	74.06	74.06
H_2O	12.50	12.50
CO_2	10.16	10.16
O_2	1.60	1.60
CO	0.78	0.78
	TOTAL	100.00

The gram-moles of C in the fuel are equal to the sum of the gram-moles of CO_2 and CO. The gram-moles of H in the fuel are equal to twice the gram-moles of H_2O. Thus,

$$C \text{ in fuel} = 10.16 + 0.78 = 10.94 \text{ gm-moles}$$

$$H \text{ in fuel} = 12.5 \times 2 = 25.0$$

The carbon-to-hydrogen ratio of the fuel is therefore:

$$C{:}H = \frac{10.94}{25.0} = 0.4376$$

If one were told this was a simple alkane hydrocarbon, then, a trial and error would yield:

$$\frac{C}{H} = \frac{7}{16} = 0.4375$$

which is the formula for heptane C_7H_{16}.

Combined Material and Energy Balances—Often problems involve both energy and material balances. In solving these, care must be taken to ensure that the material as well as the energy balances are correctly defined.

PROBLEM 9:

The coal gasification process depicted in the block flow diagram takes coal, heats it to drive off the volatile compounds, and reacts the resultant char (C) with steam (H_2O) to produce synthesis gas ($CO + H_2$) according to the reaction:

$$C + H_2O \rightarrow CO + H_2$$

The synthesis gas is reacted with a catalyst to produce methane according to the reaction:

$$CO + 3H_2 \rightarrow CH_4 + H_2O$$

To achieve the proper H_2 to CO ratio to produce methane (CH_4), a portion of the CO is removed. The volatile compounds are purified as a separate stream removing the sulfur compounds, carbon dioxide and amines as by-products. Ash residue from the coal is removed as waste.

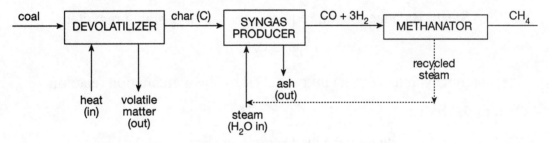

Figure 2

(a) Given 1,000 kg/hr of coal with the following analysis: fixed Carbon = 72%, volatile matter = 15%, moisture = 4%, and ash = 9%, how much steam in kilograms per hour is required to convert the fixed carbon assuming 100% conversion of the char? (b) What is the production of methane in liters/hr assuming 90% of the fixed carbon is converted? (c) How much steam in kilograms/hr is recycled from the methanator to the syngas reactor and how much new steam must be fed to the syngas reactor? (d) If the higher heating value of the coal is 7,000 kcal/kg and the higher heating value of the methane is 8.9 kcal/liter, compare the energy in the methane produced to the energy in coal fed. (e) Assume the heat required to volatilize the coal is 2,000 kcal/kg and the steam fed to the syngas reactor has an enthalpy of 720 kcal/kg. Excluding the energy value of the by-products, what is the overall energy efficiency of this process?

SOLUTION:

(a) C in $= 1,000$ kg/hr $\times 0.72$: $\dfrac{1,000 \text{ kg/hr} \times 0.72}{12 \text{ kg/kg-mole}} = 60$ kg-moles/hr of C

One mole of steam is required for each mole of char (C):

mass of steam $= 60$ kg-moles/hr $\times 18$ kg/kg-moles $= 1,080$ kg/hr

(b) The steam produces the H_2 for the methane on a mole for mole basis; and it takes 3 moles of H_2 to produce one mole of CH_4; thus:

moles of $CH_4 = 0.333 \times$ moles of steam $\times 90\% = 0.333 \times 60$ kg-moles/hr

$\times 0.9$ moles of $CH_4 = 18$ kg-moles/hr $= 18,000$ gm-moles/hr

volume of $CH_4 = 18,000$ gm-moles/hr $\times 22.4$ liters/gm-mole $= 403,200$ liters/hr

(c) Steam Balance: Steam required = steam fed–steam recycled

$$1,080 = F - R$$

The steam recycled is the steam produced by the methanation reaction. On a molar basis:

steam produced = methane produced

moles of CH_4 produced = moles of steam produced = 18 kg-moles/hr

steam recycled $= 18$ kg-moles/hr $\times$ 18 kg/kg-moles $= 324$ kgs/hr

steam fed = steam required–steam recycled

steam fed $= 1,080$ kgs/hr–324 kgs/hr $= 756$ kgs

(d) energy in coal:

$1,000$ kg $\times 7,000$ kcal/kg $= 7.00 \times 10^6$ kcal

energy in CH_4:

$403,200$ liters $\times 8.9$ kcal/liter $= 3.58 \times 10^6$ kcal

(e) Energy in $= 7 \times 10^6$ kcal $+ 2,000$ kcal/kg $\times 1,000$ kg $+ 720$ kcal/kg $\times 756$ kg

Energy in $= 9.54 \times 10^6$ kcal

$$\eta = \frac{\text{energy out}}{\text{energy in}} \times 100\% = \frac{3.58 \times 10^6 \, \text{kcal}}{9.54 \times 10^6 \, \text{kcal}} \times 100\% = 37.5\%$$

overall process energy efficiency = 37.5%

FE/EIT

FE: PM Chemical Engineering Exam

CHAPTER 8

Pollution Prevention

CHAPTER 8

POLLUTION PREVENTION

POLLUTION PREVENTION

Air Pollution—Removing air pollutants usually requires employing one of three processes:

1. scrubbing,

2. filtration, and/or

3. adsorption.

SCRUBBERS

Scrubbers are wet collection devices. There are several types of scrubbers:

> *Spray chambers*—The gas stream is impinged with water sprayed from nozzles which wet the entrained particulate matter. The gas velocity decreases as it enters the chamber and the wetted particles settle by gravity to the bottom and are removed.

> *Cyclones*—The gas stream enters all cyclones tangentially and leaves axially. The centrifugal force exerted on the gas stream causes the particles to be thrown to the interior wall; sometimes

water sprays are introduced to wet these particles making them easier to remove.

Mechanical—The water spray is generated in a restricted passage by a rotating element like a disc or drum. The restriction causes extreme turbulence enhancing contact between the particulate matter and the water.

Venturi—The gas stream is passed through a venturi tube to which water has been injected at the throat. There is an extreme pressure drop and increase in velocity of the gas stream at the throat which promotes contact between the particles and the water.

Concentration of Pollutants—In many engineering applications, the concentration of pollutants, whether they be gaseous, liquid or solid, are given in parts per million (ppm). Parts per million can be by volume or weight and the designation would be ppm_V and ppm_W respectively. The two concentrations are related by the density of the pollutant and the density of air. In most cases the concentration is based on volume (ppm_V). To obtain this value, the volume of the pollutant substance is divided by the volume it is contained within and multiplied by 1,000,000 or 10^6.

PROBLEM 1:

One gram of a substance with a density of 0.5 gm/liter is injected into a 50 cubic meter volume of air. (a) What is the concentration of this substance in parts per million by volume (ppm_V)? (b) Suppose we wanted the concentration in ppm_W? Use $\rho_{air} = 1.29$ gm/liter.

SOLUTION:

(a) First find the volume of the substance:

$$V = \frac{1 \text{ gm}}{0.5 \text{ gm/liter}} = 2 \text{ liters}$$

Concentration is therefore:

$$\text{conc. } ppm_V = \frac{2 \text{ liters}}{50 \text{ m}^3 \times 1,000 \text{ liter/m}^3} \times 10^6 = 40 ppm_V$$

(b) Mass of volume of air:

$$50 \text{ m}^3 \times 1,000 \text{ liter/m}^3 \times 1.29 \text{ gm/liter} = 64,500 \text{ gm}$$

$$\text{conc. ppm}_W = \frac{1 \text{ gm}}{64,500 \text{ gm}} \times 10^6 = 15.5 \text{ ppm}_W$$

Like all matter, waste streams come in three phases: gaseous, liquid, and solid. Minimizing or disposing of these waste streams are problems encountered by chemical engineers in all industries. What distinguishes pollution prevention problems is that the streams often contain all three phases of matter. For example, air pollution problems involve removing solid particulate matter, liquid droplets, and unwanted gases in the air. Wastewater contains unwanted solids as well as liquids and dissolved gases that must be separated and disposed of.

Exhaust Hoods—These are devices often located in work areas such as a laboratory or production rooms that prevent pollutants and contaminants from escaping the work area. This is accomplished by creating a controlled air velocity across the open area of the hood which removes the contaminants through the hood. When the process is partially enclosed, the control velocity is the average velocity through the open hood face. Control velocities *(u)* of between 0.5 and 0.75 meters/second are adequate to control contaminants for most applications. The relationship among suction opening face area *(A),* total exhaust volume rate *(Q),* and velocity *(u)* at a distance *(x)* along the centerline from the suction opening is given by:

$$u = \frac{Q}{(10x + A)}$$

Most situations require that you determine the suction opening face area *(A),* therefore:

$$A = \frac{Q - (10ux)}{u}$$

PROBLEM 2:

A laboratory hood located on the far wall in a square room with a floor area of 100 m^2 and a height of 3 meters requires 12 air changes per minute. Given a control velocity of 0.55 m/sec at the door to the room on the opposite side of the laboratory hood, what is the suction opening face area required?

SOLUTION:

First find the total volume of the room:

$$V_{room} = 100 \text{ m}^2 \times 3 \text{ m} = 300 \text{ m}^3$$

Using the 12 air changes per minute, calculate the total exhaust volume rate Q:

$$Q = 300 \text{ m}^3 \times 12 \text{ min}^{-1} = 3,600 \text{ m}^3/\text{min}$$

$$\Rightarrow Q = \frac{3,600 \text{ m}^3/\text{hr}}{60 \text{ sec/min}} = 60 \text{ m}^3/\text{sec}$$

This is a square room, so that:

$$x = (100 \text{ m}^2)^{1/2} = 10 \text{ m}$$

$$\text{Area} = \frac{60 \text{ m}^3/\text{sec} - [10 \times 0.55 \text{ m/sec} \times 10 \text{ m}]}{0.55 \text{ m/sec}}$$

$$= \frac{5 \text{ m}^3/\text{sec}}{0.55 \text{ m/sec}} = 9.1 \text{ m}^2$$

Cyclones—These devices are inertial separators without moving parts. They separate particulate matter from a gas stream by transforming the velocity of that stream into a double vortex confined within the cyclone. The gas stream spirals downward at the outside and then spirals upward on the inside of the cyclone outlet. Because of inertia and centrifugal forces, the

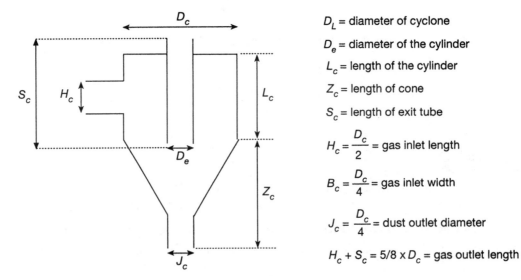

D_L = diameter of cyclone

D_e = diameter of the cylinder

L_c = length of the cylinder

Z_c = length of cone

S_c = length of exit tube

$H_c = \dfrac{D_c}{2}$ = gas inlet length

$B_c = \dfrac{D_c}{4}$ = gas inlet width

$J_c = \dfrac{D_c}{4}$ = dust outlet diameter

$H_c + S_c = 5/8 \times D_c$ = gas outlet length

Figure 1. Schematic Diagram of Cyclone

particles move to the outside wall and downward. A typical cyclone is depicted schematically in Figure 1.

The 50 percent particle cut size for a cyclone is given by:

$$D_{50\%} = \sqrt{\frac{9 \times \mu \times b}{2 \times N \times u_i \times (\rho_p - \rho_g) \times \pi}}$$

where:

$\mu \equiv$ viscosity (gm/cm-sec)

$b \equiv$ cyclone inlet width (cm)

$N \equiv$ effective turns within the cyclone

$u_i \equiv$ inlet gas velocity (cm/sec)

$\rho_p \equiv$ particle density (gm/cm^3)

$\rho_g \equiv$ gas density (gm/cm^3)

PROBLEM 3:

Calculate the 50 percent particle cut size in microns (μm) for a cyclone with 7 effective turns, an inlet width of 40 cm, and an inlet gas velocity of 1,000 cm/sec. The gas is air with a viscosity of 0.0185 gm/cm-sec and density of 0.001 gm/cm^3, and the specific gravity of the particulate matter is 1.5.

SOLUTION:

This is a straightforward problem. One must convert the specific gravity of the particulate matter to density.

$$\rho_p = 1.5 \times 1.0 \text{ gm/cm}^3 = 1.5 \text{ gm/cm}^3$$

$$D_{50\%} = \sqrt{\frac{9 \times 0.185 \text{ gm/cm-sec} \times 40 \text{ cm}}{2 \times 7 \times 1,000 \text{ cm/sec} \times (1.5 - 0.001) \text{ gm/cm}^3 \times 3.14}}$$

$$D_{50\%} = \sqrt{\frac{6.66 \text{ gm/sec}}{65,929 \text{ gm/cm}^2 - \text{sec}}}$$

$$D_{50\%} = [0.0001 \text{ cm}^2]^{1/2} = 0.01 \text{ cm}$$

$$D_{50\%} = 0.01 \text{ cm} \times 10^4 \mu\text{m/cm} = 100 \ \mu\text{m}$$

FILTRATION

Filtration—For gas filtration the filter media are prepared from fibers, aggregates, or porous substances. The media can be natural or synthetic. There are several types of filters:

Fabric or Bag Filters — used to control harmful emissions,

Fibrous Mat Filters — used in HVAC applications and as aftercleaners,

Packed Bed — aggregate filters that can operate either wet or dry, often employed to remove mists and dusts from gas streams, and

Porous Media Filters — soft or rigid and are used for high temperature gas streams.

Three key parameters for evaluating the performance of a filter are *pressure loss*, *collection efficiency,* and *lifetime*.

Sulfur Removal and Recovery—Sulfur in fuels, primarily coal, but also in fuel oils, is converted to sulfur dioxide (SO_2) at combustion temperatures. Most of the sulfur removal processes in the U.S. use some method of *flue-gas desulfurization* (FGD). In these processes, the sulfur dioxide (SO_2) is removed by a wet scrubbing process. The sulfur dioxide is reacted with either calcium, sodium, or magnesium carbonate. In the case of calcium carbonate ($CaCO_3$) or limestone, the SO_2 is converted to calcium sulfite ($CaSO_3$) according to the reaction:

$$CaCO_3 + SO_2 \rightarrow CaSO_3 + CO_2$$

Flue-gas desulfurization processes can be classified as noted in Figure 2. For the non-regenerative processes, the final products are sulfur salts of calcium and magnesium. For regenerative processes, the reactant used is recovered and used again. The final product from the flue-gas desulfurization processes is either elemental sulfur or sulfuric acid.

	Dry	**Wet**
Non-regenerative		Wet Limestone
Regenerative	Foster-Wheeler	Wellman-Lord

Figure 2

This is accomplished by the following reactions:

| Regeneration: | $CaSO_3 + CO_2 \rightarrow CaCO_3 + SO_2$ |

| Oxidation: | $SO_2 + \dfrac{1}{2}O_2 \rightarrow SO_3$ |

| Hydrolysis: | $SO_3 + H_2O \rightarrow H_2SO_4$ |

| Reduction: | $SO_2 + 2H_2 \rightarrow S + 2H_2O$ |

Another method of sulfur removal involves the recovery of sulfur from large power plants or coal gasification facilities. The *Claus Process* takes sulfur in the form of hydrogen sulfide and reacts it catalytically with sulfur dioxide to form sulfur according to the reaction:

$$2H_2S + SO_2 \rightarrow 3S + 2H_2O$$

PROBLEM 4:

(a) Coal containing 2% sulfur is burned at a power plant. Assume that the firing rate is 10,000 kg/hr and that 95% of the sulfur exits the stack gas as SO_2. How much limestone ($CaCO_3$) in kg/hr is required to remove this sulfur assuming 90% conversion efficiency? (b) If the $CaCO_3$ is regenerated, how many liters per hour of CO_2 must be reacted assuming 85% process efficiency?

SOLUTION:

(a) Basis: 10,000 kg/hr coal with 2% sulfur and 95% conversion to SO_2 (M.W. = 64):

$$SO_2 = 10,000 \text{ kg/hr} \times 0.02 \times 0.95 = 190 \text{ kg/hr}$$

$$\text{kg-moles of } SO_2 = \frac{190 \text{ kg/hr}}{64 \text{ kg/kg-mole}} = 2.97 \text{ kg-mole/hr}$$

one kg-mole of $CaCO_3$ will remove one mole of SO_2 at 100% conversion; at 90% this is:

$$\frac{1}{0.9} \times 2.97 \text{ kg-mole/hr} = 3.3 \text{ kg-mole/hr}$$

$CaCO_3$ has a M.W. of 100, thus

$$CaCO_3 = 3.3 \text{ kg-mole/hr} \times 100 \text{ kg/kg-mole} = 330 \text{ kg/hr}$$

(b) One mole of CO_2 is required to regenerate 1 mole of $CaCO_3$, but at 85% efficiency this is:

$$\frac{1}{0.85} \times 3.3 \,\text{kg-mole/hr}\ CO_2 = 3.88 \,\text{kg-mole/hr}$$

Volume of CO_2 = 3.88 kg-mole/hr × 1,000 gm/kg × 22.4 liter/gm-mole

= 86,965 liters/hr

SOLID WASTE MANAGEMENT

Solid wastes pose problems for the chemical industry almost as much as air pollution. Reducing the amount of solid waste generated is the first option and involves improving process efficiencies. However, a certain amount of solid waste material is inevitable. To dispose of this there are only two options: burn it *(incineration)* or bury it *(landfilling)*.

Incineration—The process of incineration is the thermal destruction of a volume of solid waste while producing inoffensive stack gases and a sterile residue of ash. More simply, incineration is combustion of the solid waste stream. An effective incinerator can reduce the volume of solid waste by 90% to 95%. Sometimes there is enough energy contained in the solid waste to support its own combustion. In cooling the by-products of combustion, the incineration process can produce steam which can be recovered and used in boilers or to drive turbines. Incineration can also be used to destroy hazardous waste streams, both liquid and solid.

Landfilling—Solid waste is buried under controlled conditions in sanitary landfills. This is the method most often used to dispose of municipal solid wastes (MSW). Because the waste is mostly organic and its burial deprives it of air or oxygen, the material decomposes anaerobically to produce methane (CH_4) and carbon dioxide (CO_2). The design, operation, and maintenance of sanitary landfills are usually the purview of Civil Engineering. However, in the past 20 years recovering the anaerobically produced gases from landfills has gained in popularity. This process involves Chemical Engineering principles. Control of methane migration in landfills in the U.S. is dictated by the Resource Conservation and Recovery Act (RCRA).

Landfill Gas Recovery—The decomposing refuse in landfills produces a gas mixture which ranges from 45%-55% methane. The remaining gas is primarily carbon dioxide with some water vapor and trace amounts of sulfur compounds, particularly hydrogen sulfide (H_2S). Chemically the decomposition proceeds approximately as follows:

$$(C_6H_{10}O_5)_n + nH_2O \rightarrow 3nCH_4 + 3nCO_2$$

Thus, landfill gas is a mixture of CH_4 and CO_2 in approximately equal volumes. Research sponsored by the Gas Research Institute (GRI) found that the range of landfill gas that can be produced annually per ton-in-place of refuse was between 80 SCF and 120 SCF per ton. In metric units the average would be:

100 std ft^3/ton-yr $\times$ 28.32 liter/ft^3 $\times$ 1.102 $\times$ 10^{-3} ton/kg = 3.12 liter/kg-yr

Not all landfills are technically or economically feasible for recovery. The key parameters for exploiting a landfill for energy recovery are:

- Greater than 900×10^6 kilograms,

- Minimum area of 120,000 square meters,

- Minimum depth of refuse at nine meters, and

- Two to five years of additional disposal life.

For purposes of estimating the mass of refuse in a landfill, a refuse density of 0.475 grams per cubic centimeter is used. The landfill gas recovered can be used in one of three ways:

1. Burned as a medium-Btu (4.5 kcal/liter) gas without treatment,

2. Upgraded to high-Btu (9.0 kcal/liter) gas by removing the CO_2, and

3. Burned as a medium-Btu gas to generate electricity.

The landfill gas recovery process includes vertical extraction wells, a pump or blower, and piping to connect the wells to the pump or blower. Care must be taken when installing the wells not to disturb the anaerobic conditions by introducing air into the covered and packed organic waste. A *radius of influence* is defined for the extraction well as the distance within which all gas is drawn to the well, and that no gas is drawn to the well from a distance greater than the radius of influence. Using this concept the flow rate in liters /minute to an individual well can be estimated according to the following:

$$Q_{well} = \frac{6.944 \times 10^{-7} \times R^2 \times t \times \rho \times G}{C}$$

where:

$R \equiv$ radius of influence (m)

$t \equiv$ refuse layer thickness (m)

$\rho \equiv$ refuse density (kg/m^3)

$G \equiv$ methane production rate (ml/kg-day)

$C \equiv$ fractional methane concentration in gas

The units of 6.944×10^{-7} are day-liter/ml-min.

For a series of extraction wells that overlap, the radius of influence would be one-half the inter-well distance.

PROBLEM 5:

A landfill has the following parameters: total refuse in-place = 10^8 kg, spread out over an area of 160,000 m^2, with an average depth of refuse of 12 m. (a) How many cubic meters (m^3) of methane could theoretically be recovered from this landfill annually? (b) Assume the landfill is a perfect square and 25 extraction wells are installed to recover the methane which is 50% of the landfill gas. What is the flow rate of landfill gas through one of these wells in liter/min?

SOLUTION:

(a) There are 10^8 kg of refuse from which an average 3.12 liter/kg-yr of methane can be produced, therefore:

$$\text{CH}_4 \text{ produced} = \frac{10^8 \text{kg} \times 3.12 \text{ liter/kg-yr}}{1,000 \text{ liters /m}^3} = 312,000 \text{ m}^3/\text{yr}$$

(b) For a perfect square of 160,000 m^2, each side is:

$$s = \sqrt{160,000\text{m}^2} = 400 \text{ m}$$

The 25 wells would be spaced 5×5 at a distance of:

$$R = \frac{400 \text{ m}}{5} = 80 \text{ m}$$

However actual radius of influence is half $R = 40$ m:

$$Q_{well} = \frac{\left(\begin{array}{l} 6.944 \times 10^{-7} \text{ da-l/ml-min} \times (40 \text{ m})^2 \times \\ (15 \text{ m}) \times (475 \text{ kg/m}^3) \times (3.12 \text{ l/kg-yr}) \end{array}\right)}{0.5}$$

$$Q_{well} = \frac{49.4 \text{ da-liter}^2/\text{ml-min-yr}}{365 \text{ da/yr}} \times 1,000 \text{ ml/liter}$$

$$= 135.3 \text{ liters/min}$$

FE/EIT

FE: PM Chemical Engineering Exam

CHAPTER 9

Process Control

CHAPTER 9

PROCESS CONTROL

INTRODUCTION

The area of process control relates to the modeling, analysis, and control of chemical processes. The complete, scientific procedure implemented when assessing a system can be summarized in three basic steps:

1. The development of a mathematical representation of the real process,

2. The application of design techniques and mathematical formulae to the proposed model, and

3. The interpretation of the mathematical results, with special care taken to determine the results' implications concerning the overall character of the real system, i.e., stability during response.

The primary directive of process control is to achieve an acceptable stable response. This requires the system to reject disturbances while being sensitive to setpoint changes. However, both requirements can only be met if a compromise is made between the specific response characteristics for the disturbance and the setpoint responses.

LAPLACE TRANSFORM

Usually, the governing equation that defines the behavior of output process variables as related to process inputs is a linear constant coefficient differential equation (LCCDE). In the area of process control, the

Laplace transform is a useful tool that reduces the solution of these relationships to simple algebra. This can be shown as follows:

Let $f(t)$ be a function of t for $t > 0$. Therefore, the Laplace transform of $f(t)$ denoted by $L\{f(t)\}$ is defined by:

$$L\{f(t)\} = f(s) = \int e^{-st} x f(t) dt$$

The Laplace transform of $f(t)$ is said to exist if the above integral converges for some value of s. The following table lists the Laplace transforms of some very common functions.

$f(t)$	$L\{f(t)\}$
$\delta(t)$ (unit impulse at $t = 0$)	1
$u(t)$ (unit step at $t = 0$)	$\dfrac{1}{s}$
$tu(t)$ (unit ramp at $t = 0$)	$\dfrac{1}{s^2}$
t^n (n is a positive integer)	$\dfrac{n!}{s^{n+1}}$
$e^{-\alpha t}$	$\dfrac{1}{s+\alpha}$
$te^{-\alpha t}$	$\dfrac{1}{(s+\alpha)^2}$
$e^{-\alpha t} \sin\beta t$	$\dfrac{\beta}{(s+\alpha)^2 + \beta^2}$
$e^{-\alpha t} \cos\beta t$	$\dfrac{(s+\alpha)}{(s+\alpha)^2 + \beta^2}$
$L\{(f^{(n)}(t))\}$ (n^{th} derivative)	$-f^{n-1}(0) - sf^{n-2}(0)...s^{n-1}f(0) + s^n F(s)$
$\displaystyle\int_0^t f(u)du$	$\dfrac{1}{s}F(s)$

$$t\,f(t) \qquad\qquad -\frac{dF}{ds}$$

$$\frac{1}{t}f(t) \qquad\qquad \int_0^\infty F(u)\,du$$

Table 1. Laplace Transforms of Common Functions

PROBLEM 1:

Find $y(t) = H(t)u(t)$ for the following equation:

$$\dddot{y} = \ddot{y} + 5\dot{y} + 3y + \dot{u} + 2u$$
$$y(0) = \dot{y}(0) = \ddot{y}(0) = 0$$
$$u(0) = \dot{u}(0) = 0$$

SOLUTION:

Step #1: Put the differential equation in standard format.

$$\dddot{y} - \ddot{y} - 5\dot{y} - 3y = \dot{u} + 2u$$

Step #2: Take the Laplace transform of both sides of the equation.

$$[s^3 Y(s) - \ddot{y}(0) - s\dot{y}(0) - s^2 y(0)] - [s^2 Y(s) - \dot{y}(0) - sy(0)] - 5[sY(s) - y(0)] - 3Y(s)$$
$$= [sU(s) - u(0)] + 2U(s)$$

Step #3: Use initial conditions and algebra to solve for $H(s)$.

$$[s^3 - s^2 - 5s - 3]Y(s) = [s + 2]\,U(s)$$

$$H(s) = \frac{Y(s)}{U(s)} = \frac{s+2}{s^3 - s^2 - 5s - 3}$$

Step #4: Use partial fraction expansion to simplify transfer function.

$$\frac{s+2}{s^3 - s^2 - 5s - 3} = \frac{s+2}{(s-3)(s+1)^2} = \frac{A}{(s-3)} + \frac{B}{(s+1)} + \frac{C}{(s+1)}$$

at:

$$s = 3,\ \ 5 = A(4)^2 \Rightarrow A = \frac{5}{16}$$

at:

$$s = -1, \ 1 = C(-4) \Rightarrow C = -\frac{1}{4}$$

at:

$$s = 0, \ \frac{(2)}{(-3)} = \frac{5/16}{(-3)} + \frac{B}{(1)} + \frac{-1/4}{(1)}$$

$$B = \frac{-32 + 5 + 12}{48} = -\frac{15}{48} = -\frac{5}{16}$$

$$H(s) = \frac{(5/16)}{(s-3)} + \frac{(-5/16)}{(s+1)} + \frac{(-1/4)}{(s+1)^2}$$

Step #5: Take inverse Laplace transform of $H(s)$ to get $H(t)$.

$$H(t) = \left(\frac{5}{16}\right)e^{3t} - \left(\frac{5}{16}\right)e^{-t} - \left(\frac{1}{4}\right)te^{-t}$$

$$y(t) = H(t)u(t) = \left\{\left(\frac{5}{16}\right)e^{3t} - \left(\frac{5}{16}\right)e^{-t} - \left(\frac{1}{4}\right)te^{-t}\right\} u(t)$$

PROBLEM 2:

Find $y(t)$ for the following equation:

$$\ddot{y} + 4\dot{y} + 13y = e^{-t}$$
$$y(0) = \dot{y}(0) = 0$$

SOLUTION:

Step #1: Take the Laplace transform of both sides of the equation.

$$[s^2 Y(s) - \dot{y}(0) - sy(0)] + 4[sY(s) - y(0)] + 13Y(s) = \frac{1}{s+1}$$

Step #2: Use initial conditions and algebra to solve for $Y(s)$.

$$[s^2 + 4s + 13] Y(s) = \frac{1}{s+1}$$

$$Y(s) = \frac{1}{(s+1)(s+2+3j)(s+2-3j)}$$

Step #3: Use partial fraction expansion to simplify transfer function.

$$\frac{1}{(s+1)(s+2+3j)(s+2-3j)} = \frac{A}{(s+1)} + \frac{B_1 + C_1 j}{(s+2+3j)} + \frac{B_2 C_2 j}{(s+2-3j)}$$

at:

$$s = -1, \ 1 = A(10) \Rightarrow A = \frac{1}{10}$$

at:

$$s = -2 - 3j, \ 1 = (B_1 + C_1 j)(-1 - 3j)(-6j) \Rightarrow B_1 + C_1 j = -\frac{1}{20} - \frac{1}{60}j$$

at:

$$s = -2 + 3j, \ 1 = (B_2 + C_2 j)(-1 + 3j)(+6j) \Rightarrow B_2 + C_2 j = -\frac{1}{20} + \frac{1}{60}j$$

$$Y(s) = \frac{\left(\frac{1}{10}\right)}{(s+1)} + \frac{\left(-\frac{1}{20} - \frac{1}{60}j\right)}{(s+2+3j)} + \frac{\left(-\frac{1}{20} + \frac{1}{60}j\right)}{(s+2-3j)}$$

Step #4: Use algebra to rearrange $Y(s)$'s complex terms into recognizable form.

$$Y(s) = \frac{\left(\frac{1}{10}\right)}{(s+1)} + \frac{\left(-\frac{1}{20} - \frac{1}{60}j\right)}{(s+2+3j)} + \frac{\left(-\frac{1}{20} + \frac{1}{60}j\right)}{(s+2-3j)}$$

$$= \frac{\left(\frac{1}{10}\right)}{s+1} + \frac{-\frac{s}{20} - \frac{sj}{60} + \frac{7j}{60} - \frac{6}{60} - \frac{s}{20} + \frac{sj}{60} - \frac{7j}{60} - \frac{4}{20}}{(s+2)^2 + (3)^2}$$

$$= \frac{\left(\frac{1}{10}\right)}{s+1} + \frac{-\frac{s}{10} - \frac{18}{60}}{(s+2)^2 + (3)^2}$$

$$= \frac{\left(\frac{1}{10}\right)}{s+1} + \frac{\left(-\frac{1}{10}\right)(s+2)}{(s+2)^2 + (3)^2} + \frac{\left(-\frac{1}{30}\right)(3)}{(s+2)^2 + (3)^2}$$

Step #5: Take inverse Laplace transform of $Y(s)$ to get $y(t)$.

$$y(t) = \left(\frac{1}{10}\right)e^{-t} - \left(\frac{1}{10}\right)e^{-2t}\cos(3t) - \left(\frac{1}{30}\right)e^{-2t}\sin(3t)$$

BLOCK DIAGRAMS

Linear time-invariant systems are commonly represented as a network of blocks. In the simplest system—one input and one output, one can relate the two quantities with a block diagram as in the figure below:

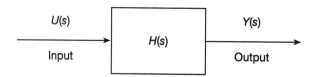

Figure 1

The general "black boxes" that relate the various system quantities represent transfer functions, e.g., $H(s)$. $H(s)$ can always be expressed as the ratio of two polynomials in the form of

$$\frac{Y(s)}{U(s)} = H(s) = \frac{M(s)}{N(s)} = k\frac{\prod\limits_{m=1}^{M}(s - z_m)}{\prod\limits_{n=1}^{N}(s - p_n)}$$

where the M zeros, z_m, and the N poles, p_n, are the roots of the numerator polynomial, $M(s)$, and the denominator polynomial, $N(s)$, respectively.

In general, transfer functions relate the system output $\{Y(s)\}$ to your input $\{U(s)\}$ and any number of process disturbances $\{D(s)\}$. This relationship is expressed as:

$$Y(s) = H(s) \times U(s) + G_d(s) \times D(s)$$

where $G_d(s)$ is the transfer function relating the process output to the process disturbance.

In even the most basic block diagrams, the output is "fed back" to the system; this creates what is termed a "closed-loop" system model:

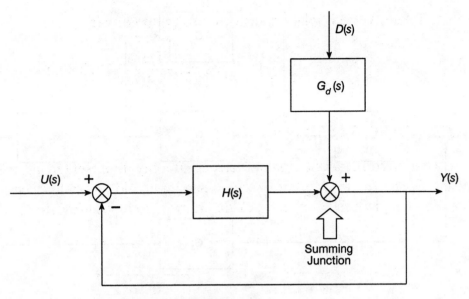

Figure 2

For single-loop feedback systems, the closed-loop transfer functions (CLTF) are given by the general expression:

$$CLTF = \frac{\pi_f}{1 + \pi_L}$$

where π_f is the product of all the transfer functions in the direct path between the output $Y(s)$ and input $U(s)$ or disturbance $D(s)$, and π_L is the product of all the transfer functions in the entire open loop.

PROBLEM 3:

$$G_1(s) = \frac{1}{s+1}$$

$$G_2(s) = \frac{3}{4s}$$

$$G_3(s) = \frac{4}{s}$$

$$G_4(s) = \frac{2}{s+2}$$

$$G_5(s) = 4$$

$$G_d(s) = \frac{1}{S^2 + 2s + 2}$$

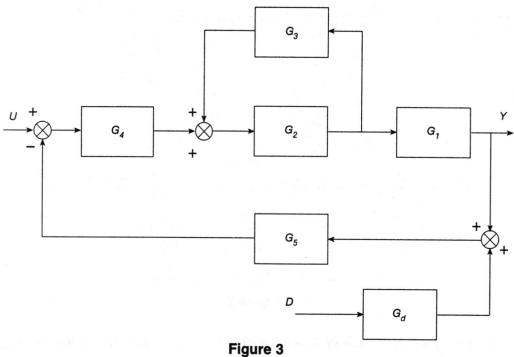

Figure 3

Find $H_1 (s) = Y(s)/U(s)$ and $H_2 (s) = Y(s)/D(s)$. (Note that the "(s)" has been dropped in the diagram for convenience.

SOLUTION:

Step #1:   Label all block inputs in the main (largest) control loop as unknown states, X_i.

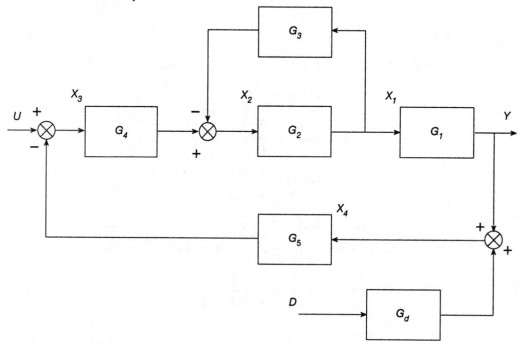

Figure 4

Step #2: Solve "backward" for Y, using states X_i.

$$Y = G_1 X_1$$
$$Y = G_1 G_2 X_2$$
$$Y = G_1 G_2 \{G_3 X_1 + G_4 X_3\}$$
$$Y = G_1 G_2 \{G_3 Y/G_1 + G_4 [U - G_5 X_4]\}$$

(Rule-of-thumb: Define all "fed-back" states, e.g., X_1, in terms of Y)

$$Y = G_1 G_2 \{G_3 Y/G_1 + G_4 [U - G_5 (Y + G_d D)]\}$$
$$Y = G_1 G_2 \{G_3 Y/G_1 + G_4 [U - G_5 Y - G_5 G_d D]\}$$
$$Y = G_1 G_2 \{G_3 Y/G_1 + G_4 U - G_4 G_5 Y - G_4 G_5 G_d D\}$$
$$Y = G_1 G_2 G_3 Y / G_1 + G_1 G_2 G_4 U - G_1 G_2 G_4 G_5 Y - G_1 G_2 G_4 G_5 G_d D$$

Step #3: Group all terms containing "Y" on equation's left-hand side, isolate H_1 and H_2.

$$Y(1 - G_2 G_3 + G_1 G_2 G_4 G_5) = (G_1 G_2 G_4) U + (-G_1 G_2 G_4 G_5 G_d)D$$

$$Y(s) = \left(\frac{G_1 G_2 G_4}{1 - G_2 G_3 + G_1 G_2 G_4 G_5}\right) U(s) + \left(\frac{-G_1 G_2 G_4 G_5 G_d}{1 - G_2 G_3 + G_1 G_2 G_4 G_5}\right) D(s)$$

$$H_1(s) = \left(\frac{G_1 G_2 G_4}{1 - G_2 G_3 + G_1 G_2 G_4 G_5}\right), \quad H_2(s) = \left(\frac{-G_1 G_2 G_4 G_5 G_d}{1 - G_2 G_3 + G_1 G_2 G_4 G_5}\right)$$

Step #4: Substitute transfer functions into equations and simplify.

$$H_1(s) = \frac{\dfrac{6}{4s(s+1)(s+2)}}{1 - \dfrac{3}{s^2} + \dfrac{24}{4s(s+1)(s+2)}}$$

$$H_1(s) = \frac{6}{4s(s+1)(s+2) - \dfrac{12}{s}(s+1)(s+2) + 24}$$

$$H_1(s) = \frac{6}{4s(s^2 + 3s + 2) - \dfrac{12}{s}(s^2 + 3s + 2) + 24}$$

$$H_1(s) = \frac{6}{4s^3 + 12s^2 - 4s - 12 - \dfrac{24}{s}}$$

$$H_1(s) = \frac{6s}{4s^4 + 12s^3 - 4s^2 - 12s - 24}$$

$$H_2(s) = \frac{-\dfrac{24}{4s(s+1)(s+2)(s^2 + 2s + 2)}}{1 - \dfrac{3}{s^2} + \dfrac{24}{4s(s+1)(s+2)}}$$

$$H_2(s) = \frac{-24}{\left(\begin{array}{c} 4s(s+1)(s+2)(s^2 + 2s + 2) \\ -\dfrac{12}{s}(s+1)(s+2)(s^2 + 2s + 2) + 24(s^2 + 2s + 2) \end{array} \right)}$$

$$H_2(s) = \frac{-24}{\left(\begin{array}{c} (4s^3 + 12s^3 + 8s)(s^2 + 2s + 2) - \\ \left(\left(12s + 36 + \dfrac{24}{s} \right)(s^2 + 2s + 2) + 24(s^2 + 2s + 2) \right) \end{array} \right)}$$

$$H_2(s) = \frac{-24}{4s^5 + 20s^4 + 28s^3 + 4s^2 - 56s - 72 - \dfrac{48}{s}}$$

$$H_2(s) = \frac{-24s}{4s^6 + 20s^5 + 28s^4 + 4s^3 - 56s^2 - 72s - 48}$$

Realize that $H_1(s)$ and $H_2(s)$ have the same block diagram "denominator" expression $(1 - G_2G_3 - G_1G_2 G_4G_5)$. Also notice that one will *always* find *one* transfer function relationship between the process output and the process input and/or disturbance. This means that all intermediate states *will not* appear in the transfer function solution.

STATE-VARIABLE MODELING

In addition to block diagrams, state-variable models are useful in describing a system's dynamic behavior. These state-variable models are particularly useful when one has a multiple-input, multiple-output system. A state-variable model is comprised of quantities required to fully describe the system behavior at any time, denoted as X. The general model for the state-variable model is given below:

$$\dot{x}(t) = Ax(t) + Bu(t) \qquad \text{(state equation)}$$

$$y(t) = Cx(t) + Du(t) \qquad \text{(output equation)}$$

where:

$x(t) = N$ by 1 state vector (N state variables)

$u(t) = R$ by 1 input vector (R inputs)

$y(t) = M$ by 1 output vector (M outputs)

$\quad A$ = system matrix

$\quad B$ = input distribution matrix

$\quad C$ = output matrix

$\quad D$ = feed-through matrix

The orders of the matrices are defined via variable definitions. This system is graphically constructed as:

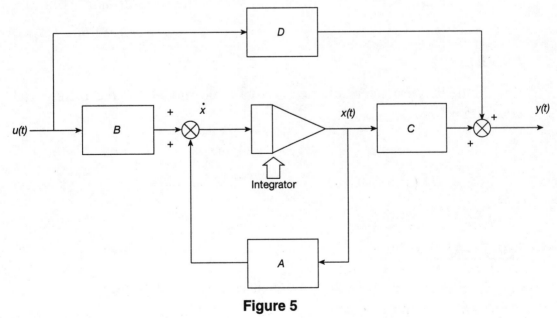

Figure 5

State-variable models can be created for open-loop or closed-loop systems. The Laplace transform of the time-invariant state equation is:

$$sX(s) - x(0) = AX(s) + BU(s)$$

from which:

$$X(s) = \phi(s)x(0) + \phi(s)BU(s)$$

where:

$$\phi(s) = [sI - A]^{-1}$$

is the resolvent matrix. *I* is an *N*-by-*N* identity matrix. The state-transition matrix:

$$\phi(t) = L^{-1}\{\phi(s)\}$$

(also defined as e^{At}) can be used to write:

$$x(t) = \phi(t)x(0) + \int_0^t \phi(t - \tau)Bu(\tau)d\tau$$

The output is obtained via the Laplace transform of the output equation, which is:

$$Y(s) = \{C\phi(s)B + D\}U(s) + C\phi(s)x(0)$$

The inverse Laplace transform of *Y(s)* yields the time-domain solution, *y (t)*.

PROBLEM 4:

Find the parameters of the state-variable model for the differential equation below:

$$\ddot{x} + 4\dot{x} + 3x = 7u(t)$$
$$y = 5x, \ (x(0) = 0)$$

Also, find $Y(s)$ and $y(t)$.

SOLUTION:

Step #1: Choose the states and find their derivative relationships:

$$x_1 = x, \ x_2 = \dot{x}$$

From the first relation, one obtains:

$$\dot{x}_1 = \dot{x} = x_2$$

And from the second relation, one obtains:

$$\dot{x}_2 = \ddot{x} = -4\dot{x} - 3x + 7u(t)$$

(Rule-of-thumb: For a set of N coupled independent differential equations, one selects S states as defined by the equation below:

$$S = \sum_{e=1}^{N} S_e$$

where S_e is the order of the eth differential equation. When S_e is an nth order differential equation, the n states chosen for S_e are:

$$\left\{ \frac{\partial^{n-1}x}{\partial t^{n-1}}, \frac{\partial^{n-2}x}{\partial t^{n-2}}, \dots \frac{\partial x}{\partial t}, x \right\})$$

Step #2: Substitute relations into general state-variable formula:

$$\begin{bmatrix} \dot{x}_1 \\ \dot{x}_2 \end{bmatrix} = \dot{x} = Ax + Bu = \begin{bmatrix} 0 & 1 \\ -3 & -4 \end{bmatrix} \begin{bmatrix} x_1 \\ x_2 \end{bmatrix} + \begin{bmatrix} 0 \\ 7 \end{bmatrix} u$$

$$y = Cx + Du = \begin{bmatrix} 5 & 0 \end{bmatrix} \begin{bmatrix} x_1 \\ x_2 \end{bmatrix} + [0]u$$

Step #3: Find $\phi(s) = |sI\text{-}A|^{-1}$:

$$sI - A = \begin{vmatrix} s & -1 \\ 3 & s+4 \end{vmatrix}$$

$$|sI - A|^{-1} = \frac{1}{s^2 + 4s + 3} \begin{vmatrix} s+4 & 1 \\ -3 & s \end{vmatrix}$$

Step #4: Use general formula to find $Y(s)$:

$$Y(s) = \{C\phi(s)B + D\}U(s) + C\phi(s)x(0)$$

$$= \left\{ [5 \quad 0] \frac{1}{s^2 + 4s + 3} \begin{vmatrix} s+4 & 1 \\ -3 & s \end{vmatrix} \begin{bmatrix} 0 \\ 7 \end{bmatrix} + [0] \right\}$$

$$U(s) + [5 \quad 0] \frac{1}{s^2 + 4s + 3} \begin{vmatrix} s+4 & 1 \\ -3 & s \end{vmatrix} [0]$$

$$= \frac{[5s + 20 \quad 5] \begin{bmatrix} 0 \\ 7 \end{bmatrix}}{s^2 + 4s + 3} U(s)$$

$$= \frac{35}{s^2 + 4s + 3} U(s)$$

Step #5: Take inverse Laplace transform to find $y(t)$:

$$y(t) = L^{-1} \left\{ \frac{35}{s^2 + 4s + 3} U(s) \right\}$$

$$\frac{35}{s^2 + 4s + 3} = \frac{A}{s+3} + \frac{B}{s+1}$$

at:

$$s = -3, \quad 35 = -2A \Rightarrow A = \frac{-35}{2}$$

at:

$$s = -1, \quad 35 = 2B \Rightarrow B = \frac{35}{2}$$

$$y(t) = \left\{ -\frac{35}{2} e^{-3t} + \frac{35^{14}}{2} e^{-t} \right\} u(t)$$

CHARACTERISTICS OF SYSTEM RESPONSE

When one knows the transfer function of the system, the system response is found by providing an input to the system. Therefore, the system response $\{R(t)\}$ is the product of the system transfer function $\{H(s)\}$ and the input forcing function $\{F(s)\}$ as shown by the coupled equations on the next page:

$$R(s) = H(s)F(s)$$

$$R(t) = L^{-1}\{R(s)\} = L^{-1}\{H(s)F(s)\}$$

This response is dependent upon the type of input forcing function, e.g., step function, ramp function, sinusoid, etc.

In approximating the system response, one finds it useful to know the initial and final values of the response. The initial and final values can be found using the initial value theorem:

$$R(0^+) = \lim_{s \to \infty} [sR(s)]$$

and the final value theorem:

$$R(\infty) = \lim_{s \to 0} [sR(s)]$$

for Laplace transforms, respectively. Note that the initial value theorem and the final value theorem only apply to stable systems.

The total system response is defined as the sum of the steady-state response and the transient response. The transient response varies with time, whereas the steady-state response does not.

There are some quick rules one can apply if a problem requires the steady-state response for a variety of forcing functions:

Unit step — The steady-state for a unit step is found by substituting 0 for s everywhere in $H(s)$. If the step has a magnitude h, multiply $H(s)$ by h.

Unit pulse — The system steady-state response is the Laplace inverse of the transfer function. That means that a pulse has no long-term effect on an engineering system.

Sinusoids — The steady-state response can be found by doing the following:

1. Substitute $j\omega$ for s in $T(s)$.

2. Convert $T(j\omega)$ into "phasor" form.

3. Convert the input sinusoid to "phasor" form.

4. Multiply $T(j\omega)$ by the input "phasor."

"Phasor" form denotes the conversion of a complex number into a magnitude-angle representation.

$$(Re) + (Im)j = P \angle Q$$

$$P = \text{magnitude} = \sqrt{(Re)^2 + (Im)^2}$$

$$Q = \text{phase} = \tan^{-1} \frac{(Im)}{(Re)}$$

PROBLEM 5:

The flowrate of reactant into a chemical reactor $\{U(s)\}$ is decreased by 0.8 m/s at $t = 0$. Find the initial value and the steady-state value for the output y if the system transfer function $H(s)$ is:

$$H(s) = \frac{Y(s)}{U(s)} = \frac{10}{(s+0.5)(s+3)}$$

SOLUTION:

Step #1: Apply initial value theorem to obtain initial value:

$$R(0^+) = \lim_{s \to \infty} [sR(s)] = \lim_{s \to \infty} [sH(s)\,U(s)]$$

$$= \lim_{s \to \infty} (\$) \left(\frac{10}{(s+0.5)(s+3)} \right) \left(-\frac{0.8}{\$} \right)$$

$$= \frac{-8}{(\infty+0.5)(\infty+3)} \cong \frac{-8}{\infty} = 0$$

Step #2: Apply final value theorem and substitute 0 for s into the equation:

$$R(\infty) = \lim_{s \to 0} [sR(s)] = \lim_{s \to 0} [sH(s)\,U(s)]$$

$$= \lim_{s \to \infty} \left[\$ \frac{10}{(s+0.5)(s+3)} \left(-\frac{0.8}{\$} \right) \right]$$

$$= \frac{-8}{(0+0.5)(0+3)} = \frac{-8}{1.5} = -5.33$$

PROBLEM 6:

$3[\sin(3t + \pi/3)]$ is applied as a sinusoidal input to a system that has a transfer function $H(s)$:

$$H(s) = \frac{-1}{5s^2 + 6s + 2}$$

What is the steady-state response?

SOLUTION:

Step #1: The angular frequency is $\omega = 3$. Substitute $j\omega$ for s in $H(s)$:

$$H(j3) = \frac{-1}{5(j3)^2 + 6(j3) + 2}$$

$$= \frac{-1}{5(-9) + 6(j3) + 2} = \frac{-1}{18j - 43}$$

Step #2: Convert $(18j–43)$ into phasor form:

$$18j - 43 = P \angle Q$$

$$P = \text{magnitude} = \sqrt{(Re)^2 + (Im)^2}$$

$$= \sqrt{(18)^2 + (43)^2} \cong 46.6$$

$$Q = \text{phase} = \tan^{-1}\frac{(Im)}{(Re)}$$

$$= \tan^{-1}\frac{(18)}{(-43)} \cong 2.745 \text{ rad} = 157.3°$$

$$18j - 43 = P \angle Q = 46.6 \angle 157.3°$$

Step #3: Find the phasor form of the transfer function:

$$H(s) = \frac{-1}{18j - 43} = \frac{-1}{46.6 \angle 157.3°}$$

$$= \left(-\frac{1}{46.6}\right) \angle (157.3°) \cong -0.0215 \angle -157.3°$$

Step #4: Convert the input sinusoid to phasor form:

$$3\left[\sin\left(3t+\frac{\pi}{3}\right)\right]=3\angle 60°$$

Step #5: Multiply transfer function phasor by input phasor to get steady-state response:

$$R(t)=\left(-0.0215\angle-157.3°\right)\left(3\angle 60°\right)$$
$$=-.0645\angle-97.3°$$

CHARACTERISTICS OF FIRST AND SECOND ORDER PROCESSES

The characteristics of many processes are a conglomeration of many time constants, each contributing to the overall process response. However, the behavior of a large number of processes can be analyzed when approximating the system model to be first or second order. The order of the process refers to the number of poles in the system transfer function, which is equal to the order of the (assumed) governing differential equation. The system order is also equivalent to the number of states one would choose to define the state-variable model.

Many observed system responses can be approximated with a first order-with-time-delay model. One can use graphical techniques to calculate the model parameters of $H(s)$, as shown in the equation below:

$$H(s)=\frac{Y(s)}{U(s)}=\frac{K_p e^{-\theta s}}{\tau s+1}$$

where:

K_p = Overall process gain

θ = Delay time

τ = First order time constant

There are many graphical techniques used to determine the model parameters. For our purposes, we will only introduce one. The first order-with-time-delay model parameters are calculated as:

$$K_p=\Delta/\delta$$

$$\tau = 1.5(t_{63\%} - t_{28\%})$$

$$\theta = t_{63\%} - \tau$$

where:

Δ = Overall change in output

δ = Overall change in input

$t_{63\%}$ = Time at which output reaches 63% of overall output change

$t_{28\%}$ = Time at which output reaches 28% of overall output change

The model parameters are found for the example response in the figure below:

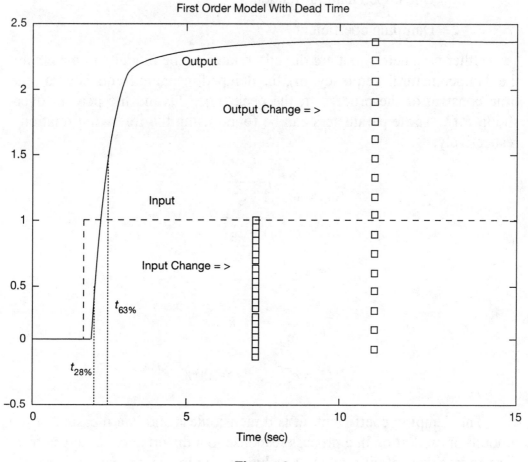

Figure 6

It is important to keep in mind that the system response must be a step change in the input in order to apply the graphical estimation technique. Note that the sampling instant was small enough to observe the dynamic behavior of the process (before it reaches steady state) and that the sampling horizon was large enough to indicate the steady-state value of the output variable.

The behavior of many other systems can be reasonably categorized as being second order. The standard form of the transfer function, *H(s)*, of second order systems is:

$$H(s) = \frac{Y(s)}{U(s)} = \frac{K_p \omega_n^2}{s^2 + 2\xi\omega_n s + \omega_n^2}$$

where:

K_p = Overall process gain

ω_n = Undamped natural frequency

ζ = Damping coefficient

Other parameters that are directly related to the model parameters are the damped natural frequency, ω_d, the damped resonant frequency, ω_p, the time constant of the process, τ, the peak time, T_p, and the percent over-shoot, *P.O.*. These parameters can be found using the following relations, respectively:

$$\omega_d = \omega_n \sqrt{1 - \zeta^2}$$

$$\omega_p = \omega_n \sqrt{1 - 2\zeta^2}$$

$$\tau = \frac{1}{\zeta\omega_n}$$

$$T_p = \frac{\pi}{\omega_d}$$

$$P.O. = e^{-\pi\zeta\sqrt{1-\zeta^2}} \times 100\%$$

The damping coefficient, ζ, is dimensionless and is a measure of the amount of oscillation in a process response to a disturbance. ζ ranges from zero to positive infinity, where a value of one means the process is critically damped. When coefficient values are less than one, the process response is characterized as being underdamped; damping coefficient values greater than one characterize overdamped processes.

For example, given a second-order process having a transfer-function *H(s)*:

$$H(s) = \frac{3^2}{s^2 + 2\zeta(3)s + 3^2}$$

The effect of underdamped ζ values on process response can be seen in the figure below:

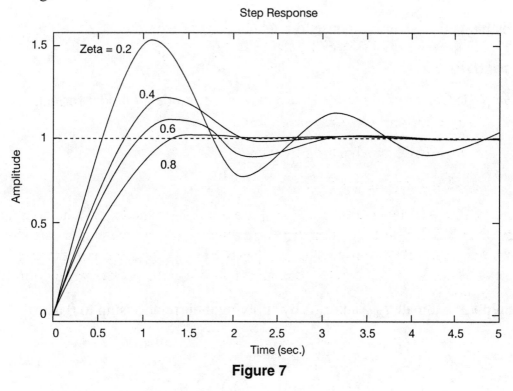

Figure 7

The effect of overdamped ζ values on process response can be seen in the figure below:

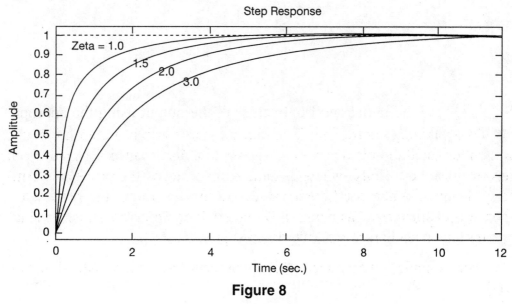

Figure 8

PROBLEM 7:

If the transfer function, $H(s)$, to a process is given to be:

$$H(s) = \frac{Y(s)}{U(s)} = \frac{5}{s+2}$$

Estimate the system response to a set change of magnitude 1.2.

SOLUTION:

Step #1: Convert $H(s)$ to the first order-with-time-delay model format.

$$H(s) = \frac{K_p e^{-\theta s}}{\tau s + 1}$$

$$\frac{5}{s+2} = \frac{\left(\dfrac{5}{2}\right) e^{-(0)s}}{\left(\dfrac{1}{2}\right)s+1}$$

Step #2: Estimate $t_{28\%}$ and $t_{63\%}$ by applying their relationship to θ and τ.

$$t_{63\%} = \theta + \tau$$

$$= (0) + \left(\frac{1}{2}\right) = \frac{1}{2}$$

$$t_{28\%} = t_{63\%} - \frac{\tau}{1.5}$$

$$= \left(\frac{1}{2}\right) - \left(\frac{1}{3}\right) = \frac{1}{6}$$

Step #3: Find the initial and final values of the output using the appropriate theorems.

$$R(0^+) = \lim_{s \to \infty} [sR(s)]$$

$$= \lim_{s \to \infty} \left[s\frac{5}{s+2}\frac{1.2}{s} \right] = \frac{6}{\infty} = 0$$

$$R(\infty) = \lim_{s \to 0} \left[s\frac{5}{s+2}\frac{1.2}{s} \right] = \frac{6}{2} = 3$$

Step #4: Use the calculated information to sketch the response. Your sketch should look like:

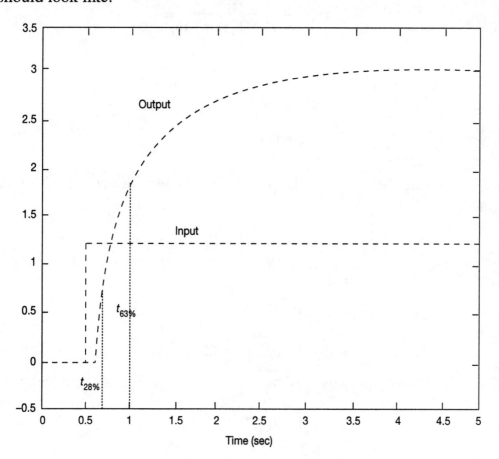

Figure 9. Sketch of First Order Model With Dead Time

PROBLEM 8:

The transfer function $H(s)$ for a given process is:

$$H(s) = \frac{Y(s)}{U(s)} = \frac{50}{s^2 + 7s + 25}$$

Determine all process parameters: K_p, ζ, ω_n, ω_d, ω_p, τ, T_p, and $P.O.$. Sketch the system response to a step input of 1.0.

SOLUTION:

Step #1: Convert $H(s)$ into the standard second-order transfer function format:

$$H(s) = \frac{K_p \omega_n^2}{s^2 + 2\zeta\omega_n s + \omega_n^2}$$

$$\frac{50}{s^2 + 7s + 25} = \frac{(2)(5)^2}{s^2 + (2)(5)(0.7)s + (5)^2}$$

$$K_p = 2.0$$

$$\zeta = 0.7$$

Step #2: Using the values of the process parameters, determine ω_d, ω_p, τ, τ_p, and *P.O.*:

$$\omega_n = 5.0$$

$$\omega_d = \omega_n\sqrt{1 - \zeta^2}$$

$$= (5)\sqrt{1 - (0.7)^2} = 3.571$$

$$\omega_p = \omega_n\sqrt{1 - 2\zeta^2}$$

$$= (5)\sqrt{1 - 2(0.7)^2} = 0.707$$

$$\tau = \frac{1}{\zeta\omega_n}$$

$$= \frac{1}{(0.7)(5)} = 0.286$$

$$T_p = \frac{\pi}{\omega_d}$$

$$= \frac{\pi}{3.571} = 0.880$$

$$P.O. = e^{-\pi\zeta\sqrt{1-\zeta^2}} \times 100\%$$

$$= e^{-\pi(0.7)\sqrt{1-(0.7)^2}} \times 100\% = 20.8\%$$

Step #3: Using ζ, one can estimate the sketch of the response to be underdamped with 20.8% overshoot. The actual response is plotted in Figure 10.

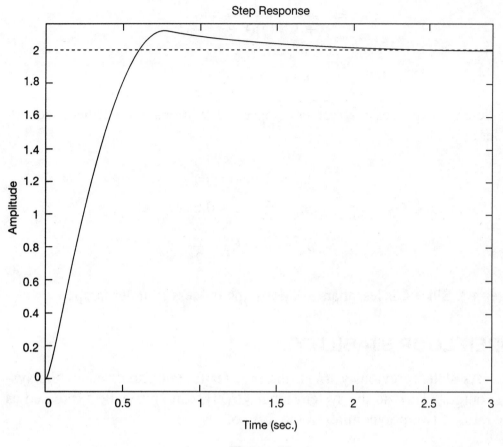

Figure 10

PROBLEM 9:

The transfer function $H(s)$ for a given process is:

$$H(s) = \frac{Y(s)}{U(s)} = \frac{1}{(s+3+4j)(s+3-4j)}$$

Determine if the process is over or underdamped.

SOLUTION:

Step #1: Convert $H(s)$ into the standard second-order transfer function format:

$$H(s) = \frac{K_p \omega_n^2}{s^2 + 2\zeta\omega_n s + \omega_n^2}$$

$$= \frac{1}{(s+3+4j)(s+3-4j)}$$

$$= \frac{1}{s^2 + 6s + 25}$$

To determine process parameters, apply the relations that define a second-order system:

$$\omega_n{}^2 = 25 \Rightarrow \omega_n = 5$$

$$2\zeta\omega_n = 6 \Rightarrow \zeta = 0.6$$

$$K_p\omega_n{}^2 = 1 \Rightarrow K_p = \frac{1}{25}$$

Step #2: Since ζ is less than 1.0, (0.6), the process is underdamped.

OPEN LOOP STABILITY

As stated previously, $H(s)$, the transfer function that relates the system output $\{Y(s)\}$ to the system input $\{U(s)\}$, can always be expressed as the ratio of two polynomials in the form of:

$$\frac{Y(s)}{U(s)} = H(s) = \frac{M(s)}{N(s)} = K \frac{\prod\limits_{m=1}^{M}(s - z_m)}{\prod\limits_{n=1}^{N}(s - p_n)}$$

The poles of the system transfer function determine the open loop stability of the system. The polynomial that is equivalent to the product of all the transfer function poles is called the *characteristic equation*. For our example above, the characteristic equation of the system would be defined as:

$$\prod_{n=1}^{N}(s - p_n) = a_N s^N + a_{N-1} s^{N-1} + \ldots + a_1 s + a_0$$

Specifically, all p_n must have negative real parts for open loop system stability. This important idea is graphically illustrated in Figure 11.

If one can easily determine all the poles of the system, then, in addition to stability, one can qualitatively sketch the system response based upon the values of the poles. There are two main attributes that define system response: stability and oscillatory behavior. When a system has all

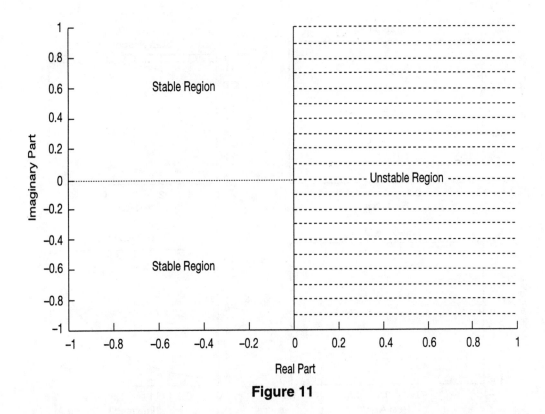

Figure 11

negative (positive) real-part roots, the response is stable (unstable). When a system possesses (does not have) complex roots, the system has oscillatory behavior (no oscillatory behavior). The four combinations of the two attributes are shown in Figure 12.

When factoring the characteristic equation of a system transfer function appears difficult, one can use the Routh test to determine system stability. To conduct the Routh stability test, one starts with the characteristic polynomial:

$$a_N s^N + a_{N-1} S^{N-1} + ... + a_1 s + a_0$$

We arbitrarily choose $a_N > 0$. If $a_N < 0$, multiply the polynomial by -1 to satisfy this condition. One first notes that a necessary condition for stability is that all coefficients in the characteristic equation must be positive. Therefore, if any coefficients are zero or less than zero, the system has at least one pole that has a positive real part, making the system unstable. If all coefficients are positive, one constructs a Routh array, as shown in Figure 14.

The Routh array has a "triangular" structure with a single element in the last row. The first two rows are the coefficients in the characteristic equation, where the first row holds either the even coefficients or the odd

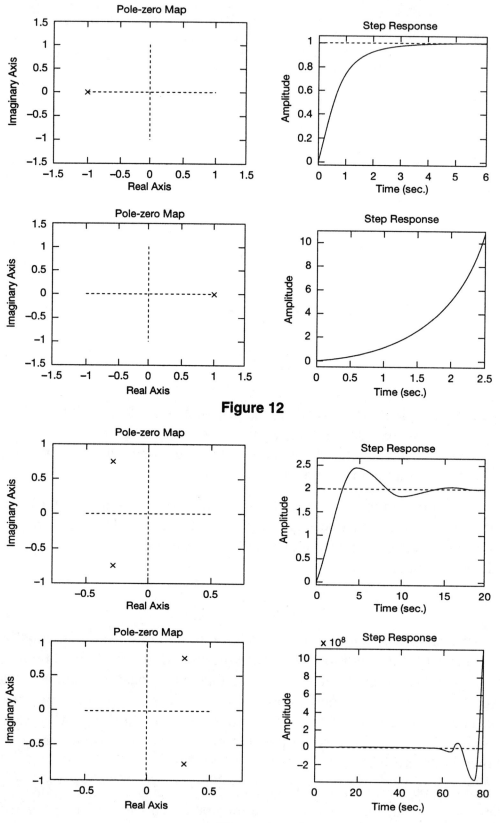

Figure 12

Figure 13

Row				
1	a_N	a_{N-2}	a_{N-4}	. . . .
2	a_{N-1}	a_{N-3}	a_{N-5}	. . . .
3	b_1	b_2	b_3	. . . .
4	c_1	c_2	. . . .	
⋮	⋮			
$N+1$	z_1			

Figure 14. Routh Array

coefficients, depending upon the value of N. Then the previously unde-fined elements are calculated from the following formula:

$$b_1 = \frac{a_{N-1}a_{N-2} - a_N a_{N-3}}{a_{N-1}}$$

$$b_2 = \frac{a_{N-1}a_{N-4} - a_N a_{N-5}}{a_{N-1}}$$

⋮

$$c_1 = \frac{b_1 a_{N-3} - a_{N-1} b_2}{b_1}$$

$$c_2 = \frac{b_1 a_{N-5} - a_{N-1} b_3}{b_1}$$

⋮

Therefore, for all roots of the characteristic equation to have negative real parts, all elements in the left hand column of its corresponding Routh array must be greater than zero. Note that the Routh test is only applicable to systems without delay terms.

155

PROBLEM 10:

Use the Routh stability criterion to determine the stability of the characteristic function:

$$-9s^3 - 16s^2 - 7s - 3$$

SOLUTION:

Step #1: Modify the characteristic function so the coefficient for the term with the highest power of s has a positive coefficient. Check if all coefficients now have a positive sign:

$$9s^3 + 16s^2 + 7s + 3$$

Step #2: Create Routh array:

$$
\begin{array}{ccc}
9 & 7 & 0 \\
16 & 3 & 0 \\
b_1 & b_2 & \\
c_1 & &
\end{array}
$$

Step #3: Calculate b_1, b_2, and c_1:

$$b_1 = \frac{[16(7) - 9(3)]}{16}$$

$$= +\frac{85}{16} = 5.31$$

$$b_2 = \frac{[16(0) - 9(0)]}{16}$$

$$= 0$$

$$c_1 = \frac{\left[\dfrac{85}{16}(3) - 16(0)\right]}{\dfrac{85}{16}}$$

$$= +3$$

Since all coefficients in the left column of the Routh array are positive, one can say that the system is open loop stable.

PROBLEM 11:

A system has a system transfer function $H(s)$ where:

$$H(s) = \frac{2(s-4)}{(s-2)(s+2)(s+3+4j)(s+3-4j)}$$

Characterize and sketch the response.

SOLUTION:

Step #1: Identify system poles.

Our system has four poles at:

$$s_1 = +2 \qquad s_2 = -2 \qquad s_3 = -3+4j \qquad s_4 = -3-4j$$

Step #2: Characterize poles.

Examining the real parts of all four poles indicates that s_1 has a positive pole. Therefore, the system is unstable. Also noticing that s_3 and s_4 are complex conjugates indicates oscillatory behavior. Now we have enough information to roughly sketch the overall response as a composite of each of the poles reaching steady state, which is shown below:

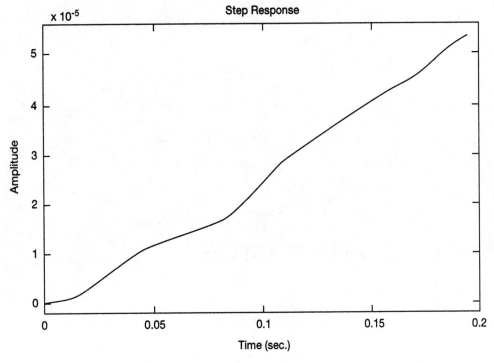

Figure 15

CLOSED LOOP STABILITY

In many systems, controllers are used to adjust system response to some desired characteristics. The two most common types of controllers are the PID and the lead (lag) controller, whose transfer functions are:

$$G_c(s) = K_c \left(1 + \frac{1}{\tau_1 s} + \tau_D s \right)$$

$$G_c(s) = K_c \left(\frac{1 + sT_1}{1 + sT_2} \right)$$

respectively,

where:

K_c = controller gain

τ_I = integral action time constant

τ_D = derivative action time constant

The ratio of T_1/T_2 determines whether the latter controller is a lead or lag controller. If T_1/T_2 is less than (greater than) one, the controller is a lead (lag) controller.

When a controller is added to the system to produce specific dynamics, the dynamics may be dependant upon the type of system. For a unity gain feedback control model:

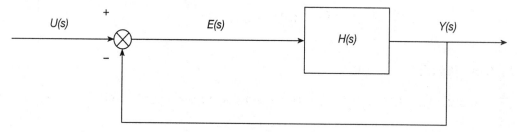

Figure 16

with the open loop transfer function defined as:

$$H(s) = \frac{K_B}{s^T} \times \frac{\displaystyle\prod_{m=1}^{M}(1 + s/\omega_m)}{\displaystyle\prod_{n=1}^{N}(1 + s/\omega_n)}$$

One can determine the type of system behavior by examining the system steady-state behavior for a variety of input disturbances. If we designate T for the type of system, then the following table illustrates the steady-state error for type zero, one, and two systems.

Steady-State Error, $e_{ss}(t)$			
Input Type	$T=0$	$T=1$	$T=2$
Unit Step	$1/(K_B+1)$	0	0
Ramp	∞	$1/K_B$	0
Acceleration	∞	∞	$1/K_B$

Table 2

One method used to evaluate controller performance is the use of frequency response analysis. The frequency response (Bode plots) of the system transfer function $H(s)$ show the system's gain margin and phase margin. Gain margin is the additional gain that will destabilize the system in a unity feedback control system. The phase margin is the additional phase that will destabilize the system. For $\omega = \omega_{180}$, the gain margin (GM) and phase margin (PM) are:

$$\angle H(j\omega_{180}) = 180°$$
$$GM = 1 / |H(j\omega_{180})|$$
$$H(j\omega_{0dB}) = 1$$
$$PM = 180° + \angle H(j\omega_{0dB})$$

PROBLEM 12:

Determine the range of K required for closed loop stability.

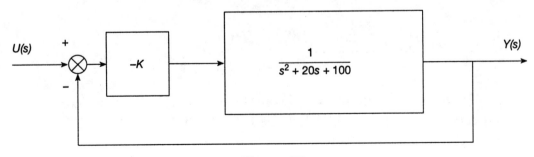

Figure 17

SOLUTION:

Step #1: Define the closed loop characteristic equation.

The closed loop characteristic equation for the system above is:

$$1 + \frac{(-K)}{s^2 + 20s + 100} = s^2 + 20s + 100 - K$$

Step #2: Apply the definition of stability to characteristic equation poles.

Using the quadratic equation, the poles of the system are defined as:

$$s_1, s_2 = \frac{-20 \pm \sqrt{400 - 400 + 4K}}{2}$$

$$= -10 \pm \sqrt{K}$$

With algebra, one obtains the complete solution as follows:

$$0 \geq -10 + \sqrt{K} \qquad 0 \geq -10 - \sqrt{K}$$

$$10 \geq \sqrt{K} \qquad -10 \leq \sqrt{K}$$

$$100 \geq K \qquad 0 \leq K$$

Therefore, the range of K required for stability is $0 \leq K \leq 100$.

PROBLEM 13:

The open loop frequency response $H(s)$ for a system as shown in Figure 18. Determine the gain margin and phase margin.

SOLUTION:

Step #1: Determine phase margin.

From the upper plot of the Bode diagram, it appears that the system has a crossover frequency (0 dB) of 0.80 rad/s. Therefore:

$$P.M. = 180° + \angle H(j\omega)$$

$$= 180° + (-80°) = 100°$$

Step #2: Determine gain margin. From the lower plot of the Bode diagram, it appears that the system reaches the critical phase (-180°) of 2.30 rad/s. Therefore, from the diagram:

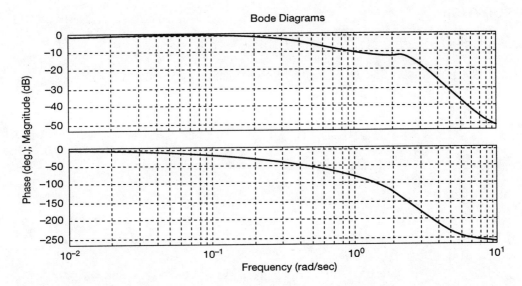

Figure 18

$$G.M. = 1 / \left| H(2.3\text{rad/s}) \right|$$
$$= 10^{-(5.1/20)}$$
$$= 0.55$$

FE/EIT

FE: PM Chemical Engineering Exam

CHAPTER 10

Process Design and Economics Evaluation

CHAPTER 10

PROCESS DESIGN AND ECONOMICS EVALUATION

PROCESS DESIGN AND ECONOMICS EVALUATION

Definitions:

Annuity — series of equal payments occurring at equal time intervals.

Capital Recovery Factor — sum that can be withdrawn each of *n* periods when *P* is invested at *i* interest.

Effective Interest Rate — exact interest rate based on original principal and a time unit of one year.

Future Worth — amount of money that a present amount will be worth at some future date based on investing it today at a given interest rate. This is also the value an annuity will have at a future date.

Interest Rate — percentage amount of interest earned by a unit of principal in a unit of time.

Principal — amount of capital on which interest is paid.

Present Worth — present amount of principal which must be deposited at a given interest rate to yield a desired amount at some future time.

Sinking Fund — a fund to which one makes a uniform series of payments at a given interest rate to achieve a future sum (F) at a given point in time.

Symbols and Mathematical Formulas:

I = interest amount

p = principal or present worth amount

i = interest rate

F = future sum of sinking fund

r = interest rate for one period

d = days in interest period

n = number of interest periods

m = number of periods in one year

R = uniform periodic payment or capital recovery factor

S = amount of principal + interest due after n periods or amount of an annuity

Simple interest:

$$S = P + I \iff S = P \times (1 + (i \times n))$$

Compound interest:

$$S = P \times (1 + i)^n$$

Effective interest rate:

$$i_{eff} = \left(1 + \frac{r}{m}\right)^m - 1$$

Present worth:

$$P = S \times \frac{1}{(1 + i)^n}$$

where $S \equiv$ amount available after n periods

Discount factor:

$$F = \frac{1}{(1+i)^n}$$

Future worth:

$$S = R \times \frac{(1+i)^n - 1}{i}$$

Sinking fund:

$$F = R \times \frac{i}{(1+i)^n - 1}$$

Amount that can be withdrawn from an annuity:

$$R = P \times \frac{i \times (1+i)^n}{(1+i)^n - 1}$$

PROBLEM 1:

In five years $250,000 is estimated to be needed to replace some plant equipment. (a) With interest rates at 5% per year, how much must be invested this year to have that sum available in five years? (b) How much must be invested each year to have this money available in five years?

SOLUTION:

(a) This is simple compound interest, except we solve for P given S.

$$S = P \times (1 + i)^n$$

$$P = \frac{S}{(1+i)^n} = \frac{\$250,000}{(1.05)^5} = \frac{\$250,000}{1.276} = \$195,882$$

(b) Here we apply the sinking fund formula with $R = \$250,000$, $i = 0.05$, and $n = 5$:

$$F = \$250,000 \times \frac{0.05}{(1.05)^5 - 1} = \$250,000 \times 0.181 = \$45,244$$

The difference in the monies invested is:

$$\$195,882 - [5 \times (\$45,244)] = -\$30,338$$

Thus, the company should invest the larger amount up front rather than invest smaller payments each year.

PROBLEM 2:

A sum of $25,000 is invested each year in an annuity which pays $6^3/_4$ percent interest. (a) At the end of twenty years, how much is the annuity worth? (b) Given that sum of money, how much can be withdrawn for fifteen years assuming the remaining sum earns interest at the rate of 4%?

SOLUTION:

(a) This is very straightforward:

$R = \$25,000$

$i = 0.0675$

$n = 20$

The future worth (s) of this annuity is:

$$s = \$25,000 \times \frac{(1.0675)^{20} - 1}{0.0675}$$

$$s = \$25,000 \times 39.894$$

$$s = \$997,339$$

(b) The amount (R) that can be withdrawn from this annuity over 15 years at 4% interest is:

$$R = \$997,339 \times \frac{0.04 \times (1.04)^{15}}{(1.04)^{15} - 1}$$

$$R = \$997,339 \times \frac{0.0726}{0.801}$$

$$R = \$89,655$$

Depreciation is the decrease in the value of an asset (equipment, building, mineral resource, etc.) due to one or more of the following causes:

- physical,
- functional, or
- depletion

Value after Depreciation:

$$V_a = V - (a \times d)$$

where:

$d \equiv$ depreciation

$V \equiv$ original value

$V_a \equiv$ value after a years or book value

$a \equiv$ years of use

There are several ways to calculate depreciation (d):

Straight-line:

$$d = \frac{V - V_s}{n}$$

where:

$V_s \equiv$ salvage value

$n \equiv$ number of years

Declining Balance or Fixed Percentage:

$$V_a = V \times (1 - f)^a$$

where:

$$f = 1 - \left[\frac{V_s}{V}\right]^{1/n}$$

$f \equiv$ fixed percentage factor

Sum-of-the-Years' Digits:

$$d_a = \frac{2 \times [n - (a+1)]}{n \times (n+1)} \times (V - V_s)$$

Total Depreciation through year a:

$$d = \sum_{i=1}^{a} d_i$$

PROBLEM 3:

A piece of equipment worth $2,000,000 has a service life of eight years with a salvage value of $100,000. (a) What is the equipment worth after five years using a straight-line depreciation method? (b) What would the depreciation in year five be using the Sum-of-the-Years' Digits method? (c) Using the Sum-of-the-Years' Digits method, what would the value of the equipment be after one year of use?

SOLUTION:

(a) Here the depreciation is:

$$d = \frac{V - V_s}{n} = \frac{\$2,000,000 - \$100,000}{8} = \$237,500$$

$$V_5 = V - a \times d = \$2,000,000 - (5 \times \$237,500) = \$812,500$$

(b)

$$d_5 = \frac{2 \times [8 - (5+1)]}{8 \times (8+1)} \times (\$2,000,000 - \$100,000) = 0.056 \times \$1,900,000$$

$$d_5 = \$105,556$$

(c)

$$d_{1=} \frac{2 \times [8 - (1+1)]}{8 \times (8+1)} \times (\$2,000,000 - \$100,000) = 0.167 \times \$1,900,000$$

$$d_1 = 0.167 \times \$1,900,000 = \$316,667$$

$$V_1 = V - d_1 = \$2,000,000 - \$316,667 = \$1,683,333$$

CAPITAL INVESTMENT

Definitions:

Break-Even Point — point of a graph of dollar amount per item versus items sold where the total product cost equals the total income.

Capitalized Cost — original cost of equipment plus the present worth of the renewable perpetuity (*perpetual annuity*).

Fixed Capital Investment — capital needed to set-up the necessary manufacturing and plant facilities.

Fixed Costs — costs that do not vary with the quantity produced.

Gross Earnings — total income minus total production costs.

Hurdle Rate — interest rate that the company deems as sufficient to risk investing in a plant or project.

Internal Rate of Return — interest rate at which the net present value of the revenues is equal to the estimated cost of the plant or project.

Net Present Value — difference between the net revenues received and the investment made in the plant or project.

Rate of Return — maximum interest rate at which money could be borrowed to finance the project under conditions where the net cash flow to the project over its life would be just sufficient to pay all principal and interest accumulated on the outstanding principal.

Sinking Fund — a separate fund into which one makes a uniform series of payments to achieve a desired future sum.

Total Investment — fixed capital investment plus working capital.

Working Capital — capital required for the operation of the plant.

(Note: Most chemical plants use an initial working capital of between 10 percent and 20 percent of total capital investment. Companies that must maintain large inventories may require 50 percent of capital investment as working capital.)

Symbols and Mathematical Formulas:

C = total annual costs except depreciation

D = total annual depreciation costs

E = gross annual earnings (before taxes)

G = gross annual income (revenue from sales)

I = annual interest

M = annual maintenance costs

N = net annual profit after taxes

O = annual operating costs

P_j = proceeds for j^{th} year

P_n = proceeds for n^{th} year ($n \equiv$ life of project)

S = total annual income/revenue

T = total annual taxes

V = project value

V_w = working capital

ϕ = tax rate

Total annual costs:

$$C = O + M + I$$

Net annual cash flow:

$$N = [(S - C) \times (1 - \phi) + \phi \times D]$$

Total annual earnings:

$$E = G - (C + D)$$

Total annual revenues:

$$S = G - \phi \times D$$

Total annual taxes:

$$T = \phi \times E = \phi \times [G - (C + D)]$$

Rate of return (i):

$$V \times (1 + i)^n - (V_s + V_w) = \sum_{j=1}^{n-1} P_J \times (1 + i)^j + P_n$$

(These calculations involve trial-and-error solutions by assuming values for i until the equation balances.)

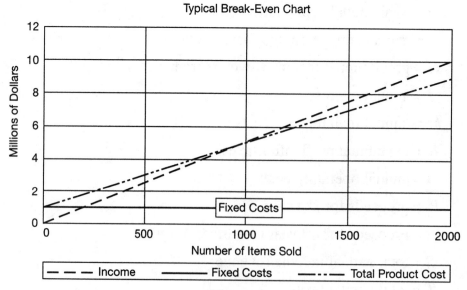

Figure 1

Methods of Evaluating Profitability:

1. *Rate of Return on Investment* — obtain a certain minimum profit before capital outlay is desirable.

2. *Discounted Cash Flow* — amount of investment that is unreturned at the end of each year during the life of the project.

3. *Present Worth* — difference between the present worth of the annual cash flows and the initial required investment.

4. *Capitalized Costs* — based upon the amount of money that must be available initially to purchase the equipment and simultaneously provide sufficient funds with interest accumulation to permit perpetual replacement of that equipment.

5. *Payout Period* — minimum length of time theoretically necessary to recover the original capital investment in the form of cash flow to the project based on total income minus all costs except depreciation.

PROBLEM 4:

The total capital investment for a proposed chemical plant is $10,000,000. The chemical plant will produce chemicals worth $8,000,000 per year. The net profits from this plant must pay off within five years, the total capital investment plus research and development costs. A rate of return after taxes of 12 percent of sales must be obtained. The income tax rate is 35 percent and half of the research and development costs are tax deductible. (a) Disregarding depreciation, what is the total amount of money the company can afford to invest in research and development to achieve the above conditions of profitability? (b) If R&D were not 50 percent tax deductible and the tax rate were 50 percent, what could the company afford to spend on R&D for the project?

SOLUTION:

(a) Let:

$X = $ R & D costs in $MM

$G = \$8MM$

$C = \$10MM$

$n = 5$ years

$\phi = 0.35$

Project Yearly Expenses =

$$\frac{\$10\text{MM} + X}{5} = 0.2(\$10 + X)\text{MM}$$

Taxable income =

$$\$8 - 0.2 \times (\$10 + 0.5 \times X)\text{MM} = \$6 - 0.1X$$

$$\text{(only 50\% of R\&D is taxable)}$$

Profit =

$$(1 - 0.35) \times [\$6 - 0.1X)\text{MM and Profit} = 0.12 \times G,$$

therefore:

$$0.12 \times (\$8\text{MM}) = 0.65 \times [\$6 - 0.1X)]\text{MM}$$

$$\$0.96\text{MM} = [\$3.9 - 0.065X]\text{MM}$$

$$X = \frac{\$(3.9 - 0.96)\text{MM}}{0.065} = \$45.23\text{MM}$$

(b) Here the taxable income =

$$\$8 - \$0.2 \times (10 + X)\text{MM} = \$6 - 0.2X$$

Profit =

$$(1 - 0.5) \times (\$6 - 0.2X)\text{MM} = [\$3.0 - 0.1X] = 0.12 \times G$$

The break-even equation becomes:

$$0.12 \times (\$8\text{MM}) = [\$3 - 0.1X)]\text{MM}$$

$$\$0.96\text{MM} = [\$3.0 - 0.1X]\text{MM}$$

$$X = \frac{\$(3.0 - 0.96)\text{MM}}{0.1} = \$20.4\text{MM}$$

COST ENGINEERING

Definitions:

Contingency — a specific provision of money or time in an estimate for undefined items which statistical studies of historical data have shown will likely be required.

Cost Estimate — a compilation for all costs of the elements of a project or effort within an agreed-upon scope.

$$\text{Element} = \text{Quantity Factor} \times \text{Cost Factor}$$

Estimate Accuracy — is a range of uncertainty reflecting likely changes in the scope of the project as the project unfolds to completion.

American Association of Cost Engineers Cost Estimate Ranges

<u>Type of Estimate</u>	<u>Positive Range</u>	<u>Negative Range</u>
Order of magnitude	+50%	–30%
Budget	+30%	–15%
Definitive	+15%	–5%

Table 1

Order of Magnitude — estimates made without detailed engineering data.

Budget — estimates made from preliminary flowsheets, layouts, and equipment details.

Definitive — estimates prepared from detailed engineering data and detail.

Determining Accuracy — Each estimate element is made up of a cost factor and a quantity factor. Both factors have uncertainties and often these uncertainties are different. In considering the overall accuracy/uncertainty of the element, the uncertainties must be multiplied according to the following:

$$(Q \pm q) \times (C \pm c) = Q \times C \pm [Q^2 \times c^2 + C^2 \times q^2]^{1/2}$$

If we take Q and C as unity, or 1, then the overall element accuracy becomes:

$$[c^2 + q^2]^{1/2}$$

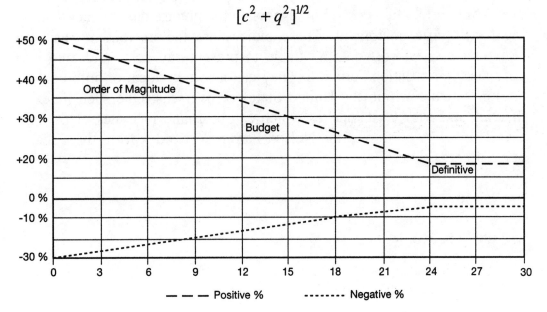

Figure 2

PROBLEM 5:

A reciprocating compressor is sized for a plant at 500 brake horse-power (bhp) with an uncertainty of ±10%. The estimated cost of this compressor including gas engine drive and installation is $2,000 per bhp with an uncertainty of ± 25%. What is the overall accuracy of the estimated cost and what are the high and low costs that would be encountered?

SOLUTION:

Using the uncertainty formula:

$$[(0.1)^2 + (0.25)^2]^{1/2} = [0.0725]^{1/2} = 0.269$$

$$\text{overall accuracy} = \pm 27\%$$

The lowest cost based on the overall accuracy is:

$$\text{Lowest cost} = (500 \times \$2,000) - 0.27 \times (500 \times \$2,000) = \$730,000$$

The highest cost based on the overall accuracy is:

$$\text{Highest cost} = (500 \times \$2,000) + 0.27 \times (500 \times \$2,000) = \$1,270,000$$

The average estimated cost is still:

$$\text{Cost}_{avr} = 500 \times \$2,000 = \$1,000,000$$

Cost Estimating Indexes — Order of Magnitude and Budget estimates are usually done by using indexes. This is particularly so when estimating installation costs, but also when the precise design data is lacking for specific equipment. These indices are factors that are used to convert the latest cost data available to present-day costs and take into consideration inflation/deflation. They can also take location into consideration whether within the United States or overseas. One such index is the Nelson-Farrar Cost Indexes which can be found in issues of *Oil and Gas Journal*. A portion of the Nelson-Farrar Cost Index from the December 1, 1997 issue is on the next page.

Refinery Construction: (1946 base year)

Item	1962	1976	1994	1996
Pumps, compressors	222.5	538.6	1,278.2	1,354.5
Electrical machinery	189.5	287.2	560.5	561.7
Heat exchangers	183.6	478.5	690.7	793.3
Instruments	214.8	466.4	887.6	932.3
Miscellaneous (average)	198.8	423.8	851.1	903.5
Labor	258.8	729.4	1,664.7	1,753.5

Oil & Gas Journal, December 1, 1997, page 60

Table 2. Nelson-Farrar Cost Indexes

PROBLEM 6:

A refinery has cost data for plants it constructed in 1976 and 1994 which give:

Heat Exchanger (1976) = $76,000

Electric Motor (1994) = $3,500

Pump (1994) = $35,000

You are to use these for a budget estimate for replacing an electric motor-driven pump and heat exchanger system of similar size as those used in 1976 and 1994. What would the total cost of the system be in 1996 dollars?

SOLUTION:

Heat Exchanger Index =

$$\frac{(1996)}{(1976)} = \frac{793.3}{478.5} = 1.658 \times \$76,000 = \$126,008$$

Electric Motor Index =

$$\frac{(1996)}{(1994)} = \frac{561.7}{560.5} = 1.002 \times \$3,500 = \$3,507$$

Pump Index =

$$\frac{(1996)}{(1994)} = \frac{1,354.5}{1,278.2} = 1.06 \times \$35,000 = \$37,100$$

Adding the costs:

$$\$126,008 + \$3,507 + \$37,100 = \$166,615$$

Rounding off gives a budget estimated cost = $166,600

FE/EIT

FE: PM Chemical Engineering Exam

CHAPTER 11

Process Equipment Design

CHAPTER 11

PROCESS EQUIPMENT DESIGN

PROCESS EQUIPMENT DESIGN

Cylindrical Process Vessels — Most vessels in the chemical process industry are cylindrical in shape with a preferred length to diameter ratio (*L/D*) of around three. However, the *L/D* ratio is usually a function of space available. In designing such vessels, the volume is known and the engineer must calculate the diameter and length.

$$V = \frac{\pi \times (D^2)}{4} \times L,$$

rearranging terms $\quad \Rightarrow D = \sqrt{\dfrac{4 \times V}{\pi \times L}}$

If the *L/D* ratio is known, then $L = \text{ratio} \times D$, and:

$$D = \sqrt{\frac{4 \times V}{\pi \times \text{ratio}}}$$

PROBLEM 1:

It is required to store 10,000 liters of 85% sulfuric acid in a cylindrical vessel whose *L/D* ratio will be four. What is the diameter in meters and volume in cubic meters of this vessel?

SOLUTION:

$$L/D = 4 \Rightarrow L = 4 \times D$$

and therefore:

$$V = \pi D^3$$

$$D = \sqrt[3]{\frac{10,000 \times 10^{-3}}{3.14}}$$

$$D = [3.183]^{1/3}$$

$$D = 1.47\,\text{m}$$

$$V = \times \pi \times D^3 = \times 3.14 \times (1.47)^3 = 10\,\text{m}^3$$

The ASME Boiler and Pressure Vessel Code, Section VIII, Division 1 specifies the required thickness of the shell of the vessel. The ASME formula for thickness is:

$$t = \frac{P \times R}{[(S \times E) - 0.6 \times P]}$$

where:

$P \equiv$ design pressure (psig)

$R \equiv$ inside radius of shell (inch)

$S \equiv$ maximum allowable stress (psi)

$E \equiv$ joint efficiency fraction

$t \equiv$ thickness (inch)

Values for S, maximum allowable stress, are given for various materials. Joint efficiencies are also given for various conditions.

Material	Spec.	Grade	Comp.	Stress (psi)
Carbon Steel	SA201	A	C, Si	55,000
		B	C. Si	60,000
	SA212	A	C. Si	65,000
		B	C, Si	70,000
	SA283	A	C, Si	45,000
		B	C, Si	50,000
Low-alloy Steel	SA302	B	Mn, $\frac{1}{2}$Mo	80,000
	SA387	B	1Cr, $\frac{1}{2}$Mo	60,000
Alloy-Steel	304	stainless	18Cr, 8Ni	75,000
	316	stainless	Cr, Ni, Mo	70,000
Nickel Plate	SB162		Ni	55,000
Nickel <3/16-inch	SB334		Ni-Mo-Cr	115,000
Aluminum	SB209	ASTM 990A		11,000
	SB209	ASTM GM41A		40,000

Table 1. Maximum Allowable Stress Values

	Degree of Examination		
Type of Joint	Full X-ray	Spot Exam	None
Butt, double welded	1.00	0.85	0.70
Butt, single welded	0.90	0.80	0.65
Double-fillet lap joint	---	---	0.55
Single-fillet lap joint	---	---	0.50

Table 2. Maximum Allowable Joint Efficiencies

PROBLEM 2:

For the previous problem assume that the vessel will be constructed of 316 stainless steel with single-welded butt joints that are spot examined. Also assume a working pressure of 50 psig. (a) What is the required thickness in centimeters of the cylindrical shell? (b) Given that 316 stainless steel has a specific gravity of 7.86, what is the mass in kilograms of the cylindrical shell of the vessel not including any nozzles or supports?

SOLUTION:

(a) For this situation $P = 50$ psig, from the tables above $S = 70,000$ psi and $E = 0.8$.

$$R = 0.5 \times D = 1.47 \, \text{meters} \times 0.5 = 0.735 \, \text{m} \times 39.37 \, \text{in/m} = 28.94 \, \text{in}$$

$$t = \frac{P \times R}{[(S \times E) - 0.6 \times P]} = \frac{50 \times 28.94}{[(70,000 \times 0.8) - 0.6 \times 50]} = \frac{1446.85}{55,970}$$

$$\text{thickness} = 0.026 \, \text{inch} \times 2.54 \, \text{cm/in} = 0.066 \, \text{cm}$$

(b) Find the surface area of the steel that was fabricated into the vessel.

$$A_{\text{suf}} = \pi \times D \times L = 3.14 \times 1.47 \, \text{m} \times 5.88 \, \text{m} = 27.155 \, \text{m}^2$$

$$V_{\text{steel}} = A_{\text{suf}} \times t = 27.155 \, \text{m}^2 \times 0.066 \, \text{cm} \times 10^4 \, \text{cm}^2/\text{m}^2 = 1.792 \times 10^4 \, \text{cm}^3$$

$$M = 7.86 \, \text{gm/cm}^3 \times 1.792 \times 10^4 \, \text{cm}^3 = 14.09 \times 10^4 \, \text{gm}$$

Mass of Vessel Shell = 14.09×10^4 gm $\times 10^{-3}$ kg/gm = 140.9 kgs

PROBLEM 3:

A cylindrical carbon steel tank with a diameter of 33 centimeters will be used to store compressed natural gas (CNG) at a design pressure of 3,600 psig with a safety factor of 1.25. The tank will be of SA212 Grade B carbon steel, butt double-welded, and 100% X-rayed. What is the thickness in centimeters required?

SOLUTION:

$$P = 3,600 \times 1.25 = 4,500 \, \text{psig}$$

$$S = 70,000 \, \text{psi}$$

$$E = 1.00$$

$$R = 33 \, \text{cm} \times 0.5 \times 0.394 \, \text{in/cm} = 6.5 \, \text{in}$$

$$t = \frac{P \times R}{[(S \times E) - 0.6 \times P]} = \frac{4,500 \times 6.5}{[(70,000 \times 1) - 0.6 \times 4,500]} = \frac{29,250}{67,300}$$

$$\text{thickness} = 0.435 \, \text{inch} \times 2.54 \, \text{cm/in} = 1.104 \, \text{cm}$$

Pressure Relief Valves — Valves which relieve pressure beyond a specified limit and reclose upon return to normal operating conditions. An important factor in sizing these valves is the time it takes to relieve the overpressure condition. When the gas or vapor in a pressure vessel is released such that the pressure ratios are greater than or equal to 0.53, then its velocity will be sonic and *choking conditions* occur. For release to the atmosphere, *choking flow* occurs as follows:

$$\text{choking flow} = \frac{p_o}{p_i} \geq 0.53 \Rightarrow \text{for } p_i = 14.7 \text{ psia,}$$

$$\Rightarrow P_o \quad 0.53 \times 14.7 = 7.79$$

When gas or vapor is released into the atmosphere under maximum flow rate at pressures above 191 kPa (27.74 psia) *choking conditions* occur which will last until the pressure in the vessel reduces to 191 kPa. For an ideal gas the *choking flowrate* is:

$$W_{\max} = 1.29 \times d^2 \times \sqrt{\frac{k \times M}{T_1} \times \left(\frac{3.6}{k+1}\right)^{(k+1/k-1)}}$$

where:

$d \equiv$ relief valve diameter (cm)

$k = C_p/C_v \equiv$ ratio of specific heats

$M \equiv$ molecular weight of the gas or vapor (gm/gm-mole)

$T_1 \equiv$ absolute temperature (K) upstream of the relief valve

To size a pressure relief valve that vents to the atmosphere, it is necessary to calculate W_{max} in terms of d^2, then determine the amount of gas or vapor released between the relief pressure and 191 kPa. The mass of gas or vapor released is:

$$\Delta m = \frac{M \times V}{R \times T_1} \times [p_r - 191 \text{ kPa}]$$

A time of release must be specified and is usually between one and ten seconds, depending on the volume of the vessel (V).

PROBLEM 4:

For the vessel we have been using in Problems 1 and 2, design a relief valve such that it releases at 345 kPa gauge to the atmosphere at a temperature of 30°C. The time of release should be seven seconds. The vapor is considered a 60%-40% mixture of sulfuric acid and water with a k value = 0.5. However, only 25% of the volume would be vapor.

SOLUTION:

$M = 0.6 \times 100$ gm/gm-mole $+ 0.4 \times 18$ gm/gm-mole $= 67.2$ gm/gm-mole

$p_r = 345$ kPa

$R = 8.306$ Pa-m^3/ gram-mole-K

$T_1 = (273 + 30)$K

$V = 0.25 \times 10$ m$^3 = 2.5$ m^3

$$\Delta m = \frac{M \times V}{R \times T_1} \times [p_r - 191]\text{kPa}$$

$$= \frac{67.2\,\text{gm/gm-mole} \times 2.5\,\text{m}^3}{8.306 \times 10^{-3}\,\text{kPa-m}^3/\text{gm-mole-K} \times 303\text{K}} \times [345 - 191]\text{kPa}$$

$$\Delta m = \frac{25,872\,\text{gm-kPa-m}^3/\text{gm-mole}}{2.517\,\text{kPa-m}^3/\text{gm-mole}} = 10,279\,\text{gm}$$

$$W_{max} = \frac{10,279\,\text{gm} \times 0.25}{7\,\text{sec}}$$

mass flow rate $= W_{max} = 367$ gm/sec

$$W_{max} = 12.9 \times d^2 \times \sqrt{\frac{k \times M}{T_1} \times \left(\frac{3.6}{k+1}\right)^{(k+1/1-k)}}$$

$$= 12.9 d^2 \times \sqrt{\frac{0.5 \times 62.7}{303} \times \left(\frac{3.6}{1.6}\right)^3}$$

$$W_{max} = 12.9 d^2 \times [0.1035 \times (2.25)^3]^{1/2} = 14.004 \times d^2$$

$$d = \sqrt{\frac{1}{14.004}} \times 367\,\text{gm/sec} = 5.12\,\text{cm}$$

Shell and Tube Heat Exchangers — A heat exchanger is a device used to transfer heat from one fluid to another. Major types of heat exchangers include:

Chiller — cools a process stream by evaporating a refrigerant and used where process temperatures are lower than attainable with water.

Cooler — cools process stream by exchanging heat with air or water.

Condenser — condenses vapors by exchanging heat with water or some other media.

Heater — heats a process stream by condensing steam.

Reboiler — connects to the bottom of a distillation column to boil bottom liquids and supply heat to the column.

Steam Generator — produces steam for use elsewhere in the process by combustion of any type of fuel.

Waste Heat Boiler — produces steam by using hot waste gas or liquid from the process.

Vaporizer — heater which vaporizes part of a liquid process stream.

These heat exchangers are classified by their type of construction.

Fixed-Tubesheet — straight tubes secured at both ends in tube–sheets welded to the shell.

U-Tube — both ends of U-shaped tubes are fastened to a single stationary tubesheet.

Floating Head — there are four subtypes in this category:

1. *Outside-Packed Stuffing Box* — shellside fluid is sealed by rings of packing compressed within a stuffing box by a packing ring follower. Used for shellside temperatures of 600°F and 600 psig.

2. *Outside-Packed Lantern Ring* — shellside and tubeside fluids are each sealed by separate rings of packing separated by a lantern ring. Limited to 500°F and 150 psig.

3. *Pull-Through Bundle* — a separate head is bolted directly to a floating tubesheet.

4. *Inside Split Backing-Ring* — floating cover is secured against the floating tubesheet by bolting it to a split backing-ring.

The Tubular Exchanger Manufacturers Association (TEMA) defines three classes of heat exchangers:

1. *Class "R"* — specified for the generally severe requirements of the petroleum and related applications. Designed and fabricated for safety and durability.

2. *Class "C"* — specified for moderate requirements of commercial and process general applications. Designed and fabricated for economy and overall compactness.

3. *Class "B"* — specified for chemical process service. Designed for maximum economy and compactness.

The preliminary design and sizing of shell and tube heat exchangers involve specifying the tube diameter and length, and assuming an overall heat transfer coefficient (U). Properties of the shellside and tubeside fluids are available and used to calculate the heat transferred. For shell and tube heat exchangers, the log mean temperature (ΔT_{lm}) must be calculated so that the overall heat transfer area (A) can then be determined. Once this is known, then the number of tubes is found by dividing their surface area into the overall heat transfer area.

PROBLEM 5:

It is necessary to reduce the temperature of a 10,000 kg/hr stream of methanol from 50°C to 30°C using cooling water on the shell side of a counterflow shell and tube heat exchanger. Cooling water is available at 20°C. The cooling water flow rate is 15,000 kg/hr. The heat capacity (C_p) of methanol is 0.62 cal/gm-°C. What would the outlet temperature of the cooling water be, and what is the log mean temperature difference? The tube length is 150 cm and the diameter is 2 cm. Assume an overall heat transfer coefficient of 120 cal/hr-cm²-°C. Calculate the overall heat transfer area and number of tubes.

SOLUTION:

First calculate the heat transferred by the methanol:

$$Q = 10,000 \, \text{kg/hr} \times 10^3 \, \text{gm/kg} \times 0.62 \, \text{cal/gm-°C} \times (50 - 30)°C$$
$$Q = 124 \times 10^6 \, \text{cal/hr}$$

We know the mass flow of the cooling water and its C_p (= 1.0 cal/gm-°C), thus we find the temperature rise of the cooling water as follows:

$$Q = m \times C_p \times \Delta T \Rightarrow \Delta T = \frac{Q}{m \times C_p}$$

$$\Delta T = \frac{124 \times 10^6 \text{ cal/hr}}{15,000 \text{ kg/hr} \times 10^3 \text{ gm/kg} \times 1.0 \text{ cal/gm-}^{\circ}\text{C}}$$

$$\Delta T = 8.27^{\circ}\text{C}$$

The outlet temperature of the cooling water is:

$$20^{\circ}\text{C} + 8.3^{\circ}\text{C} = 28.3^{\circ}\text{C}$$

We can now calculate the log mean temperature (ΔT_{lm}).

$$\Delta T_{lm} = \frac{\Delta T_{\text{max}} - \Delta T_{\text{min}}}{\ln \dfrac{\Delta T_{\text{max}}}{\Delta T_{\text{min}}}} = \frac{(50 - 20) - (30 - 28.3)}{\ln \dfrac{30}{1.7}}$$

$$= \frac{30 - 1.7}{\ln(17.65)} = \frac{28.3}{2.87} = 9.86$$

$$\Delta T_{lm} = 9.86^{\circ}\text{C}$$

Knowing the ΔT_{lm} enables us to calculate the overall heat transfer area.

$$Q = U \times A \times \Delta T_{lm} \Rightarrow A = \frac{Q}{U \times \Delta T_{lm}} = \frac{124 \times 10^6 \text{ cal/hr}}{120 \text{ cal/hr-cm}^2\text{-}^{\circ}\text{C} \times 9.86^{\circ}\text{C}} = 104,800 \text{ cm}^2$$

The overall heat transfer area is 104,800 cm².

The tubes have diameters of 2 cm and lengths of 150 cm; therefore, each tube has a surface area of:

$$A_{suf} = \pi \times D \times L = 3.14 \times 2 \text{ cm} \times 150 \text{ cm} = 942.5 \text{ cm}^2$$

$$\text{number of tubes} = \frac{\text{Area}}{A_{suf}} = \frac{104,800 \text{ cm}^2}{942.5 \text{ cm}^2\text{/tube}} = 111.2 \text{ tubes}$$

$$\text{actual number of tubes} = 112$$

Electric Motors — Electric motors are used to power most rotating equipment in chemical plants. Thus, a chemical engineer should have a passing knowledge of what these are and how to size them. For a pump, the horsepower required is given by:

$$hp_{pump} = \frac{Q \times \Delta p}{1,715 \times \eta_{pump}}$$

where:

$Q \equiv$ flow rate (gal/min)

$\Delta p \equiv$ differential pressure (psi) which is sometimes given in feet as head

and

$\eta_{pump} \equiv$ pump efficiency

The electrical power (kilowatts) required by that pump can also be calculated from the flow rate and pressure.

$$Power = \frac{0.00043 \times Q \times \Delta p}{\eta_{pump}}$$

This electrical power is related to voltage and current as follows:

$$Power = 0.001732 \times V \times I \times \cos\phi \times \eta_{motor}$$

where:

$V \equiv$ voltage (volts)

$I \equiv$ current (amperes)

$\cos \phi \equiv$ power factor

The power factor ($\cos\phi$) is used for three-phase power which is required for motors above $^1/_3$ horsepower. The three-phase squirrel cage induction motor is the workhorse of the chemical industry. For this type of motor, motor speeds are fairly constant and will vary a maximum of 5 percent from no load to full load. Motor speeds are available only for 900, 1,200, 1,800, and 3,600 revolutions per minute (RPMs), with 1,800 RPM as the most economical and popular speed.

PROBLEM 6:

For the heat exchanger in the previous problem, a pump is required to deliver the cooling water to the exchanger. The pressure difference is 150 kPa and the mass flow rate is 15,000 kg/hr. The pump has an efficiency of 85% and is three-phase with a power factor of 0.707. (a) What is the horsepower of this motor? (b) How much power in kilowatts does this motor require and how much current is drawn by the motor assuming it has a 95% efficiency and 440 volts are supplied?

SOLUTION:

(a) Flow rate:

$$Q = 15,000 \, \text{kg/hr} \times 10^3 \, \text{gm/kg} \times 1 \, \text{cm}^3/\text{gm} \times 10^{-3} \text{liter/cm}^3 = 15,000 \, \text{liter/hr}$$

$$Q = \frac{15,000 \, \text{liter/hr}}{60 \, \text{min/hr}} \times 0.2642 \, \text{gal/liter} = 66 \, \text{gal/min}$$

$$\Delta p = 150 \, \text{kPa} \times 0.145 \, \text{psi/kPa} = 21.75 \, \text{psi}$$

$$hp_{\text{pump}} = \frac{Q \times \Delta p}{1,715 \times \eta} = \frac{66 \times 21.75}{1,715 \times 0.85} = 0.9855$$

For all intents and purposes this is a one horsepower motor.

(b) $$\text{Power} = \frac{0.00043 \times Q \times \Delta p}{\eta} = \frac{0.00043 \times 66 \times 21.75}{0.85} = 0.726 \, \text{kilowatts}$$

You can also convert hp to kw by multiplying by 0.7457 and dividing by the motor efficiency:

$$\text{Power} = \frac{0.7457 \, \text{kw/hp} \times 1 \, \text{hp}}{0.95} = 0.785 \, \text{kw}$$

This would be a better value to use:

$$\text{Power} = 0.001732 \times V \times I \times \cos\phi \times \eta_{\text{motor}} \Rightarrow I = \frac{577.4 \times \text{Power}}{V \times \cos\phi \times \eta_{\text{motor}}}$$

$$I(\text{current}) = \frac{577.4 \times 0.785}{440 \times 0.707 \times 0.95} = \frac{453.26}{295.5} = 1.53 \, \text{amps}$$

PROBLEM 7:

A reciprocating compressor is rated for 50 brake horsepower. Specify the electric motor drive for this compressor assuming the motor has an efficiency of 90%. Calculate the current required assuming 440 volts and a power factor of 0.866.

SOLUTION:

$$\text{Power} = \frac{50 \, \text{hp} \times 0.7457 \, \text{kw/hp}}{0.9} = 41.4 \, \text{kilowatts}$$

$$I(\text{current}) = \frac{577.4 \times 41.4}{440 \times 0.866 \times 0.9} = \frac{24,075.6}{342.9} = 70.2 \, \text{amps}$$

FE/EIT

FE: PM Chemical Engineering Exam

CHAPTER 12

Process Safety

CHAPTER 12

PROCESS SAFETY

PROCESS SAFETY

Chemical Releases—The U.S. Environmental Protection Agency (US EPA) has established regulations regarding the accidental release of hazardous chemicals. These hazardous chemicals are listed by US EPA and include 77 toxic substances, 63 flammable materials, and certain high explosives. A partial list of some of the key substances and their threshold quantity (*TQ*) are given in the table on the next page. US EPA has published *Risk Management Program (RMP) for Accidental Chemical Release* in the Federal Register under Combined Federal Regulations (CFR) 40 CFR Part 68. The basic functions of the Risk Management Program are:

- *Hazard-Assessment Program* — identify and analyze potential on-site and off-site impacts of worst case accidental release scenarios

- *Prevention Program* — technology and management for handling the listed substances

- *Emergency-Response Program* — mitigate the impact of any accidental release

- *Management System* — implementation of the overall risk-management program.

Toxic Chemical	Threshold lbs	Endpoint mg/liter
Ammonia (anhydrous)	10,000	0.14
Chlorine	2,500	0.0087
Hydrochloric Acid (30%)	15,000	0.030
Nitric Acid (80%)	15,000	0.026
Phosgene	500	0.00081
Propylene Oxide	10,000	0.59
Sulfur Dioxide (anhydrous)	5,000	0.0078

Table 1. Partial List Of RMP Chemicals

The following flammable chemicals all have threshold quantities of 10,000 pounds and an overpressure limit of one pound per square inch: carbon monoxide, ethane, hydrogen, methane, and propane.

The US EPA developed worst case estimates for worker exposure to chemical substances. For inhalation exposure, the amount of contaminant within a room can be calculated for both open and containerized operations involving chemicals.

For open operations:

$$C = 74,542 \times k \times p_{vap} \times \left(\frac{18}{M}\right)^{1/3}$$

For containerized operations:

$$C = 4,590 \times k \times p_{vap} \times \left(\frac{18}{M}\right)^{1/3}$$

where:

$C \equiv$ concentration of contaminate (ppm)

$k \equiv$ dimensionless factor to account for non-ideal mixing which ranges from 0.1 to 0.5,

$M \equiv$ molecular weight of liquid chemical (gm/gm-mole)

$p_{vap} \equiv$ vapor pressure of chemical (atm)

PROBLEM 1:

Chlorobenzene (C_6H_5Cl M.W. = 112.5) is being filled into drums at 20°C for which the vapor pressure of chlorobenzene is less than 10 mm Hg. Assuming a non-ideal mixing factor of 0.4, what would be the concentration (ppm_v) in the surrounding area?

SOLUTION:

$$p_{vap} = \frac{10 \text{ mm Hg}}{760 \text{ mm Hg/atm}} = 0.0132 \text{ atm}$$

$$k = 0.4$$

$$M = 112.5$$

$$C = 4,590 \times k \times p_{vap} \times \left[\frac{18}{M}\right]^{1/3} = 4,590 \times 0.4 \times 0.0132 \times \left[\frac{18}{112.5}\right]^{1/3}$$

$$C = 24.16 \times [0.16]^{1/3} = 13.1 \text{ ppm}_v$$

Carbon Monoxide — is the most toxic of the common air pollutants and as a by-product of combustion is potentially present at excess levels in many industrial spaces. The toxicity of carbon monoxide is due to the fact that it bonds to hemoglobin in the blood nearly 200 times more readily than oxygen. In Figures 1 and 2, the health effects associated with various concentrations of carbon monoxide versus time are plotted.

Various U.S. government agencies, including the US EPA and the Occupational Health and Safety Administration (OSHA), have promulgated safe levels of carbon monoxide concentrations which are listed in Table 2 below.

Agency	Maximum 8-hour average (ppm_v)	Maximum 1-hour average (ppm_v)
US EPA	9	35
OSHA	50	200 (15 minutes)
ASHRAE*	9	35

* recommended limits for office buildings and commercial spaces

Table 2. Ambient Air Quality Standards for Carbon Monoxide

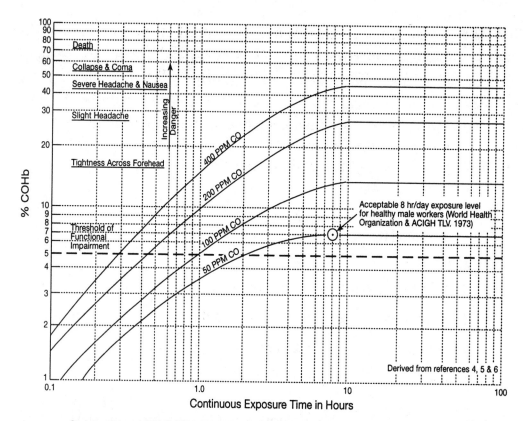

Carboxyhemoglobin (COHb) formation and range of physiological effects as a function of carbon monoxide exposure for adults engaging in light work activities

Figure 1[1]

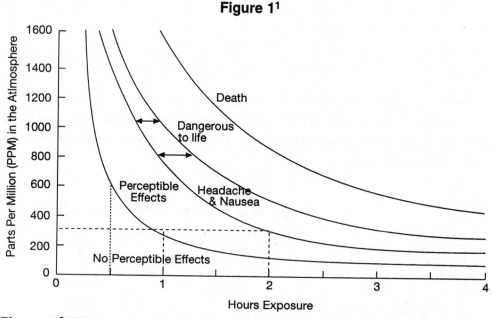

Figure 2.[2] Effects of Carbon Monoxide for a Given Time on Human Beings

1. Adams, D. E. and Bullerdiek, W. A., "Safety Devices for Gas-Fired Appliances," report prepared for the U.S. Consumer Products Safety Commission, May 1980.

2. Ibid.

Not only is carbon monoxide a health hazard, it is also a combustible gas with a wide flammability limit of between 12.5% and 74.2% in air. Contrast this with methane whose flammability limits are between 5% and 15%.

Indoor Air Quality — a mathematical expression relating the indoor concentration of a pollutant with the outdoor concentration, the rate of emissions generated and the ventilation rate is:

$$C_i = C_o + \frac{S}{A \times V}$$

where:

$C_i \equiv$ indoor concentration of pollutant (ppm$_v$)

$C_o \equiv$ outdoor concentration of pollutant (ppm$_v$)

$S \equiv$ rate of indoor pollutant emission (cm^3/min)

$A \equiv$ ventilation rate (min^{-1})

$V \equiv$ volume of space (m^3)

Note that 10^6 cm^3/m^3 means that the fractional term is already in ppm$_v$.

PROBLEM 2:

The outdoor concentration of carbon monoxide in New York City is 5 ppm$_v$. A warehouse space that is 50 m by 30 m and has a height of 5 m uses forklifts that emit carbon monoxide at a rate of 25 liters/min. The ventilation for the warehouse is 5 air changes per hour. What would the concentration of carbon monoxide be on the warehouse floor and does this meet OSHA requirements?

SOLUTION:

$$V = 50 \text{ m} \times 30\text{m} \times 5 \text{ m} = 7,500 \text{ m}^3$$

$$S = 25 \text{ liters/min} \times 10^3 \text{ cm}^3\text{/liter} = 25,000 \text{ cm}^3\text{/min}$$

$$C_o = 5 \text{ ppm}_v$$

$$A = \frac{5 \text{ hr}^{-1}}{60 \text{ min/hr}} = 0.0833\text{/min}$$

$$C_i = C_o + \frac{S}{A \times V} = 5 + \frac{25,000 \text{ cm}^3/\text{min}}{0.0833/\text{min} \times 7,500 \text{ m}^3} = 5 + 40$$

$$C_i = 45 \text{ ppm}_v$$

This is close to, but still less than, the OSHA eight-hour maximum concentration standard.

Incineration — is the combustion process of thermally reducing the volume of solid and/or liquid waste, while producing inoffensive gases and sterilized residue. An effectively operated and well-maintained incinerator can reduce the volume of solid waste by as much as 95%. For the incineration of hazardous wastes, the Resource Conservation and Recovery Act (RCRA) specifies regulations for their safe operation. Some of the standards that must be met by hazardous waste incinerators are:

- Particulate emissions ≤ 0.08 grains per dry standard cubic foot (180 milligrams/cm^3)

- Hydrochloric acid (HCl) emissions ≤ 4 pounds per hour (≈1,800 gms/hr)

- Carbon monoxide emissions ≤ 100 ppm$_v$

- Destruction and reduction efficiency (DRE) of 99.99% as defined:

$$DRE = \frac{W_{in} - W_{out}}{W_{in}} \times 100\%$$

where:

W_{in}, W_{out} = mass feed and emission rates given in kg/hr.

Organic wastes often have heating values sufficient to support combustion and, therefore, auxiliary fuel is required only to initiate combustion. On the other hand, inorganic components of the waste, which are mostly metals, cannot be thermally destroyed, only oxidized. For metals, the incineration process converts them to their oxidized state and they are removed as ash. Some metal salts may have boiling points lower than the temperature of the incineration process, in which case they would vaporize and exit in the flue gas. These vaporized salts can be removed by air pollution equipment on the exit end of the stack. However, high metal content wastes are not good candidates for incineration.

The largest number of hazardous waste incinerators in operation today are liquid injection incinerators. These are usually refractory-lined chambers, cylindrical in cross section. Depending on the heating value of the fuel, they may be equipped with a secondary burner to aid in combustion. Liquid injection incinerators operate at temperatures between 1,000°C and 1,700°C and have residence times of between 0.005 and 2.5 seconds.

PROBLEM 3:

A hazardous waste incinerator has feed mixture and emissions listed below:

Compound	Formula	M.W.	HHV kcal/kg	INLET kg/hr	OUTLET gm/hr
Benzene	C_6H_6	78	2,082	1,000	50
Toluene	C_7H_8	92	2,108	500	10
Total Particulates					500

Calculate the DRE (destruction and reduction efficiencies). Assuming 150% excess air is required for combustion, how many liters per hour of air must be supplied? What will the stack gas flow rate be in cubic meters per hour? What will the particulate loading be for the flue gas in milligrams/m³? Benzene has a vapor density of 0.033 gm/cm³. What is the concentration of benzene in the stack gas in ppb$_v$?

SOLUTION:

The DREs for each are:

$$DRE_{C_6H_6} = \frac{1,000 - 50 \times 10^{-3}}{1,000} \times 100\% = 99.995\%$$

$$DRE_{C_7H_8} = \frac{500 - 10 \times 10^{-3}}{500} \times 100\% = 99.998\%$$

The two combustion reactions are:

$$C_6H_6 + 7.5\,O_2 \rightarrow 6CO_2 + 3H_2O$$

$$C_7H_8 + 9O_2 \rightarrow 7CO_2 + 4H_2O$$

For every mole of benzene burned, 7.5 moles of oxygen are required, and likewise for every mole of toluene burned, 9 moles of oxygen are required.

$$\text{benzene moles} = \frac{10^6 \text{ gms/hr}}{78 \text{ gm/gm-mol}} = 12{,}821 \text{ gm-mol/hr}$$

$$\text{toluene moles} = \frac{5 \times 10^5 \text{ gms/hr}}{92 \text{ gm/gm-mol}} = 5434.8 \text{ gm-mol/hr}$$

$$O_2 \text{ for benzene} = 7.5 \times 12{,}821 \text{ gm-mol/hr} = 96{,}154 \text{ gm-mol/hr}$$

$$O_2 \text{ for toluene} = 9 \times 5{,}434.8 \text{ gm-mol/hr} = 48{,}913 \text{ gm-mol/hr}$$

$$\text{Total } O_2 = 145{,}067 \text{ gm-mol/hr}$$

$$\text{Total } O_2 = 145{,}067 \text{ gm-mol/hr} \Rightarrow$$

$$\text{air req'd} = \frac{145{,}067 \text{ gm-mol/hr}}{0.21 \, O_2/\text{air}} = 690{,}795 \text{ gm-mol/hr}$$

150% excess air =

$$1.5 \times 690{,}795 \text{ gm-mol/hr} \times 22.4 \text{ liters/gm-mol} = 23.21 \times 10^6 \text{ liter/hr}$$

The composition of the flue gas is found as follows:

	From benzene gm-mols/hr	From toluene gm-mols/hr	Total gm-mols/hr
CO_2:	$12{,}821 \times 6 = 76{,}926 +$	$5435.8 \times 7 = 38{,}050.6 =$	$114{,}976.6$
H_2O:	$12{,}821 \times 3 = 38{,}463 +$	$5435.8 \times 4 = 21{,}743.2 =$	$60{,}206.2$

Assuming the nitrogen goes through unreacted:

$$N_2 = \frac{23.21 \times 10^6 \text{ liter/hr} \times 0.79}{22.4 \text{ liters/gm-mol}} = 818{,}567 \text{ gm-mol/hr}$$

The excess oxygen is:

$$150\% - 100\% = 50\% = 0.5.$$

This assumes that this oxygen does not react with N_2 or benzene and toluene.

$$O_{2xs} = 0.5 \times 145,067 \text{ gm-mol/hr} = 72,534 \text{ gm-mol/hr}$$

Develop a chart/table for the flue gas:

Component	gm-mol/hr	%
Nitrogen	818,567	76.8
Carbon Dioxide	114,976.6	10.8
Water	60,206.2	5.6
Oxygen	72,534	6.8
	1,066,284	100.0

Flue gas flow rate = 1,066,284 gm-mol/hr $\times$ 22.4 liters/gm-mol = 23.88×10^6 liter/hr

Flue gas flow rate =

$$23.88 \times 10^6 \text{ liter/hr} \times 10^{-3} \text{ m}^3/\text{liter} = 23,885 \text{ m}^3/\text{hr}$$

Particulate loading =

$$\frac{500 \text{ gm/hr}}{23,885 \text{ m}^3/\text{hr}} \times 10^3 \text{ mg/gm} = 20.93 \text{ mg/hr}$$

Benzene concentration =

$$\frac{50 \text{ gm/hr}}{0.033 \text{ gm/cm}^3 \times 23,885 \text{ m}^3/\text{hr}} = 0.0634 \text{ cm}^3/\text{m}^3$$

Noting that $cm^3/m^3 = 10^6 = ppm_v$ and $ppm_v = 10^3 \text{ ppb}_v$

$$\text{Benzene concentration} = 63.4 \text{ ppb}_v$$

Odor Control — "The public's perception is that an unpleasant odor indicates the presence of harmful chemical substances. Local regulatory authorities are more likely to be notified and asked to act on odor problems than on most other environmental issues."[3] Odor is human sense experience and therefore highly subjective. Essentially volatile chemicals interact with the olfactory system causing impulses to be transmitted to the brain. The odor detection threshold is the minimum concentration at which an odor is detectable. The odor recognition threshold is the minimum concentration at which an odor is recognized as something specific. Table 3 lists some chemicals, their odor threshold, and their health limits as well as a description of the odor.

3. Siegell, Jeffrey H., "Solve Plant Odor Problems," pp. 35–41, *Chemical Engineering Progress*, January 1996.

There are several procedures for reducing and/or eliminating odor problems:

- process modification

- dilution

- masking

- oxidation

  - incineration

  - dry gas oxidation

  - wet chemical absorption/scrubbing

- adsorption

Chemical	Detection Threshold ppm$_v$	Health Limits 8-hour ppm$_v$	Odor Description
Ammonia	17	25	Irritating
Butadiene	0.45	10	Rubber
Chlorine	0.01	0.5	Bleach
Chlorobenzene	1.3	10	Almond
Diisopropyl Amine	0.13	5	Fishy
Hydrogen Sulfide	0.0005	10	Rotten eggs
Methyl Ethyl Ketone	10	200	Sweet/sharp
Methyl Mercaptan	0.0005	0.5	Rotten cabbage
Naphthalene	0.027	10	Tar/creosote
Phenol	0.047	5	Medicinal
Toluene	2.8	100	Sour/burnt

**Table 3. Detection Thresholds and Health Exposure Limits
for Odorous Chemical Compounds**

One method of odor control is by chemical absorption. The odorous substance is absorbed into the liquid solution and reacts to form non-odorous and less noxious compounds. The pH of the solution is often very critical to absorption and the oxidation reaction. Some of the odorous chemicals and chemicals used to absorb them are listed in Table 4.

Odor Chemical	Absorption Chemical
Amines ($-NH_2$)	HCl or H_2SO_4
Cyanide (HCN)	H_2O_2 (hydrogen peroxide)
Hydrogen Sulfide (H_2S)	NaOCl

Mercaptans (RSH)	NaOH (pH 11)
Organic Sulfides (RS)	$KMnO_4$
Phenol	H_2O_2

Table 4

Some typical oxidation reactions are shown below.

$$H_2S + 4NaOCl + 2NaOH \rightarrow 4NaCl + Na_2SO_4 + 2H_2O$$

$$H_2S + NaOCl \rightarrow NaCl + S\downarrow + H_2O \text{ (at low pH)}$$

$$2 NH_3 + 3 NaOCl \rightarrow N_2 + 3NaCl + 2H_2O$$

PROBLEM 4:

A flue gas stream with a flow rate of 500 standard m³/min containing 100 ppm$_v$ of H_2S is cooled to 80°C, then sent to an absorption column containing a 10% solution of sodium hypochlorite (NaOCl – MW = 74.5) with a density of 1 gm/cm³. (a) Assuming the solution reacts with all of the H_2S, what is the flow of the sodium hypochlorite absorption solution in liters/min? (b) If this were a low pH solution of NaOCl, how much sulfur could be recovered in kilograms per day according to the reaction $H_2S + NaOCl \rightarrow NaCl + S\downarrow + H_2O$?

SOLUTION:

(a) Flue gas is at 80°C, therefore:

$$22.4 \text{ liter/gm-mole} \times \frac{(273 + 80)K}{273K} = 28.96 \text{ liter/gm-mole}$$

Calculate the gm-moles of H_2S:

$$\frac{100 \times 10^{-6} \times 500 \, m^3/min \times 10^3 \, l/m^3}{28.96 \, l/gm\text{-}mole} = 1.726 \, gm\text{-}mol/min$$

According to the reaction:

$$H_2S + 4NaOCl + 2NaOH \rightarrow 4NaCl + Na_2SO4 + 2H_2O$$

4 moles of NaOCl react with 1 mole of H_2S, therefore:

$$1.726 \text{ gm-mol/min} \times 4 \times 74.5 \text{ gm/gm-mole} = 514 \text{ gm/min}$$

The solution is 10% NaOCl,

$$NaOCl = \frac{514 \, gm/min}{0.1} \times 1 \, cm^3 /gm \times \frac{1 \, liter}{1,000 \, cm^3} = 5.14 \, liters \, /min$$

(b) We have 1.726 gm-mol/min of H_2S, thus assuming 100% reaction and recovery,

$$S \ recovered = \frac{1.726 \, gm\text{-}mol/min \times 1,440 \, min/day}{32 \, gm/gm\text{-}mol \ S \times 1,000 \, gm/kg} = 0.078 \, kg/day$$

This is not a very great amount and thus this process would not be practical for this situation.

FE/EIT

FE: PM Chemical Engineering Exam

CHAPTER 13

Transport Phenomena

CHAPTER 13

TRANSPORT PHENOMENA

TRANSPORT PHENOMENA

Basic Equations of Hydrostatics:

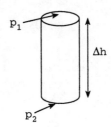

Figure 1

$$\frac{dp}{dh} = -\rho \times g \Rightarrow \frac{dp}{\rho} = g \times dh \Rightarrow \frac{dp}{\rho} = g \times dh = \text{constant}$$

$$p_2 - p_1 = \rho \times \frac{g}{g_c} \times \Delta h$$

where:

$dp \equiv$ differential pressure (gm_f/cm^2)

$Dh \equiv$ differential elevation (cm)

$\rho \equiv$ density (gm/cm^3)

$g =$ gravitational acceleration ($g = 980$ cm/sec^2)

$g_c \equiv$ gravitational constant (980 gm-cm/gm$_f$-sec^2) defined earlier.

Note:

$$\frac{g}{g_c} = \frac{980\,\text{cm/sec}^2}{980\,\text{gm-cm/gm}_f\text{-sec}^2} = 1\,\text{gm}_f/\text{gm}$$

Pascal's Law — The pressure of a static fluid at any point is the same in all directions.

PROBLEM 1:

A column of water is contained and completely fills a vessel 10 meters high open to the atmosphere. Water has a density of 1 gm/cm³. Atmospheric pressure is 101 kPa. What is the pressure in kPa at the bottom of the column?

SOLUTION:

$$p_2 - p_1 = \rho \times g/g_c \times \Delta h \Rightarrow p_2 = p_1 + (\rho \times g \times \Delta h)$$

$$\rho \times g \times \Delta h = 1\,\text{gm/cm}^3 \times 1\,\text{gm}_f/\text{gm} \times 1{,}000\,\text{cm} = 1{,}000\,\text{gm}_f/\text{cm}^2 = 1\,\text{kg}_f/\text{cm}^2$$

$$1.097 \times 10^{-5}\,\text{kg}_f/\text{cm}^2 = 1\,\text{Pa} \Rightarrow 91.16 \times 10^3\,\text{Pa-cm}^2/\text{kg}_f$$

$$\rho \times g \times \Delta h = 1\,\text{kgm}_f/\text{cm}^2 \times 91.16 \times 10^3\,\text{Pa-cm}^2/\text{kg}_f = 9.12 \times 10^4\,\text{Pa} = 91\,\text{kPa}$$

$$p_2 = 101\ \text{kPa} + 91\ \text{kPa} = 192\ \text{kPa}$$

Reynolds Number — This is a dimensionless number used in fluid flow that relates diameter, velocity of flow, density and viscosity.

$$N_{RE} = \frac{D \times u \times \rho}{\mu}$$

Where:

D = pipe diameter

u = average fluid velocity

ρ = fluid density

μ = viscosity of fluid

For $N_{Re} < 2{,}000$ there is Laminar Flow

For $N_{Re} > 4{,}000$ there is Turbulent Flow

And $2,000 > N_{Re} < 4,000$ defines a Transition Region between Laminar and Turbulent Flow.

Continuity Equation — for incompressible fluids (liquids under most circumstances) the volumetric flow rate remains constant over large ranges of pressure and temperature, therefore

$$Q = \text{constant} \Rightarrow Q = u_1 \times A_1 = u_2 \times A_2$$

For circular pipes the continuity equation can be related to the squares of the diameters.

$$u_1 \times (D_1)^2 = u_2 \times (D_2)^2$$

PROBLEM 2:

Water at 20°C is flowing in a pipe with a diameter of 5 cm at 20 cm/sec. It then enters a smaller pipe with a diameter of 2 cm. Water has a density of 1 gm/cm^3 and a viscosity of 0.0103 gm/cm-sec at this temperature. What is velocity of the water in the smaller pipe? What are the N_{re}s of the water flows?

SOLUTION:

The squares of the diameters of the two pipes are found:

$$(D_1)^2 = (5\text{cm})^2 = 25 \text{ cm}^2$$

$$(D_2)^2 = (2\text{cm})^2 = 4 \text{ cm}^2$$

$$u_1 \times (D_1)^2 = u_2 \times (D_2)^2 \Rightarrow u_2 = \frac{20 \times 25}{4} = 125 \text{ cm/sec}$$

$$N_{re} = \frac{5\,\text{cm} \times 10\,\text{cm/sec} \times 1\,\text{gm/cm}^3}{0.0103\,\text{gm/cm-sec}} = 9,709$$

$$N_{re} = \frac{2\,\text{cm} \times 125\,\text{cm/sec} \times 1\,\text{gm/cm}^3}{0.0103\,\text{gm/cm-sec}} = 24,271$$

Bernoulli Equation — Referring to Figure 2, this equation relates the energy of a fluid in motion.

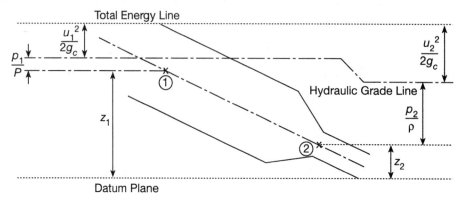

Figure 2. Bernoulli Equation

$$a_1 + \frac{p_1}{\rho} + \frac{u_1^2}{2g_c} = z_2 + \frac{p_2}{\rho} + \frac{u_2^2}{2g_c} + f_L$$

where:

$g_c \equiv$ gravitational constant (980 gm-cm/gm$_f$-sec^2) defined earlier

$f_L \equiv$ head loss (cm of water)

For a straight run of pipe $z_1 = z_2 = 0$ and Bernoulli's Equation becomes:

$$\frac{p_1}{\rho} + \frac{u_1^2}{2g_c} = \frac{p_2}{\rho} + \frac{u_2^2}{2g_c} + f_L$$

Solving for u_2 with $f_L = 0$:

$$u_2^2 = u_1^2 + 2g_c \times \frac{p_1 - p_2}{\rho}$$

This equation is valid for liquids where the density does not vary with pressure to any appreciable extent. The equation cannot be used with gases or compressible fluids.

The units of pressure (p) are usually given in Pa or kPa and must be converted as follows:

Pa $\times$ 1.0197$\times$10^{-2} gm$_f$/cm^2-Pa or kPa $\times$ 10.97 gm$_f$/cm^2-kPa

When divided by ρ, which is given in gm/cm^3, the (p/ρ) term becomes:

$$\frac{p}{\rho} = \frac{\text{Pa} \times 1.1097 \times 10^{-2} \, \text{gm}_f/\text{cm}^2 - \text{Pa}}{\text{gm/cm}^3} = \frac{\text{gm}_f - \text{cm}}{\text{gm}}$$

PROBLEM 3:

Water with a density of 1gm/cm^3 flowing in a pipe at a velocity 500 cm/sec exerts a pressure of 100 kPa. Further down the pipe the pressure is measured at 90 kPa, what is the velocity of the water at that second point?

SOLUTION:

Calculate pressure drop divided by density:

$$\frac{p_1 - p_2}{\rho} = (100 - 90)\,\text{kPa} \times 109.7\,\text{gm}_f/\text{cm/gm}$$

$$u_2{}^2 = (500\,\text{cm/sec})^2 + 2 \times 980\,\text{gm-cm/gm}_f\text{-sec}^2 \times 109.7\;\text{gm}_f\text{-cm/gm}$$

$$u_2{}^2 = 250{,}000\ \text{cm}^2/\text{sec}^2 + 215{,}012\ \text{cm}^2/\text{sec}^2 = 465{,}012\ \text{cm}^2/\text{sec}^2$$

$$u_2 = \sqrt{465{,}012\,\text{cm}^2/\text{sec}^2} = 682\,\text{cm/sec}$$

Frictional Head Loss — This is the head loss due to friction flow of a fluid flowing in a full pipe or duct. The formula for head loss (h_L) is:

$$H_L = f \times \frac{L \times u^2}{2g \times D}$$

where:

$L \equiv$ length of pipe (cm)

$D \equiv$ diameter of pipe (cm)

$u \equiv$ velocity (cm/sec)

$g \equiv$ gravitational acceleration (980 cm/sec^2)

The dimensionless friction factor f is dependent upon the N_{Re}. The Moody Diagram plots f versus N_{Re} for various pipe types and roughness factors.

Flow resistance for turbulent flow in various pipe fittings such as elbows, valves and tees, is expressed in equivalent lengths. These are added together to get an overall equivalent length to use in the formula for h_L above.

$$L_{eq} = \sum L_i$$

Pumping of Fluids — Bernoulli's equation can be written for pumps as follows:

$$H = h_d - h_s + \frac{u_d{}^2 - u_s{}^2}{2g_c}$$

where:

H = total fluid head

h_d = head at pump

h_s = head at pump suction

If pump suction and discharge nozzle are the same size (diameter), then $u_d = u_s$, and

$$H = h_d - h_s$$

When suction lift is involved is h_d negative.

Net Positive Suction Head (NPSH) — The absolute pressure available at the pump suction flange (cm of liquid above the vapor pressure of liquid at pumping temperature).

Sonic or Acoustic Velocity — This is the velocity of sound (a) in a fluid and, for an ideal gas, is determined by:

$$a = \sqrt{\frac{g_c \times k \times R \times T}{M}}$$

The g_c and R terms can be combined to a single constant, $C = g_c \times R$:

$$C = 9.8 \times 10^{-3} \text{ kg-m/kg}_f\text{-sec}^2 \times 8.47 \times 10^5 \text{ kg}_f\text{-m/kg-mole-K}$$

$$C = 8.306 \times 10^3 \text{ kg-m}^2/\text{kg-mole-sec}^2\text{-K}$$

$$a = \sqrt{\frac{k \times C \times T}{M}}$$

where:

$k = C_p/C_v \equiv$ ratio of specific heats

$T \equiv$ absolute temperature of the fluid (K)

$M \equiv$ molecular weight of the gas (gm/gm-mole)

Mach Number (N_{Ma}) — is the ratio of the fluid velocity to the acoustic velocity.

$$N_{Ma} = \frac{u}{a}$$

PROBLEM 4:

A supersonic jet fighter plane is flying at a velocity of 500 meters per second in air at -10K. What is the Mach Number (N_{Ma}) of this velocity?

SOLUTION:

Need to determine the velocity of sound in air at -10K:

$$a = \sqrt{\frac{k \times C \times T}{M}}$$

$$= \sqrt{\frac{1.4 \times 8.306 \times 10^3 \, kg\text{-}m^2/kg\text{-}mole\text{-}sec^2\text{-}K \times 263K}{28.84 \, kg/kg\text{-}mole}}$$

$$a = \sqrt{10.6043 \times 10^4 \, m^2/sec^2} = 325.6 \, m/sec$$

$$N_{Ma} = \frac{u}{a} = \frac{500 \, m/sec}{325.6 \, m/sec} = 1.54$$

Nozzles — For a given set of upstream conditions, the flow rate of gas from a nozzle will increase, for a decrease in the absolute pressure ratio, until the linear velocity in the throat reaches sonic velocity. The value of p_2/p_1 for which sonic velocity is just attained is called the critical pressure ratio. For an ideal gas in a frictionless nozzle the critical pressure ratio (r_c) for diameter ratios < 0.2 is:

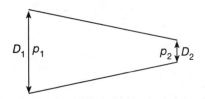

Figure 3

$$r_c = \left(\frac{2}{k+1}\right)^{k/(k-1)} \text{ for } \frac{D_2}{D_1} < 0.2$$

To attain gas velocity greater than sonic, a convergent-divergent nozzle must be used.

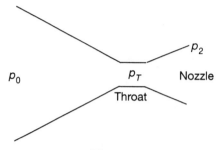

Figure 4

In the diffuser portion, the pressure is increasing, the velocity is decreasing and the cross-sectional area is decreasing. In the throat, the velocity reaches sonic velocity. In the nozzle the pressure decreases, the velocity increases becoming supersonic and the cross-sectional area increases.

Bernoulli's Equation for Compressible Flow — This equation can be applied to compressible flow, however the density (ρ) is not constant and will change with pressure. The heights above the datum plane and the fluid head have negligible effects for compressible flow. Thus:

$$\frac{p_1}{\rho_1} + \frac{u_1^2}{2g_c} = \frac{p_2}{\rho_2} + \frac{u_2^2}{2g_c}$$

Particle Flow — Whenever a particle is suspended in a fluid, there is relative motion between the particle and the fluid, and the fluid exerts a drag force (F_d) on the particle.

$$F_d = \frac{C \times A_p \times u^2 \times \rho}{2g_c}$$

where:

A_p = projected cross-sectional area of the particle in the direction of flow

ρ = density of the fluid

C = dimensionless drag coefficient which for spherical particles is:

$$C = \frac{24}{N_{\text{Re}}}$$

Thus, for spherical particles settling by gravity there is a terminal velocity (u_t) given by:

$$u_t = \sqrt{\frac{4 \times g \times D_p \times (\rho_p - \rho)}{\rho \times C}}$$

where:

D_p = diameter of the spherical particle

ρ_p = density of the particle

For N_{Re} between 1,000 and 200,000 the drag coefficient is constant ($C = 0.44$) for spheres, and the terminal settling velocity is given by:

$$u_t = \sqrt{\frac{(8909\,\text{cm/sec}^2) \times D_p \times (\rho_p - \rho)}{\rho}}$$

PROBLEM 5:

What is the terminal settling velocity in m/sec of a particle with a diameter of 5 cm and density of 1 gm/cm^3 in air with a viscosity of 0.0185 gm/cm-sec and density of 0.0012 gm/cm^3?

SOLUTION:

Use the special formula for u_t:

$$u_t = \sqrt{\frac{8,909\,\text{cm/sec}^2 \times 5\,\text{cm} \times (1 - 0.0012)\,\text{gm/cm}^3}{0.0012\,\text{gm/cm}^3}}$$

$$= \sqrt{\frac{44,491\,\text{gm/cm-sec}^2}{0.0012\,\text{gm/cm}^3}}$$

$$u_t = \sqrt{37.07 \times 10^6\,\text{cm}^2/\text{sec}^2} = 6,088\,\text{cm/sec} = 60.88\,\text{m/sec}$$

Check the N_{Re} using the value of u_t obtained above.

$$N_{\text{Re}} = \frac{5 \times 6,088 \times 0.0012}{0.0185} = 1,974$$

The N_{Re} is within the range of 1,000 to 200,000.

FE/EIT

FE: PM Chemical Engineering Exam

Practice Test 1

FUNDAMENTALS OF ENGINEERING EXAMINATION
TEST 1

(Answer sheets appear in the back of this book.)

TIME: 4 Hours
             60 Questions

> **DIRECTIONS**: For each of the following questions and incomplete statements, choose the best answer from the four answer choices. You must answer all questions.

1. A reversible reaction of the type $A \underset{kr}{\overset{kf}{\rightleftharpoons}} B$ has a forward rate constant of 2×10^{-2} and a reverse rate of 4 min^{-1}. What fraction of reactant A is converted at equilibrium?

   (A) 2×10^{-2} (C) 0.005

   (B) 1.000   (D) 0.050

2. A metallic material with a mass of 50 grams and a temperature of 70°C is immersed in a bath of water having a mass of 200 grams and a temperature of 10°C. After attaining equilibrium with no heat lost to the surroundings, the water with the immersed metal has a temperature of 28°C. What is the specific heat (C_p) of the metallic material in cal/gm-°C?

   (A) 1.19   (C) 2.33

   (B) 1.71   (D) 9.33

3. A mixture of hydrocarbon vapors contains five grams of benzene (MW = 78) and three grams of toluene (MW = 92) and two grams of xylene (MW = 106). Assuming the vapors behave as ideal gases, what volume in liters will be occupied by this mixture at 175°C and 0.5 atmosphere pressure?

(A) 0.2

(C) 3.3

(B) 0.8

(D) 8.5

4. A material containing 5 percent water is dried to 1 percent water in a hot-air dryer. The air fed to the dryer contains 0.5 percent water. Moist air leaving the dryer contains 2 percent water. How much air in kilograms per hour (kg/hr) is required to dry 100 kg/hr of wet material assuming 100% efficiency?

(A) 261.4

(C) 266.7

(B) 260.1

(D) 272.0

5. A liquefied petroleum gas (LPG) has the following composition:

$$C_3H_8 = 30\%, \ C_4H_{10} = 60\%, \ \text{and} \ N_2 = 10\%$$

What is the mass ratio of dry air to fuel for 100% combustion of this fuel?

(A) 7.5%

(C) 21.5%

(B) 20.3%

(D) 35.7%

6. A liquid-to-liquid counterflow heat exchanger heats cold fluid from 20°C to 80°C. Assuming the hot fluid enters at 200°C, and exits at 120°C, what is the log mean temperature difference for the heat exchanger?

(A) 31

(C) 109

(B) 93

(D) 213

7. A liquid chemical is stored in an elevated tank above the floor of a process area. A vertical pipe is to be installed from the bottom of this tank to a mixer on the process floor. The pipe is essentially frictionless and the bottom of the tank is five meters from the discharge of the pipe to the mixer. What is the minimum pipe diameter (in centimeters) that will allow a flow rate of five liters per second into the mixer?

(A) 1.9   (C) 3.0

(B) 8.0   (D) 80.2

Questions 8–10 are based on the following:

A bus garage has a total volume of 10,000 m^3. Tailpipe emissions from buses in this garage have one percent CO and the rate of these emissions can reach a flow of 200,000 liters/hr. It is necessary to maintain the concentration of CO in the garage at or below 50 ppm$_v$. This is done with ventilation equipment which exchanges air in the facility. The terminology is air changes per hour (ach) and is equivalent to the number of times a volume of air equal to the volume of the facility is exchanged per hour.

8. If there were no air changes, what would be the concentration in ppm$_v$ of CO in the garage facility?

(A) 20   (C) 200

(B) 196   (D) 2,000

9. How many air changes per hour will be required to reduce the CO concentration to 50 ppm$_v$?

(A) 3   (C) 5

(B) 4   (D) 30

10. For the bus garage, suppose the concentration of CO was mandated not to exceed 20 ppm$_v$, how many air changes would be required to achieve this concentration?

(A) 7.5   (C) 10.0

(B) 9.0   (D) 11.0

11. One kilogram of nitrogen with an initial volume of three cubic meters and a pressure of 20 bars expands according to pV^n = constant to a final volume of 15 cubic meters and a pressure of three bars. The value of n is most nearly?

(A) 1.40   (C) 0.29

(B) 1.18   (D) 1.33

Questions 12–15 are based on the diagram below.

For this process ideal gas is compressed at constant volume from stage 1 to stage 2. Stage 2 to stage 3 is adiabatic isentropic and stage 3 to stage 1 is a decrease in volume at constant pressure. The following values apply:

$p_1 = 1$ atm

$V_1 = V_2 = 1$ liter

$T_1 = 20°C$

$V_3 = 3$ liters

$k = 1.4$

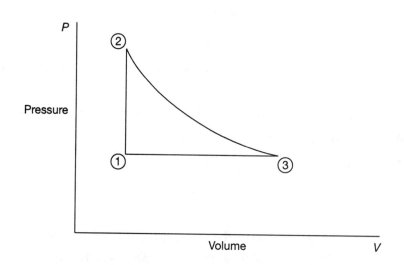

12. What is the heat supplied to the process in calories?

(A) 4.6   (C) 53.5

(B) 40.9   (D) 80.1

13. What is the heat rejected in calories?

(A) –7.0   (C) +7.0

(B) –62.3   (D) +62.3

14. What is the percent efficiency of the cycle?

(A) 23.4%   (C) 34.3%

(B) 30.5%   (D) 100%

15. What is the corresponding Carnot efficiency of the process?

    (A) 23.4%

    (B) 26.9%

    (C) 65.7%

    (D) 78.4%

16. One kilogram of water is injected into a 20 liter volume vessel which is maintained at a temperature of 200°C. At 200°C, the specific volumes of liquid and vapor are respectively V_{liq} = 0.11 liter/kilogram and V_{gas} = 126 liter/kilogram. What percent of water will be evaporated in the vessel?

    (A) 99%

    (B) 84%

    (C) 16%

    (D) 8%

Questions 17–19 are based on the following:

A copper casing having a mass of 100 kilograms and a temperature of 500°C is quenched in a 500 kilogram bath of oil where the initial temperature is 25°C. The specific heat of the copper is $C_{p/Cu}$ = 0.386 kJ/kg-K, and the specific heat of the oil is $C_{p/oil}$ = 0.193 kJ/kg-K. Assume no heat is lost to the surroundings.

17. What is the change in entropy of the casing in kcal/K?

    (A) –12.1

    (B) –22.3

    (C) –20.7

    (D) +20.7

18. What is the total entropy for the system in kcal/K?

    (A) 13.9

    (B) 36.2

    (C) 49.6

    (D) 225.1

19. What is the total work lost by the system in kcal/K?

    (A) 10,787

    (B) 6,950

    (C) 5,840

    (D) 4,142

Questions 20–22 are based on the following:

Methanol is produced from synthesis gas, a mixture of CO and H_2 according to the following reaction:

$$CO + 2H_2 = CH_3OH$$

This synthesis gas is, in turn, usually made from the Water Gas Shift Reaction:

$$CH_4 + H_2O = CO + 3H_2$$

20. How many m^3 of CH_4 are required to produce 1,000 liters of CH_3OH, which has an approximate density of 1 gm/cm³, assuming 90% over-all process efficiency and that CH_4 behaves as an ideal gas?

    (A) 630   (C) 778

    (B) 700   (D) 803

21. The cost of CH_4 is $0.10 per m^3 and represents 30 percent of the total cost to manufacture CH_3OH. Assuming a 20 percent profit margin, what is the price that must be charged per liter of CH_3OH?

    (A) $0.09   (C) $0.28

    (B) $0.26   (D) $0.31

22. The current price of CH_4 is $0.10 per m^3. Assuming the conditions of Question 21, how much more will have to be charged for a liter of CH_3OH if the price is raised one cent to $0.11 per m^3?

    (A) $0.008   (C) $0.031

    (B) $0.012   (D) $0.340

Questions 23 and 24 are based on the following:

Solid carbon (C) is reacted with steam (H_2O) to form a synthesis gas (H_2 and CO) according to the reaction:

$$C(s) + H_2O = CO + H_2$$

At 700K and 100 atmospheres pressure, this reaction produces synthesis gas for which the mole fraction of H_2 is 0.77.

23. What is the equilibrium constant for this reaction under the above conditions?

(A) 0.59   (C) 2.58

(B) 1.00   (D) 11.21

24. What is the partial pressure of H_2 in atmospheres if the final pressure is 150 atmospheres?

(A) 50   (C) 115

(B) 65   (D) 150

Questions 25 and 26 are based on the following:

Henry's Law states that the equilibrium value of the mole fraction of gas dissolved in liquid is directly proportional to the partial pressure of that gas above the liquid surface. In mathematical terms this is:

$$Y_i = \frac{1}{H} \times p_i$$

where:

H = Henry's Law constant

Y_i = mole fraction of gas dissolved in that liquid

p_i = partial pressure

25. For CO_2 at 25°C, the Henry's Law constant, $1/H = 6 \times 10^{-3}$ moles/ atm. If the partial pressure of CO_2 in 25°C air at 760 mmHg pressure is 50 mmHg, how much CO_2 in grams per liter can be dissolved in that water?

(A) 0.0004   (C) 0.0170

(B) 0.0010   (D) 0.9600

26. For CH_4 at 5°C the Henry's Law constant is, 4×10^{-5} mole/atm. At 5°C and one atmosphere pressure a solution of water contains 0.001 gram/liter of methane. What is the partial pressure of CH_4 in mmHg above the solution?

   (A) 1.19

   (B) 19.00

   (C) 21.40

   (D) 342.00

Questions 27–29 are based on the following:

A 2,000 Megawatt per hour coal-fired power plant uses pulverized coal as its boiler fuel. The coal has a heating value of 25,000 kJ/kg and contains 3% by weight of sulfur and 15% by weight of ash. The power plant operates at a thermal efficiency of 35% and has an annual capacity factor of 70%. For this type of plant 0.5 kilograms of ash are emitted in the stack gases per kilogram of ash present in the feed coal. An electrostatic precipitator (ESP) removes 99.5% of the particulate matter produced.

27. What is the rate of fly ash in kilograms per hour discharged after the stack gas has passed through the ESP?

   (A) 76

   (B) 216

   (C) 309

   (D) 432

28. How many kilograms per hour of sulfur dioxide (SO_2) are discharged from the plant?

   (A) 17,280

   (B) 24,690

   (C) 34,560

   (D) 49,370

29. Since the amount of SO_2 emitted is unacceptable, it is proposed to install a limestone ($CaCO_3$) scrubber prior to the ESP. This scrubber operates with 10 percent excess $CaCO_3$ and will remove 85 percent of the SO_2 generated. How many kilograms of $CaCO_3$ will be required?

   (A) 27,000

   (B) 29,700

   (C) 54,000

   (D) 59,400

Questions 30–32 are based on the following:

A process boiler wastes 500 kilograms per hour of water to a sewer at a temperature of 80°C. Assume yearly boiler operation of 3,500 hours with a boiler feedwater temperature of 20°C, a C_p for water of 1 cal/gm-°C, and fuel cost of $0.30 per million Joules of energy.

30. How much heat in kilocalories per hour is being lost by this process?

    (A) 30

    (B) 40

    (C) 30,000

    (D) 40,000

31. Given the fuel cost and hours of operation, how much money can be saved annually by recycling the waste water as boiler feedwater?

    (A) $1,250

    (B) $131,800

    (C) $175,400

    (D) $329,900

32. Assume the piping and pumping for the waste water recycle system cost $200,000 to design, purchase, and install. With money available at 8 percent interest, what is the pay back time for the system?

    (A) 0.66

    (B) 1.75

    (C) 1.52

    (D) 2.00

Questions 33 and 34 are based on the following:

A flat furnace wall is constructed in two layers of different bricks. The inner layer is 10 cm wide and constructed with brick having a thermal conductivity of 0.28 cal-cm/m²-min-°C. The outer layer is 20 cm wide with bricks having a thermal conductivity of 1.0 cal-cm/m²-min-°C. The temperature at the face of the inner wall is 700°C and the temperature at the face of the outer wall is 80°C.

33. What is the heat loss through this composite wall in cal/min?

    (A) −11.13

    (B) 7.61

    (C) +11.13

    (D) −22.25

34. What is the temperature in °C at the interface between the two composite layers?

    (A) 428
    (C) 303

    (B) 589
    (D) 390

Questions 35 and 36 are based on the following:

A vapor stream enters a tray in a distillation column at a rate of 100 kg-mole/hr and has a composition of 30 mole percent benzene and 70 mole percent xylene. Liquid flows onto the tray at a rate of 150 kg-mole/hr with a composition of 40 mole percent benzene and 60 mole percent xylene. Under these conditions the composition of the vapor leaving the tray contains 1.3 times the fraction of benzene as the liquid leaving the tray.

35. What is the mole fraction of benzene leaving the tray as liquid?

    (A) 0.24
    (C) 0.40

    (B) 0.32
    (D) 0.42

36. What is the mole fraction of benzene leaving the tray as vapor?

    (A) 0.24
    (C) 0.40

    (B) 0.32
    (D) 0.42

Questions 37 and 38 are based on the following:

The solubility of sodium nitrate ($NaNO_3$) in water at 10°C is 44.5 percent by weight and at 40°C it is 51.4 percent by weight.

37. What is the percentage saturation of a solution containing 49 percent by weight of $NaNO_3$ at 40°C?

    (A) 49%
    (C) 95%

    (B) 91%
    (D) 100%

38. How may grams of $NaNO_3$ can be crystallized from a 49 percent solution of one kilogram mass by reducing its temperature from 40°C to 10°C?

    (A) 69
    (C) 101

    (B) 81
    (D) 124

Questions 39 and 40 refer to the following:

Water at 20°C flows through a tube with a diameter of 0.5 cm at velocity of 2 m/sec. The viscosity of the water at this temperature is 1×10^{-3} poise and its density is 1 gm/cm^3.

39. Is the water flowing through the tube doing so under conditions of laminar flow, transition range flow, or turbulent flow?

   (A) laminar

   (B) transition range

   (C) turbulent

   (D) none of the above

40. What is the maximum flow velocity in cm/sec for which laminar flow can occur, if other conditions remain the same?

   (A) 0.02

   (B) 0.04

   (C) 2.00

   (D) 4.00

Questions 41 and 42 are based on the following:

A mixture of nitrogen and oxygen at –190°C and 100 kPa is in perfect solution and its vapor behaves as an ideal gas. The vapor pressure of nitrogen and oxygen are given as:

$$p_{N_2} = 136.7 \text{ kPa}$$
$$p_{O_2} = 30.1 \text{ kPa}$$

41. What is the mole fraction of nitrogen in the liquid phase?

   (A) 0.60

   (B) 0.66

   (C) 0.73

   (D) 0.82

42. What is the mole fraction oxygen in the vapor phase?

   (A) 0.10

   (B) 0.22

   (C) 0.30

   (D) 0.90

Questions 43–45 refer to the following:

A furnace fired with a hydrocarbon fuel has the following dry-stack analysis:

$CO_2 = 12\%$

$O_2 = 7\%$

$N_2 = 81\%$

43. What is the weight percent of carbon, C, in the fuel?

    (A) 70.5%   (C) 93.5%

    (B) 88.2%   (D) 96.6%

44. What is the percent of excess air for this combustion process?

    (A) 0%   (C) 48%

    (B) 33%   (D) 81%

45. Including excess air, how many liters of air are supplied per gram of fuel?

    (A) 3.08   (C) 10.00

    (B) 4.85   (D) 14.90

46. At 25°C, O_2 has a solubility in water of 2×10^{-5} mole/gm-mole. How many milliliters of O_2 can be dissolved in 1,000 liters of water at 25°C and 1 atmosphere pressure?

    (A) 10   (C) 40

    (B) 20   (D) 90

Questions 47 and 48 refer to the following:

Water is to be heated from 20°C to 80°C by condensing steam on the shell side of a shell and tube heat exchanger. The water flow rate is 100 kg/hr. Steam at 0.2 kPa and 150°C is to be condensed to saturated water at 0.1 MPa and 100°C.

47. Approximately how many kg/hr of steam will have to be condensed to achieve this heat transfer assuming 100% efficiency and no fouling of the heat exchanger?

(A) 2.5

(C) 49.0

(B) 11.0

(D) 271.0

48. For an overall heat transfer coefficient of $U = 2,350$ cal/hr-m^2-°C, what is the heat transfer area in m^2 of the tube side of the heat exchanger?

(A) 0.17

(C) 31.90

(B) 7.67

(D) 42.60

49. The reaction $CH_4 + 2O_2 = CO_2 + 2H_2O$ has a heat of reaction of 890 kilojoules per gram mole. What is the enthalpy in kJ/gm for the combustion of one gram of methane (CH_4)?

(A) 11.1

(C) 890.0

(B) 55.5

(D) 14,240

50. A lubricating nipple for a bearing has a diameter of 2 mm and a length of 10 mm. Oil having a viscosity of 10 poise and a density of 0.8 gm/cm^3 must be forced through this nipple. How much pressure in kPa must be exerted on this oil to force it through the nipple at a flow rate of 100 cm^3/hr?

(A) 1.4

(C) 27.8

(B) 22.2

(D) 22,200

Questions 51 and 52 are based on the following:

A reaction vessel contains the following gases: 0.1 mole of CO, 0.15 mole of steam (H_2O), 0.2 mole of CO_2, and 0.3 mole of H_2. These gases are in equilibrium according to the reaction:

$$CO + H_2O = CO_2 + H_2$$

51. What is the equilibrium constant for the condition?

(A) 0.25

(C) 2.25

(B) 0.44

(D) 4.00

52. If the equilibrium constant does not change, what will be the final concentration of CO_2 if one adds 0.05 moles of H_2O to the reactants?

(A) 0.015

(C) 0.215

(B) 0.200

(D) 0.267

53. A water pipe with an inside diameter of 20 cm furnishes water through a network of smaller pipes to a faucet having a diameter of 2 cm. If water flows from that faucet at a velocity of 5 cm/sec, what is the average velocity in cm/sec it produces in the main water pipe?

(A) 0.05

(C) 0.50

(B) 0.10

(D) 5.00

54. A rounded hole of 0.5 cm diameter is punched into the side wall of a large cylindrical drum at a point 0.75 meter from the top of the liquid level in the drum. At the beginning of this situation, how many liters/hour of fluid will flow from the hole?

(A) 27

(C) 187

(B) 74

(D) 265

55. A process under design which does not experience extreme temperatures requires temperature sensors at several hundred locations throughout the production line. Of the following temperature sensing systems, the most cost-effective would be

(A) thermocouples with manual monitoring.

(B) fiber optic sensors with a central computer monitoring system.

(C) optical pyrometers with a central computer monitoring system.

(D) mercury thermometers with a technician with manual monitoring.

56. When sampling material from a process, which of the following is *not* a primary consideration to ensure accurate and characteristic measurement?

(A) Sampling location

(B) Sample return location

(C) Condition of sample transport to analysis instrument

(D) Sampling frequency

57. For which of the following is computer process control generally least useful?

(A) Equipment maintenance

(B) Real-time data acquisition

(C) Auxiliary process control

(D) Automatic control for a manually supervised process

58. The equilibrium adsorption of benzene vapor on a certain activated charcoal at 33°C is reported as follows:

Benzene vapor adsorbed, cm^3(STP)/g charcoal	15	25	40	50
Partial pressure benzene, mm Hg	0.0010	0.0045	0.0251	0.1150

By Linear Interpolation between the closest adjacent points, estimate the equilibrium partial pressure of benzene when 30 cm^3 (STP) of benzene is adsorbed per gm of charcoal.

(A) 0.0148 mmHg

(C) 0.0169 mmHg

(B) 0.0320 mmHg

(D) 0.0114 mmHg

59.

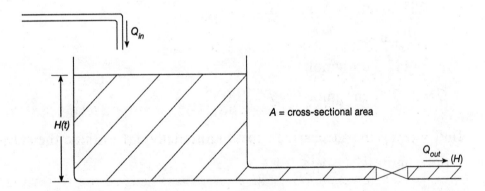

A mass balance over a continuous flow tank shown in the figure above yields:

$$A \times \left(\frac{dH}{dt} \right) = Q_{in} - Q_{out}$$

Given that:

$$A = 0.5 \text{ m}^2$$

$$Q_{in} = 0.7 \text{ m}^3/\text{s}$$

$$Q_{out} = 0.98 \times H \text{m}^3/\text{s}$$

$$H_0 = 0.5 \text{ m at } t_0 \text{s}$$

Using the Simple Euler First-Order method with an increment time (Δt) of 2 s, find the liquid level in the tank at $t = 2$ s. The Euler formula is:

$$H_{i+1} = H_i + (\Delta t) \times \left(\frac{dH}{dt}\right)_i$$

(A) 0.528 m
(C) 0.472 m
(B) 0.514 m
(D) 0.486 m

60. The Virial Equation of State truncated to three terms is given as:

$$Z = \frac{PV}{RT} = 1 + \frac{B}{V} + \frac{C}{V^2}$$

This equation can be written in the form $V = f(V)$.

Given that:

$R = 83.14 \text{ cm}^3 \text{ bar gmol}^{-1}\text{K}^{-1}$,

$P = 10 \text{ bar}$

$B = -242.5 \text{ cm}^3\text{gmol}^{-1}$

$C = 25{,}200 \text{ cm}^6\text{gmol}^{-2}$ at $T = 100°C$

find V using the successive substitution method. Continue the substitutions until $|V_{i+1} - V_i| \le 0.1$.

(A) 522.1 cm^{3}gmol^{-1}
(C) 2,847.5 cm^{3}gmol^{-1}
(B) 3,101.9 cm^{3}gmol^{-1}
(D) 3,334.5 cm^{3}gmol^{-1}

TEST 1

ANSWER KEY

1.	(C)	16.	(C)	31.	(B)	46.	(B)
2.	(B)	17.	(B)	32.	(B)	47.	(B)
3.	(D)	18.	(A)	33.	(A)	48.	(D)
4.	(A)	19.	(D)	34.	(C)	49.	(B)
5.	(B)	20.	(C)	35.	(B)	50.	(B)
6.	(B)	21.	(D)	36.	(D)	51.	(D)
7.	(B)	22.	(C)	37.	(B)	52.	(C)
8.	(B)	23.	(C)	38.	(B)	53.	(A)
9.	(A)	24.	(B)	39.	(C)	54.	(D)
10.	(B)	25.	(D)	40.	(D)	55.	(B)
11.	(B)	26.	(C)	41.	(B)	56.	(B)
12.	(D)	27.	(B)	42.	(A)	57.	(A)
13.	(B)	28.	(C)	43.	(C)	58.	(D)
14.	(A)	29.	(D)	44.	(C)	59.	(A)
15.	(B)	30.	(C)	45.	(D)	60.	(C)

DETAILED EXPLANATIONS
OF ANSWERS

TEST 1

1. **(C)**

$$A \underset{kr}{\overset{kf}{\rightleftharpoons}} B$$

$$k_f = 2 \times 10^{-2} \, \text{min}^{-1}$$

$$k_r = 4 \, \text{min}^{-1}$$

$$r = k_f \times C_A - k_r \times C_B$$

At equilibrium $r = 0$, therefore:

$$k_f \times C_A = k_r \times C_B$$

$$k_{eq} = \frac{k_f}{k_r} = \frac{2 \times 10^{-2} \, \text{min}^{-1}}{4 \, \text{min}^{-1}} = 5 \times 10^{-3}$$

$$C_B = k_{eq} \times C_A = 5 \times 10^{-3} \times C_A$$

0.005 or 0.5% of A is converted.

Answer choice (A) is the forward reaction rate k_f. Answer choice (B) assumes that all of reactant A is converted, and choice (D) is too high by a factor of 10.

2. **(B)**

Heat lost by metal = heat gained by the water.

$$50 \text{gm} \times C_p \times (70 - 28)°\text{C} = 200 \text{gm} \times 1.0 \text{cal/gm-}°\text{C} \times (28 - 10)°\text{C}$$

Rearranging terms and solving for C_p:

$$C_p = \frac{3,600 \, \text{cal}}{2,100 \, \text{gm-}°\text{C}} = 1.71 \text{cal/gm-}°\text{C}$$

Answer choice (A) divides the mass of metal material by its temperature loss. Answer choice (C) simply divides the temperature loss of the metal by the temperature gain of the water, and answer choice (D) reverses the temperature gain of the water and metal.

3. **(D)**

Constituent	Mass grams	MW	gm-mole
benzene	5	78	0.064
toluene	3	92	0.033
xylene	2	106	0.019
		Total	0.116

Since the vapor mixture is an ideal gas, $pV = nRT$.

$$V = \frac{n \times R \times T}{p}$$

$$= \frac{0.116\,\text{gm-mole} \times 82.06\,\text{atm-cm}^3/\text{gm-moleK} \times (175 + 273)\text{K}}{0.5\,\text{atm}}$$

$$V = 8519\ \text{cm}^3 = 8.5\ \text{liters}$$

Answer choice (A) uses $R = 1.987$ whose dimensions are cal/gm-moleK. Answer choice (B) is low by a factor of 10, and answer choice (C) was calculated using °C instead of K.

4. **(A)**

Let X = kg/hr of dry air fed.

Water balance: Water In = Water Out

$$0.05 \times 100 + 0.005 \times \frac{X}{0.995} = 0.01 \times 100 + 0.2 \times \frac{X}{0.98}$$

$$5 + 0.00503 \times X = 1.0 + 0.02041 \times X$$

Rearranging terms:

$$0.01538 \times X = 4$$

$$X = 260.1$$

This is the dry air fed to the dryer, so that you must add the water in that air which is 0.5%.

$$260.1 + 0.005 \times 260.1 = 261.4$$

Answer choice (B) is the total dry air without the water. Answer choice (C) is solved from the following equation: $0.05 \times 100 + 0.005 \times X = 0.01 \times 100 + 0.02 \times X$. Answer choice (D) compounds the error from choice (C) by adding 2 percent water.

5. **(B)**

Basis: 1 gm-mole of fuel gas

The combustion reaction yields only CO_2 and H_2O as by-products.

$$\text{moles of C per mole of gas} = 0.3 \times 3 + 0.6 \times 4 = 3.3 \text{ moles}$$

$$\text{moles of H per mole of gas} = 0.3 \times 8 + 0.6 \times 10 = 8.4 \text{ moles}$$

$$O_2 \text{ required} = 3.3 + 0.5 \times 8.4 = 7.5 \text{ moles}$$

air = 21% O_2, therefore

$$\text{air} = \frac{7.5 \text{ moles}}{0.21} = 35.7 \text{ moles}$$

$$\text{weight of fuel gas} = 0.3 \times 44 + 0.6 \times 58 + 0.1 \times 28 = 50.8 \text{ gm}$$

$$35.7 \text{ moles of air} \times (0.21 \times 32 + 0.79 \times 28) = 1029.6 \text{ gm}$$

$$\text{ratio of air:fuel} = \frac{1029.6 \text{ gm}}{50.8 \text{ gm}} = 20.3\%$$

Answer choice (A) is moles of O_2, required. Answer choice (C) did not add N_2 to the fuel gas, and answer choice (D) is the moles of air required, or volume ratio.

6. **(B)**

$$\Delta(T_{lm}) = \frac{(T_{Ho} - T_{Co}) - (T_{Hi} - T_{Ci})}{\ln\frac{(T_{Ho} - T_{Co})}{(T_{Hi} - T_{Ci})}}$$

$$\Delta(T_{lm}) = \frac{(120 - 80) - (200 - 20)}{\ln\frac{(120 - 80)}{(200 - 20)}} = \frac{-140}{\ln(0.222)} = \frac{-140}{-1.5}$$

$$\Delta(T_{lm}) = 93$$

Answer choice (A) used the exponential in the numerator. Answer choice (C) used $(T_{Ho} - T_{Ci})$, and answer choice (D) used the $\log_{10}$ instead of ln.

7. **(B)**

Flow is by gravity and frictionless, therefore:

$$u = \sqrt{2 \times g \times h}$$

where:

$$g = 9.8 \text{ m/sec}^2$$

$$u = \sqrt{2 \times 9.8 \text{ m/sec}^2 \times 5 \text{ m}}$$

$$u = \sqrt{98 \text{ m}^2/\text{sec}^2}$$

$$u = 9.9 \text{ m/sec}$$

Flow is $Q = u \times A$ where A = cross-sectional area of the pipe, thus:

$$A = \frac{Q}{u} = \frac{5 \text{ l/sec} \times 10^{-3} \text{ m}^3/\text{l}}{9.9 \text{ m/sec}} = 0.005 \text{ m}^2$$

$$D = \sqrt{4 \times A/\pi} = \sqrt{4 \times 0.005 \text{ m}^2/3.14} = \sqrt{0.0064 \text{ m}^2}$$

$$D = 0.0798 \text{ m} \times 100 \text{ cm/m} = 7.98 \text{ cm} \approx 8.0$$

Answer choice (A) was derived using $g = 32.2 \text{ ft/sec}^2$, which is the gravitational acceleration in engineering units, answer choice (C) neglected to use the factor of 2 in determining velocity, and answer choice (D) did not convert l to m^3.

8. **(B)**

Basis: 1 hour time frame.

$$CO = \frac{200,000 \text{ liters/hr} \times 10^{-3} \text{ m}^3/\text{liter} \times 0.01 \times 1 \text{ hr}}{10,000 \text{ m}^3 + (200,000 \text{ liters/hr} \times 10^{-3} \text{ m}^3/\text{liter} \times 1 \text{ hr})} \times 10^6 \text{ ppm}_v$$

$$= 196 \text{ ppm}_v$$

Answer choice (A) did not consider volume of emissions and is low by a factor of 10, answer choice (C) did not consider volume of emissions, and (D) did not consider volume of emissions and is high by a factor of 10.

9. **(A)**

Basis: 1 hour time frame.

$$\frac{200,000\,\text{liters/hr} \times 10^{-3}\,\text{m}^3/\text{liter} \times 0.01}{10,000\,\text{m}^3 + (200,000\,\text{liters/hr} \times 10^{-3}\,\text{m}^3/\text{liter} \times 1\,\text{hr}) + V_{ach}} \times 10^6 = 50$$

Rearranging terms and solving for V_{ach}:

$$V_{ach} = \frac{(2 \times 10^6 - 5 \times 10^5)\text{m}^3}{50} = \frac{15 \times 10^5\,\text{m}^3/\text{hr}}{50} = 30,000\,\text{m}^3/\text{hr}$$

$$\text{Air changes} = \frac{30,000\,\text{m}^3/\text{hr}}{10,000\,\text{m}^3} = 3 \text{ air changes per hour}$$

Answer choice (B) took 200 ppm$_v$ and divided it by 50 ppm$_v$. Answer choice (C) added the term 5×10^5 to the numerator of the V_{ach} expression and answer choice (D) is high by a factor of 10.

10. **(B)**

Basis: 1 hour time frame.

$$\frac{200,000\,\text{liters/hr} \times 10^{-3}\,\text{m}^3/\text{liter} \times 0.01}{10,000\,\text{m}^3 + (200,000\,\text{liters/hr} \times 10^{-3}\,\text{m}^3/\text{liter} \times 1\,\text{hr}) + V_{ach}} \times 10^6 = 20$$

Rearranging terms and solving for V_{ach}:

$$V_{ach} = \frac{(2 \times 10^6 - 2 \times 10^5)\text{m}^3/\text{hr}}{20} = \frac{18 \times 10^5\,\text{m}^3/\text{hr}}{20} = 90,000\,\text{m}^3/\text{hr}$$

$$\text{Air changes} = \frac{90,000\,\text{m}^3/\text{hr}}{10,000\,\text{m}^3} = 9 \text{ air changes per hour}$$

Answer choice (A) took 50 ppm$_v$ and divided it by 20 ppm$_v$ and multiplied this by 3, the correct answer from the previous question. Answer choice (C) took 50 ppm$_v$ and divided it by 20 ppm$_v$ then multiplied this by 4, the incorrect answer from the previous question. Answer choice (D) added 2×10^5 to the numerator.

11. **(B)**

Given the initial and final conditions of p and V and noting that $pV^n =$ constant. Therefore:

$$p_1 V_1^n = p_2 V_2^n = 20 \times (3)^n = 3 \times (15)^n$$

$$\frac{20}{3} = \left[\frac{15}{3}\right]^n \Rightarrow 6.67 = 5^n$$

Using logarithmic notation:

$$\log_{10}(6.67) = n \times \log_{10}(5)$$

$$n = \frac{\log_{10}(6.67)}{\log_{10}(5)} = \frac{0.829}{0.669} = 1.18$$

Answer choice (A) is the ratio of C_p/C_v for nitrogen, which is 1.4, and (C) is the value of k for nitrogen based on that ratio according to

$$\frac{C_p - C_v}{C_p}$$

Answer choice (D) divides $p_1 V_1$ by $p_2 V_2$.

12. **(D)**

$$\text{For } Q = 0, p_2 \times V_1^k = p_1 \times V_3^k$$

Rearranging terms:

$$p_2 = 1 \, \text{atm} \times \left[\frac{3 \, \text{liters}}{1 \, \text{liter}}\right]^{1.4} = 1 \times 4.6 = 4.6 \, \text{atm}$$

For $V = $ constant:

$$Q = \frac{\Delta(pV)}{k-1} = \frac{(4.6 \times 1) - (1 \times 1)}{1.4 - 1} = \frac{3.6}{0.4} = 9.0 \text{ atm-liters}$$

$$Q = 9.0 \text{ atm-liters} \times 8.9 \, \text{cal/atm-liters} = 80.1 \, \text{calories}$$

Answer choice (A) is $P_2 \times V_1$ and answer choice (B) is the same only converted to calories. Answer choice (C) is $\Delta(pV)^k$ converted to calories.

13. **(B)**

For p = constant:

$$Q = \frac{k}{k-1} \times p \times (V_1 - V_3) = \frac{1.4}{1.4-1} \times 1\,\text{atm} \times (1-3)\,\text{liters} = -7\,\text{atm-liters}$$

$$Q = -7\,\text{atm-liters} \times 8.9\,\text{cal/atm-liters} = -62.3\,\text{cal}$$

Answer choice (A) is atm-liters. Answer choice (C) is choice (A) with a positive sign and answer choice (D) is choice (B) with a positive sign.

14. **(A)**

$$\eta = \frac{Q_{in} - Q_{out}}{Q_{in}} \times 100\% = \frac{81.3 - 62.3}{81.3} \times 100\% = 23.4\%$$

Answer choice (B) divides by Q_{out} while choice (C) uses 7.0 and 4.6 as the respective quantities of heat, and choice (D) assumes 100% efficiency.

15. **(B)**

Carnot efficiency is based on T_{in} and T_{out}; therefore, one needs to calculate T_2 and T_3.

$$T_2 = T_1 \times \frac{p_2}{p_1} = (20 + 273) \times \frac{4.6}{1} = 1{,}348\text{K}$$

$$T_2 = 1{,}348 - 273 = 1{,}074°\text{C}$$

$$\text{For } Q = 0, \ T_3 = T_2 \times \left[\frac{V_1}{V_2}\right]^{(k-1/k)} = 1{,}348 \times \left[\frac{1}{3}\right]^{0.286} = 985\text{K}$$

$$T_3 = 985 - 273 = 712°\text{C}$$

$$\eta_{car} = \frac{T_2 - T_3}{T_2} = \frac{1{,}348 - 985}{1{,}348} \times 100\% = 26.9\%$$

Answer choice (A) assumes Carnot efficiency is the same as the process efficiency. Answer choices (C) and (D) use 20°C as the base temperature and T_2 and T_3, respectively, as the higher temperatures.

16. **(C)**

Total volume of liquid and gas in the vessel is the sum of the products of the mass of the liquid and gas times their respective specific volumes.

$$V_{tot} = m_{liq} \times V_{liq} + m_{gas} \times V_{gas} = 1 \text{ liter}$$

$$m_{liq} + m_{gas} = 1 \text{ kg}$$

$$(1 - m_{gas}) \times 0.11 + m_{gas} \times 126 = 20 \text{ liter}$$

$$125.89 \times m_{gas} = 19.89 \text{ liter}$$

$$m_{gas} = \frac{19.89 \text{ liter}}{125.89 \text{ liter/kg}} = 0.158 \text{ kg}$$

$$\% \text{ evaporated} = \frac{0.158 \text{ kg}}{1.00 \text{ kg}} \times 100\% \approx 16$$

Answer choice (A) assumes most of the water evaporates. Answer choice (B) used V_{gas} with the $(1 - m_{gas})$ term, and answer choice (D) used 10 liters for volume.

17. **(B)**

First find the equilibrium temperature of the entire system.

$\Delta Q = 0$: heat lost by copper casing = heat gained by the oil

$$Q_{cu} = 100 \text{ kg} \times 0.386 \text{ kJ/kg-K} \times (500 - T)\text{K}$$

$$Q_{oil} = 500 \text{ kg} \times 0.193 \text{ kJ/kg-K} \times (T - 25)\text{K}$$

$$Q_{cu} = Q_{oil}$$

Combining these equations and solving for T,

$$19,300 - 38.6 \times T = 96.5 \times T - 2,412.5$$

$$135.1 \times T = 21,712.5$$

$$T = \frac{21,712.5}{135.1} = 160.7°\text{C}$$

$$\Delta S_{Cu} = m \times C_{p/Cu} \times \ln \frac{T_2}{T_1} = 100 \times 0.386 \times \ln \frac{(160.7 + 273)}{(500 + 273)}$$

$$\Delta S_{Cu} = 38.6 \times \ln (0.561) = 38.6 \times (-0.578) = -22.3 \text{ kcal/K}$$

Answer choice (A) used the incorrect signs for the two equations. Answer choices (C) and (D) are based on T_1, not T_2, as °C not K with (D) having the wrong sign.

18. **(A)**

$$\Delta S_{oil} = m \times C_{p/oil} \times \ln \frac{T_2}{T_1} = 500 \times 0.193 \times \ln \frac{(160.7+273)}{(25+273)}$$

$$\Delta S_{oil} = 96.5 \times \ln(1.455) = 96.5 \times 0.375 = +36.2 \, \text{kcal/K}$$

Note the positive sign.

$$\Delta S_{tot} = \Delta S_{Cu} + \Delta S_{oil} = -22.3 + 36.2 = 13.9 \, \text{kcal/K}$$

Answer choice (B) is ΔS_{oil}. Answer choice (C) is based on ΔS_{Cu}, answer choice (A) in the previous question, and answer choice (D) uses °C rather than K.

19. **(D)**

$$\Delta W = T_0 \times \Delta S_{tot} = (25 + 273)\text{K} \times 13.9 \, \text{kcal/K}$$

$$\Delta W = 4,142 \, \text{kcal}$$

Answer choice (A) is based on $\Delta S_{tot} = 36.2$ as given in answer choice (B) for Question 18. Answer choice (B) uses °C instead of K, and answer choice (C) uses $\Delta S_{tot} = 49.6$ as given in answer choice (C) for Question 18.

20. **(C)**

It takes 1 mole of CO to produce 1 mole of CH_3OH. It also takes 1 mole of CH_4 to produce 1 mole of CO and 3 moles of H_2 although only 2 moles are needed. Therefore, at 90% overall efficiency,

$$\text{mole of } CH_4 = \frac{\text{mole of } CH_3OH}{0.9}$$

Each gm-mole of CH_4 is 22.4 liters. One gm-mole of CH_3OH weighs 32 grams, and 1 liter = 1,000 cm^3. Thus:

$$1,000 \, \text{liters of } CH_3OH = \frac{1,000 \, \text{liter} \times 1,000 \, \text{cm}^3/\text{liter} \times 1 \, \text{gm/cm}^3}{32 \, \text{gm/gm-mole}}$$

$$= 31,250 \, \text{gm-mole}$$

$$\text{mole of } CH_4 = \frac{31{,}250 \text{ gm-mole}}{0.9}$$

$$= 34{,}722 \text{ gm-mole}$$

$$CH_4 = 34{,}722 \text{ gm-mole} \times 22.4 \text{ liters/gm-mole} \times 10^{-3} \text{ m}^3/\text{liter}$$

$$= 778 \text{ m}^3$$

Answer choice (A) used $0.9 \times$ mole of CH_3OH. Answer choice (B) did not convert cm³/liter or m³/liter or divide by 0.9, and answer choice (D) used 31 gm/gm-mole as MW for CH_3OH.

21. **(D)**

This is fairly straightforward but requires the answer from Question 20.

$$\$0.10/\text{m}^3 \times 0.778 \text{ m}^3/\text{liter } CH_3OH = \$0.0778/\text{liter}$$

$$\text{cost per liter } CH_3OH = \frac{\$0.0778/\text{liter}}{0.3} \times 1.2 = \$0.31$$

Answer choice (A) was not divided by 0.3. Answer choice (B) was not multiplied by 1.2, and answer choice (C) used 700 m³/liter CH_3OH.

22. **(C)**

Price increase for CH_4:

$$\$0.01/\text{m}^3 \times 0.778 \text{ m}^3/\text{liter } CH_3OH = \$0.0078/\text{liter } CH_3OH$$

$$\text{added cost per liter } CH_3OH = \frac{\$0.00778/\text{liter}}{0.3} \times 1.2 = \$0.031$$

Answer choice (A) is simply the increase in price $\times$ 0.778 m³/liter, answer (B) is the increase in price $\times$ 1.2, and (D) is the new price charged.

23. **(C)**

Let X = CO and H_2 formed. Thus, the mole fraction of water reacted is $1 - X$, therefore:

$$K_{eq} = \frac{(CO) \times (H_2)}{(H_2O)} = \frac{X^2}{(1 - X)}$$

We are given $H_2 = 0.77$, which means that CO is also 0.77, so that:

$$K_{eq} = \frac{(0.77)^2}{(1-0.77)} = \frac{0.593}{0.23} = 2.58$$

Answer choice (A) is X^2, answer choice (B) uses $X = 0.617$, and answer choice (D) uses $(1 - X)^2$ for the denominator.

24. **(B)**

For the concentrations given, 1 mole of H_2O reacts to form 0.77 mole each of CO and H_2. Thus, the total number of moles in equilibrium is:

$$X_{tot} = 0.77 \times 2 + (1 - 0.77) = 1.77$$

$$p_{H_2} = \frac{0.77}{1.77} \times 150 \text{ atm} = 65 \text{ atm}$$

Answer choice (A) assumes all of reactants and products are in equal mole fractions. Answer choice (C) multiplies the mole fraction of H_2 by the total pressure, and answer choice (D) is the total pressure.

25. **(D)**

$$p_{CO_2} = \frac{50 \text{ mmHg}}{760 \text{ mmHg/atm}} = 0.0658 \text{ atm}$$

$$Y_{CO_2} = \frac{1}{H} \times p_{CO_2} = 6 \times 10^{-3} \text{ moles/atm} \times 0.658 \text{ atm} = 3.95 \times 10^{-4} \text{ moles}$$

One gram-mole of $CO_2 = 44$ grams, thus

$$\frac{3.95 \times 10^{-4} \text{ moles} \times 44 \text{ grams } CO_2/\text{mole} \times 1{,}000 \text{ cm}^3/\text{liter}}{18 \text{ grams } H_2O/\text{mole} \times 1 \text{ cm}^3/\text{gram}}$$

$$= 0.96 \text{ grams/liter}$$

Answer choice (A) is the concentration of CO_2 in moles. Answer choice (B) is in grams/cm^3, and answer choice (C) does not use the molecular weight of H_2O in determining the concentration.

26. **(C)**

Determine the moles of CH_4 in solution with CH_4 having a molecular weight of 16 gm/mole:

$$\frac{0.001 \text{ gm CH}_4/\text{liter} \times 18 \text{ grams H}_2\text{O/mole} \times 1 \text{ cm}^3/\text{gram}}{1,000 \text{ cm}^3/\text{liter} \times 16 \text{ gm CH}_4/\text{mole}}$$

$$Y_{\text{CH}_4} = 1.125 \times 10^{-6} \text{ mole CH}_4$$

$$p_{\text{CH}_4} = \frac{1.125 \times 10^{-6} \text{ mole CH}_4}{4 \times 10^{-5} \text{ mole/atm}} = 0.028 \text{ atm}$$

$$p_{\text{CH}_4} = 0.028 \text{ atm} \times 760 \text{ mm Hg/atm} = 21.4 \text{ mm Hg}$$

Answer choices (A) and (B) did not use the molecular weight of H_2O in determining the concentration. Answer choice (B) also did not use the molecular weight of CH_4, and answer choice (D) did not divide by the molecular weight of CH_4.

27. **(B)**

The first step is to calculate the rate of coal fired per hour.

rate of fire (kg/hr) =

$$\frac{2,000 \text{ MW} \times 0.7 \times 3.6 \times 10^6 \text{ kJ/MW-hr}}{25,000 \text{ kJ/kg} \times 0.35} = 576,000 \text{ kg/hr}$$

The amount of ash produced and emitted in the stack gas is:

Ash produced =

576,000 kg/hr × 0.15 ash/coal × 0.5 kg/kg = 43,200 kg ash/hr

The ESP removes 99.5% of this ash, therefore

43,200 kg ash/hr × (1 – 0.995) = 216 kg/hr

Answer choice (A) did not use 35% efficiency. Answer choice (C) did not use capacity factor of 70%. Answer choice (D) did not use 0.5 kg/kg for ash in stack gas.

28. **(C)**

For SO_2 the reaction is:

$$S + O_2 = SO_2$$

S in coal = 576,000 kg/hr × 0.03 S/coal = 17,280 kg S/hr

$$\frac{17,280 \text{ kg S/hr}}{32 \text{ kg/mole}} = \frac{SO_2}{64 \text{ kg/mole}}$$

$$SO_2 = 2 \times 17,280 \text{ kg S/hr} = 34,560 \text{ kg/hr}$$

Answer choice (A) did not convert the S to SO_2. Answer choice (B) used coal feed that did not use capacity factor of 70% and also failed to convert the S to SO_2. Answer choice (D) used coal that did not use capacity factor of 70%.

29. **(D)**

The chemical reaction in the scrubber is:

$$SO_2 + CaCO_3 + \frac{1}{2} O_2 = CaSO_4 \downarrow + CO_2$$

For every mole of SO_2 removed, it requires one mole of $CaCO_3$ and this generates one mole of $CaSO_4$ gypsum sludge. Thus:

$$\frac{34,560 \text{ kg/hr}}{64 \text{ kg/mole } SO_2} \times 100 \text{ kg/mole } CaSO_4 \times 1.1 = 59,400 \text{ kg/hr}$$

Answer choice (A) used 17,280 kg/hr for SO_2 removed and did not consider 10% excess $CaCO_3$. Answer choice (B) is answer choice (A) with 10% excess, and answer choice (C) did not consider 10% excess $CaCO_3$.

30. **(C)**

$$Q_{lost} = m \times C_p \times \Delta T$$

$$= 500 \text{ kg/hr} \times 1.0 \text{ cal/gm-°C} \times 1,000 \text{ gm/kg} \times 1 \text{ kcal/1,000 cal}$$

$$\times (80\text{-}20)°C$$

$$Q_{lost} = 30,000 \text{ kcal/hr}$$

Answer choice (A) did not account for Kg/gm in the answer. Answer choice (B) did not use Kg/gm and used 80°C for the temperature difference. Answer choice (D) used 80°C for the temperature difference.

31. **(B)**

$$3,500 \text{ hr/yr} \times 30,000 \text{ kcal/hr} \times \$.30/10^6 \text{ J} = \$31.5 \text{ kcal/J-yr}$$

$$\$31.5 \text{ kcal/J-yr} \times 4.184 \times 10^3 \text{ J/kcal} = \$131,800$$

Answer choice (A) used conversion for J/BTU. Answer choice (C) used 40,000 kcal/hr as Q_{lost}, and answer choice (D) used 8,640 hrs/yr.

32. **(B)**

Let n = payback in years. The incurred cost for the recycle system is equivalent to the savings during that period.

$$\$200,000 \times (1.08)^n = \$131,800 \times n$$

Converting this expression to logarithms:

$$\log_{10}(200,000) + \log_{10}(1.08) \times n = \log_{10}(131,800) + \log_{10}(n)$$
$$5.3010 + n \times 0.0334 = 5.1199 + \log_{10}(n)$$

Rearranging terms:

$$\log_{10}(n) - n \times 0.0344 = 0.1811$$

Need to do a trial and error with estimated values of n.

Let $n = 1.5$

$$\log_{10}(1.5) - 1.5 \times 0.0334 = 0.1811 \Rightarrow$$
$$0.1761 - 0.0501 = 0.12662 \neq 0.1811$$

Let $n = 2$

$$\log_{10}(2) - 2 \times 0.0334 = 0.1811 \Rightarrow$$
$$0.3010 - 0.0201 = 0.2809 \neq 0.1811$$

Let $n = 1.75$

$$\log_{10}(1.75) - 1.75 \times 0.0334 = 0.1811 \Rightarrow$$
$$0.2430 - 0.0505 = 0.1846 \cong 0.1811$$

Therefore the payback time is approximately 1.75 years, or one year and nine months.

Answer choice (A) divides \$131,800 by \$200,000, while choice (C) is the reciprocal, and choice (D) assumes that the system is paid back in two years.

33. **(A)**

Assume an area of 1 m^2. The conductive heat transfer equation is:

$$q = \frac{-\Delta T}{\Sigma \dfrac{k}{k \times \Delta}}$$

$$\Sigma \frac{x}{k \times A} = \frac{10}{0.28 \times 1} + \frac{20}{1.0 \times 1} = 55.7 \, \text{min-} °\text{C/Cal}$$

$$q = \frac{-(700-80)°\text{C}}{55.7 \, \text{min-}°\text{C/cal}} = -11.13 \, \text{Cal/min}$$

Answer choice (B) was calculated by transposing the thermal conductivities and with a positive sign indicating heat gained. Answer choice (C) was calculated without the negative sign, and answer choice (D) is double answer choice (A).

34. **(C)**

We know the inner wall temperature T_{iw} = 700°C and we calculated the heat transferred in the previous question. Therefore:

$$\frac{q}{A} = \frac{k(T_x - T_{iw})}{x}$$

Rearranging terms:

$$T_x = \frac{q \times x}{k \times A} + 700°\text{C}$$

$$= \frac{-11.13 \, \text{cal/min} \times (10 \, \text{cm})}{0.28 \, \text{cal-cm/m}^2\text{-min-}°\text{C} \times 1 \, \text{m}^2} + 700°\text{C} = 303°\text{C}$$

Answer choice (A) uses answer choice (B) from Question 33 to calculate the temperature. Answer choice (B) uses $k = 1.0$, and answer choice (D) is the midpoint between 700°C and 80°C.

35. **(B)**

Let Y = mole fraction of benzene in vapor, and X = mole fraction of benzene in liquid.

$$Y = 1.3 \times X$$

Material Balance In:

$$\text{benzene in liquid} = 150 \text{ kg-mole/hr} \times 0.4 = 60 \text{ kg-mole/hr}$$
$$\text{benzene in vapor} = 100 \text{ kg-mole/hr} \times 0.3 = 30 \text{ kg-mole/hr}$$
$$\text{Total benzene} = 90 \text{ kg-mole/hr}$$

Material Balance Out:

$$\text{benzene in liquid} = 150 \times X$$
$$\text{benzene in vapor} = 100 \times Y$$

Total benzene is therefore:

$$150 \times X + 100 \times (1.3X) = 90$$
$$280 \times X = 90$$

$$X = \frac{90}{280} = 0.32$$

Answer choice (A) benzene in liquid fraction is total liquid plus vapor. Answer choice (C) is benzene in liquid as fraction of total liquid, and answer choice (D) is benzene in vapor rather than liquid.

36. **(D)**

From the previous question, $Y = 1.3 \times X$ and we found $X = 0.32$, therefore:

$$Y = 1.3 \times 0.32 = 0.42$$

Answer choice (A) benzene in liquid fraction is total liquid plus vapor. Answer choice (B) is benzene leaving the tray as liquid, and answer choice (C) is benzene in liquid as fraction of total liquid.

37. **(B)**

At 40°C a saturated solution of $NaNO_3$ contains 51.4% by weight, therefore

$$\% \text{ saturation} = \frac{\text{wgt \% solute}}{\text{wgt \% solvent}} \times \frac{\text{wgt solvent at solubility}}{\text{solubility \%}}$$

For 49% saturation by weight there are:

$$\frac{49\%}{51\%} = \frac{\text{wgt of solute}}{\text{wgt of solvent}} = 0.961$$

$$\frac{\text{wgt solvent at solubility}}{\text{solubility \%}} = \frac{(1 - 0.514)}{0.514} = 0.946$$

$$\% \text{ saturation} = 0.961 \times 0.946 = 0.906 \times 100\% = 91\%$$

Answer choice (A) is the given percent solution, while answer choice (C) simply divides this solution percent by the percent saturation, and answer choice (D) assumes the solution is saturated.

38. **(B)**

Let X = yield of $NaNO_3$ crystals in grams.

Mass $NaNO_3$ at 40°C = $NaNO_3$ in solution at 10°C + $NaNO_3$ crystallized

$$1{,}000 \times 0.49 = (1{,}000 - X) \times 0.445 + X$$

Rearranging terms:

$$X = \frac{(490 - 445)}{(1 - 0.445)} = 81 \text{ grams}$$

Answer choice (A) is the saturation difference between 40°C and 10°C for a 1 kg solution. Answer choice (C) results from dividing (490 − 445) by 0.445, and answer choice (D) uses the saturation amount 514 grams instead of 490 grams.

39. **(C)**

Calculate the Reynolds Number:

$$N_{Re} = \frac{D \times u \times \rho}{\mu}$$

where:

ρ = density
μ = viscosity (1 poise = 0.1 gm-sec/m)

$$N_{Re} = \frac{0.005 \text{ m} \times 2 \text{ m/sec} \times 1 \text{ gm/cm}^3 \times 10^6 \text{ cm}^3/\text{m}^3}{0.1 \text{ gm/m-sec}} = 100{,}000$$

Since $N_{Re} > 4{,}000$ this is turbulent flow.

40. **(D)**

For laminar flow $N_{Re} < 2{,}000$, therefore:

$$N_{Re} = \frac{0.005 \text{ m} \times u_{lam} \times 1 \text{ gm/cm}^3 \times 10^6 \text{ cm}^3/\text{m}^3}{0.1 \text{ gm-sec/m}} = 2{,}000$$

Rearranging terms:

$$u_{lam} = \frac{2,000 \times 0.1 \text{ gm-sec/m}}{0.005 \text{ m} \times 1 \text{ gm/cm}^3 \times 10^6 \text{cm}^3/\text{m}^3} = 0.04 \text{ m/sec}$$

$$u_{lam} = 0.04 \text{ m/sec} \times 100 \text{ cm/m} = 4.0 \text{ cm/sec}$$

Answer choice (A) used $N_{Re} = 1,000$ and did not convert m to cm. Answer choice (B) did not convert m to cm and answer choice (C) used $N_{Re} = 1,000$.

41. **(B)**

Let X = mole fraction of nitrogen in liquid. Total pressure = sum of partial pressure of constituents and this is 100 kPa.

Therefore:

$$100 = 136.7 \times X + 30.1 \times (1 - X)$$

Rearranging terms:

$$X = \frac{(100 - 30.1)}{(136.7 - 30.1)} = 0.66$$

Answer choice (A) is $100/(136.7 + 30.1)$. Answer choice (C) is $100/136.7$ and answer choice (D) is $136.7/(136.7 + 30.1)$.

42. **(A)**

Let X_{N_2} = nitrogen in the vapor phase and X_{O_2} = oxygen in the vapor phase.

$$X_{N_2} = \frac{136.7}{100} \times 0.66 = 0.902$$

$$X_{O_2} = 1 - X_{N_2} = 1 - 0.902 = 0.098 \approx 0.10$$

Answer choice (B) is $30/136.7$, while answer choice (C) is $30.1/100$, and answer choice (D) is the mole fraction of nitrogen in the vapor phase.

43. **(C)**

Basis: 1,000 liters of stack gas with stack gases which behave as ideal gases with a molecular volume of 22.4 liters/gm-mole.

Constituent	Fraction	Liters	gm-mole
CO_2	0.12	120	5.36
O_2	0.07	70	3.13
N_2	0.81	810	36.16
Totals	1.00	1,000	44.65

$C + O_2 = CO_2$, therefore, $C = 5.36$ gm-mole and $O_2 = 5.36$ gm-mole. air = 79% N_2, and 21% O_2. Thus:

$$air = \frac{36.16 \text{ gm-mole}}{0.79} = 45.77 \text{gm-mole}$$

$$O_2 \text{ supplied} = 45.77 \text{ gm-mole} \times 0.21 = 9.61 \text{ gm-mole}$$

$$\text{excess } O_2 = 9.61 - 5.36 = 3.13 \text{ gm-mole}$$

Let $X = O_2$ for H_2O:

$$O_2 \text{ supplied} = O_2 \text{ for } CO_2 + \text{excess } O_2 + O_2 \text{ for } H_2O$$

$$9.61 = 5.36 + 3.13 + X$$

$$X = 1.12 \text{ gm-mole}$$

$$H_2 + \frac{1}{2}O_2 = H_2O:$$

Therefore,

$$H_2 = 2 \times 1.12 \text{ gm-mole} = 2.24 \text{ gm-mole}$$

Constituent	gm-mole	MW	grams	wgt %
C	5.36	12	64.32	93.5
H	2.24	2	4.48	6.5
Total			68.80	100.0

$$C\% = \frac{64.32}{68.80} \times 100\% = 93.5$$

Answer choice (A) did not convert gm-moles to grams. Answer choice (B) did not consider excess air, and answer choice (D) used molecular weight of 1 for H_2.

44. (C)

From the solution to Question 43 we found that the excess oxygen was 3.13 gm-moles. The total O_2 required for combustion was likewise found to be:

$$\frac{3.13}{0.21} = 14.905 \text{ gm-moles}$$

Thus, the excess air is:

$$\% \text{ excess air} = \frac{14.905}{(45.77 - 14.905)} \times 100\% = 48\%$$

Answer choice (A) is no excess air. Answer choice (B) computes the excess air divided by the total air supplied, and answer choice (D) is the percent of N_2.

45. (D)

From the solution to Question 43 we found that 45.77 gm-moles of air are supplied.

$$45.77 \text{ gm-moles} \times 22.4 \text{ liters/gm-mole} = 1,025.3 \text{ liters}$$

We also found that 68.8 grams of fuel are supplied to produce 1,000 liters of stack gas. Therefore:

$$\frac{1,025.3 \text{ liters air}}{68.8 \text{ grams fuel}} = 14.9 \text{ liters/gram}$$

Answer choice (A) is based upon excess air while choice (B) is based on O_2 supplied, and answer choice (C) is based on the air required without excess air.

46. (B)

A gram-mole of ideal gas occupies 22.4 liters at standard conditions of 25°C and 1 atmosphere pressure.

$$O_2 \text{ in solution} = 2 \times 10^{-5} \text{ moles/gm-mole} \times \frac{1,000 \text{ liters}}{22.4 \text{ liters/gm-mole}}$$

$$= 8.93 \times 10^{-4} \text{ gm-mole}$$

$$O_2 \text{ in solution} = 8.93 \times 10^{-4} \text{ gm-mole} \times 22.4 \text{ liters/gm-mole} \times 1,000 \text{ ml/liter} = 20 \text{ ml}$$

Answer choice (A) multiplies the solubility by the ratio of the molecular weights of water:oxygen. Answer choice (C) like choice (A) uses the ratio but inverts it (i.e., oxygen:water), and answer choice (D) is the result in gm-moles $\times$ 100,000.

47. **(B)**

$$Q_{liq} = 100 \text{ kg/hr} \times 1.0 \text{ cal/gm-}°C \times (80 - 20)°C \times 1,000 \text{ gm/kg}$$

$$Q_{liq} = 6,000,000 \text{ cal/hr}$$

$$Q_{liq} = 6,000 \text{ kcal/hr} \times 4.184 \times 10^{-3} \text{ J/kcal} = 25,100 \text{ kJ/hr}$$

From steam tables given:

steam at 0.2 MPa & 150°C - enthalpy = 2,768.8 kJ/kg

water at 0.1 MPa & 100°C - enthalpy = 419.0 kJ/kg

steam at 0.1 MPa & 100°C - enthalpy = 2,676.1 kJ/kg

ΔH_{evap} at 0.1 MPa & 100°C - enthalpy = 2,257.0 kJ/kg

$$Q_{stm} = 25,100 \text{ kJ/hr} = m_{stm} \times (h_{stm} - h_{wat}) = m_{stm} \times (2,768.8 - 419) \text{ kJ/kg}$$

$$m_{stm} = \frac{25,100 \text{ kJ/hr}}{2,349.8 \text{ kJ/kg}} = 10.7 \text{ kg/hr}$$

Answer choice (A) did not convert the 6,000 kcal to kJ. Answer choices (C) and (D) used the heat of vaporization and the heat of saturated steam, respectively.

48. **(D)**

$$Q = U \times A \times \Delta T$$

from the solution to 47 we found Q = 6,000,000 cal/hr

$$A = \frac{Q}{U \times \Delta T}$$

$$A = \frac{6,000,000 \text{ cal/hr}}{2,350 \text{ cal/hr-m}^2°C \times (80 - 20)^2}$$

$$A = 42.6 \text{m}^2$$

Answer choice (A) uses 25,100 for Q, answer choice (B) converts the temperature difference to K, and answer choice (C) uses 80°C as the temperature difference.

49. **(B)**

Calculate the molecular weight of methane: C = 12.03 and H = 1.008.

$$1 \times 12.03 + 4 \times 1.008 = 16.04$$

$$\frac{890 \text{ kJ/gm-mole}}{16.04 \text{ gm/gm-mole}} = 55.5 \text{ kJ/gm}$$

Answer choice (A) divides by the sum of the molecular weights for both CH_4 and $2O_2$. Answer choice (C) does not divide by the molecular weight, and (D) multiplies by the molecular weight.

50. **(B)**

Note: 1 Pa-sec = 1 poise.

Therefore, $\mu = 10$ Pa-sec. (This conversion may not be that well known, but it simplifies the calculation tremendously. The alternative is to use 1 poise = 1 gm/cm-sec, and then you need to use $g_c = 980$ gm_f-sec^2/gm-cm to get the pressure in force terms – gm_f/cm^2 then convert to kg_f/cm^2 and 9.8×10^4 kg_f/cm^2 = 1 Pa.)

The flow rate is:

$$Q = 100 \text{ cm}^3/\text{hr} \times 1 \text{ hr}/3{,}600 \text{ sec} \times 0.8 \text{ gm/cm}^3 = 0.022 \text{ gm/sec}$$

$$Q = 2.22 \times 10^{-2} \text{ gm/sec}$$

For laminar flow:

$$Q = \frac{\rho \times r^4 \times \Delta p}{8 \times \mu \times L}$$

Rearranging terms:

$$\Delta p = \frac{8 \times Q \times \mu \times L}{\rho \times r^4} = \frac{8 \times 2.22 \times 10^{-2} \text{ gm/sec} \times 10 \text{ Pa-sec} \times 1 \text{ cm}}{0.8 \text{ gm/cm}^3 \times (0.1 \text{ cm})^4}$$

$$\Delta p = 22{,}200 \text{ Pa}$$

$$\Delta p = 22{,}200 \text{ Pa} \times 1 \text{ kPa}/1{,}000 \text{ Pa} = 22.2 \text{ kPa}$$

Answer choice (A) used $r = 0.2$ cm, answer choice (C) does not convert flow to gm/sec, and answer choice (D) is the answer in Pa.

51. **(D)**

$$K_{eq} = \frac{(CO_2) \times (H_2)}{(CO) \times (H_2O)} = \frac{0.2 \times 0.3}{0.1 \times 0.15} = 4.00$$

Answer choice (A) inverts the relation with the reactants in the numerator. Answer choice (B) is $(CO) \times (CO_2)/(H_2) \times (H_2O)$, and answer choice (C) is the reciprocal of choice (B).

52. **(C)**

Let $X =$ additional moles of H_2 formed. For every mole of H_2 formed, one mole of CO_2 will also be formed, and one mole of CO will be consumed. Therefore, the equilibrium equation becomes:

$$K_{eq} = \frac{(0.2 + X) \times (0.3 + X)}{(0.1 - X) \times (0.2)} = 4.00$$

$$X^2 + 1.3X - 0.02 = 0$$

This is a quadratic equation $aX^2 + bX + c$, and can be solved by:

$$X = \frac{-b \pm \sqrt{b^2 - 4ac}}{2a}$$

$$X = \frac{-1.3b \pm \sqrt{(1.3)^2 - 4(1)(-0.02)}}{2(1)}$$

$$X = \frac{-1.3 \pm \sqrt{1.77}}{2} = \frac{-1.3 \pm 1.33}{2} = \frac{+0.03}{2} = 0.015$$

$$\text{and } \frac{-2.63}{2} = -1.315$$

The logical answer is:

$$X = 0.015$$

$$CO_2 = 0.2 + 0.015 = 0.215$$

Answer choice (A) is the added CO_2, answer choice (B) assumes there is no increase in CO_2, and answer choice (D) solved for X in the following: $X \times 0.3/(0.1) \times (0.2) = 4.00$

53. **(A)**

This is incompressible fluid flow for which the volumetric flow rates must be identical, therefore:

$$A_1 u_1 = A_2 u_2$$

$$A_1 = \frac{\pi \times (20 \text{ cm})^2}{4} = 314.2 \text{ cm}^2$$

$$A_2 = \frac{\pi \times (2 \text{ cm})^2}{4} = 3.14 \text{ cm}^2$$

$$u_1 = 5 \text{ cm/sec}$$

$$u_2 = u_1 \times \frac{A_2}{A_1} = 5 \text{ cm/sec} \times \frac{3.14 \text{ cm}^2}{314.2 \text{ cm}^2} = 0.05 \text{ cm/sec}$$

Answer choice (B) divides the diameters, not their squares, while choice (C) is off by a factor of 10, and choice (D) assumes that the velocity is the same.

54. **(D)**

$$Q = C \times A \times \sqrt{2 \times g \times h}$$

C for a rounded hole is 0.98

$g = 980 \text{ cm/sec}^2$

$h = 0.75 \text{ m} = 75 \text{ cm}$

$$A = \frac{\pi \times (0.5 \text{ cm})^2}{4} = \frac{0.7854 \text{ cm}^2}{4} = 0.196 \text{ cm}^2$$

$$Q = 0.98 \times 0.196 \text{ cm}^2 \times \sqrt{2 \times 980 \text{ cm/sec}^2 \times 75 \text{ cm}}$$

$$= 0.192 \text{ cm}^2 \times \sqrt{147,000 \text{ cm}^2/\text{sec}^2}$$

$$Q = 73.6 \text{ cm}^3/\text{sec} \times \frac{3,600 \text{ sec/hr}}{1,000 \text{ cm}^3/\text{l}} = 265 \text{ l/hr}$$

Answer choice (A) did not convert h to cm, answer choice (B) did not convert to l/hr, and answer choice (C) did not use two in the square root term.

55. **(B)**

The two components to consider are the temperature sensors and the monitoring system. Optical pyrometers are by far more expensive than the other sensors and require manual calibration, eliminating answer choice (C). Labor cost associated with manual monitoring would be excessive with hundreds of sensors, eliminating answer choices (A) and (D). A computer monitoring system would be much more cost effective and accurate, and would lend itself to a better quality control procedure.

56. **(B)**

The sampling location (A) is important because process inhomogeneities or spatial variations will cause material variations. Sample return location (and method) (B), if this is done at all, may be important to ensure non-contamination or to simply salvage some product, but does not affect measurement, so this is the best answer. Condition of sample transport to the analysis instrument (C) is important because the sample should not be altered significantly en route. For example, a significant change in temperature may give an erroneous result. Finally, answer choice (D) sampling frequency is important to ensure a characteristic sample, while not expending excessive effort on analysis.

57. **(A)**

Although data collected by a computer may be one factor used in determining when equipment maintenance is required (A), it is generally not the purpose of computer process control and when utilized does not result in as much benefit or cost savings as the other choices. Real-time data acquisition (B) is an important use of computers for the purpose of process control. Auxiliary control of a process using computers (C), along with some other control for default or safety, is a common use for computers in processing. Automatic computer control (D) is also widely used for processes supervised at some level by workers or managers. The least useful of the choices for computer process control is therefore (A).

58. **(D)**

Answer choice (D) is correct.

Linear interpolation between any two points i and j is given by:

$$Y = Y_i + \frac{(X - X_i)}{(X_j - X_i)} \times (Y_j - Y_i)$$

where:

$$X's = \text{Benzene vapor adsorbed, cm}^3\text{(STP)/g charcoal}$$

$$Y's = \text{Partial pressure benzene, mm Hg}$$

Hence:

$$Y = 0.0045 + \frac{(30-25)}{(40-25)} \times (0.0251 - 0.0045)$$

$$= 0.0114 \text{ mmHg}$$

Answer choice (A) is the average of the partial pressures at 25 cm^3(STP)/g and 40 cm^3(STP)/g benzene vapor adsorption and is therefore incorrect. Answer choice (B) is incorrect because it takes $Y_i = 0.0251$ mm Hg instead of 0.0045 mm Hg. Answer choice (C) is incorrect because it makes a numerical error in calculating

$$\frac{(X - X_i)}{(X_j - X_i)} \text{ as } = \frac{15}{25}.$$

59. **(A)**

Answer choice (A) is correct.

Applying the Euler formula we get:

$$H_{i+1} = H_i + (\Delta t) \times \frac{(0.7 - 0.98\sqrt{H_i})}{0.5}$$

so that, at the end of 2 s:

$$H_1 = H_0 + (\Delta t) \times \frac{(0.7 - 0.98\sqrt{H_o})}{0.5}$$

$$= 0.5 + (2) \times \frac{(0.7 - 0.98\sqrt{0.5})}{0.5}$$

$$= 0.528 \text{ m}$$

Answer choice (B) is obtained if one does not consider the area in the computation of *dH/dt* and is an incorrect choice. Answer choices (C) and (D) are incorrect calculations.

60. **(C)**

Answer choice (C) is correct.

Let us take

$$V_1 = V_{initial\ guess} = V_{ideal\ gas} = \frac{RT}{P} = 3{,}102\ \text{cm}^3\text{gmol}^{-1}$$

The Virial EOS in iterative form is written as:

$$V_{i+1} = \frac{RT}{P}\left(1 + \frac{B}{V_i} + \frac{C}{V_i^2}\right)$$

$$= \frac{83.14 \times 373.1}{10}\left(1 - \frac{242.5}{V_i} + \frac{25{,}200}{V_i^2}\right)$$

Iteration	R.H.S.	L.H.S.	$|V_{i+1} - V_i|$
$i = 1$	$V_1 = 3{,}102.0\ \text{cm}^3\text{gmol}^{-1}$,	so that, $V_2 = 2{,}867.6\ \text{cm}^3\text{gmol}^{-1}$	234.4
$i = 2$	$V_2 = 2{,}867.6\ \text{cm}^3\text{gmol}^{-1}$,	so that, $V_3 = 2{,}849.2\ \text{cm}^3\text{gmol}^{-1}$	18.4
$i = 3$	$V_3 = 2{,}849.2\ \text{cm}^3\text{gmol}^{-1}$,	so that, $V_4 = 2{,}847.6\ \text{cm}^3\text{gmol}^{-1}$	1.6
$i = 4$	$V_4 = 2{,}847.6\ \text{cm}^3\text{gmol}^{-1}$,	so that, $V_5 = 2{,}847.5\ \text{cm}^3\text{gmol}^{-1}$	0.1

Therefore, the answer is (C) 2,847.5 cm³gmol⁻¹. Answer choice (A) is incorrect because it is obtained if $T = 100$ K is used in the calculations. Answer choice (B) is the ideal gas volume and is therefore incorrect, especially since the pressure is as high as 10 bar. Answer choice (D) is incorrect as it is obtained if the negative sign of (B) is not considered.

FE/EIT

FE: PM Chemical Engineering Exam

Practice Test 2

FUNDAMENTALS OF ENGINEERING EXAMINATION

TEST 2

(Answer sheets appear in the back of this book.)

TIME: 4 Hours
60 Questions

DIRECTIONS: For each of the following questions and incomplete statements, choose the best answer from the four answer choices. You must answer all questions.

Questions 1 and 2 refer to the following:

The Steam-Iron Reaction:

$$3Fe + 4H_2O \rightarrow Fe_3O_4 + 4H_2$$

is used to produce H_2 commercially.

1. How many kgs of Fe are required to produce 1,000 liters of H_2?

   (A) 0.09   (C) 2.60

   (B) 1.88   (D) 5.25

2. How many kgs of steam are required to produce 1,000 liters of H_2?

   (A) 0.80   (C) 2.60

   (B) 1.88   (D) 3.21

3. Air has a heat capacity of $C_p = 1.0$ kJ/kg-K and a density of 0.0013 gm/cm^3 at 25°C. If the temperature in a 30 m^3 room increases by 5°C, assuming adiabatic conditions, approximately how much heat in kcal must have been added to get this temperature increase?

(A) 39   (C) 185

(B) 47   (D) 195

Questions 4–6 are based on the following:

For a crack in a pipeline, gas loss can be calculated if the area of the crack (A_v), gas pressure drop across the crack (Δp), and gas density (ρ) are known.

$$Q = 5.1 \times 10^{-2} \times C_d \times A_v \times \frac{[\Delta p]^{1/2}}{\rho}$$

For $N_{Re} > 2{,}000$, $C_d = 0.6$, Q is in m³/hr, A_v is in mm², Δp is in mbar, and ρ is in kg/m³.

4. A natural gas pipeline that has gas at a pressure of 3.5 MPa has a crack 1,000 mm² in it which is leaking gas to the atmosphere, 1 bar pressure. Assume the density of methane at 3.5 MPa is 25 kg/m³. What is the flow rate of the gas leak in liters/min?

(A) 37.6   (C) 3,762

(B) 226   (D) 225,690

5. Assume the methane leaking from the pipe behaves as an ideal gas and that its higher heating value is 30 kJ/m³. If this leaking gas were to ignite, approximately how much heat would be released in kJ/min?

(A) 4   (C) 1,881

(B) 113   (D) 6,768

6. Radiation is normally between 30 percent and 40 percent of the heat release. Heat flux (q_T) is defined as the rate of heat transferred per unit area per unit time and expressed in cal/cm²-sec. According to the *Fire Litigation Handbook*, humans can tolerate an absorbed energy heat flux of 0.1 cal/cm²-sec for approximately 12 seconds. The formula for radiant heat flux is given by:

$$q_T = \frac{H_{rad}}{4 \times \pi \times r^2}$$

where r = distance in cm.

Approximately what is the distance at which $q_T = 0.1$ cal/cm²-sec for a gas leak which ignites and generates 20,000 cal/min of heat and H_{rad} is 40% of the heat generated?

(A) 10   (C) 20

(B) 18   (D) 212

Questions 7 and 8 refer to the drawing below.

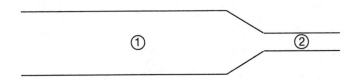

The horizontal pipe in the drawing has a constriction in it. Water with a density of 1 gm/cm^3 is flowing through it at 25°C. At Point 1 the diameter is 10 cm and at Point 2 it is 3 cm. At Point 1 the velocity is 1 cm/sec and the pressure is 200 kPa.

7. What is the velocity in cm/sec at Point 2?

(A) 0.09   (C) 3.33

(B) 1.00   (D) 11.11

8. What approximately is the pressure at Point 2 in kPa?

(A) 0   (C) 194

(B) 78   (D) 200

Questions 9–11 are based on the following situation.

Chlorine gas (Cl_2) is produced in an oxidizing furnace according to the reaction:

$$2\,HCl + \frac{1}{2}O_2 \rightarrow H_2O + Cl_2$$

For this process 1,000 liter/hr of pure HCl is fed at 250°C and 1 atmosphere pressure. This gas is contacted with pure O_2 whose feed rate is 20 percent in excess of stoichiometric. The reaction goes to completion and the product gases are at 300°C and 0.8 atmosphere pressure. Pure O_2 costs $5 per liter, but at 20 percent in excess of stoichiometric the reaction is essentially 100 percent. Oxygen (O_2) at 98 percent purity at a cost of $4 per liter is available, but this reaction must be at 30% in excess of stoichiometric. The cost to remove steam from the product is $0.15 per liter. Assume all gases behave as ideal gases even H_2O and that all H_2O goes to steam.

9. How many liters/hr of pure O_2 must be fed to the furnace?

   (A) 140

   (B) 168

   (C) 300

   (D) 336

10. What is the cost differential in $/hr using 98 percent O_2 rather than pure O_2?

    (A) $0

    (B) $112

    (C) $140

    (D) $168

11. What is the cost differential in $/hr to remove steam using 98 percent O_2 rather than pure O_2?

    (A) $42

    (B) $55

    (C) $75

    (D) $84

Questions 12 and 13 are based on the following:

The solubility product for $BaCO_3$ (MW = 197.35) is $K_{sp} = 8 \times 10^{-9}$ mole per liter.

$$Ba^{++} + CO_3^{=} \rightarrow BaCO_3 \downarrow$$

12. How many milligrams (mg) of $BaCO_3$ can be dissolved in one liter of pure water?

    (A) 0

    (B) 8.1×10^{-6}

    (C) 0.0016

    (D) 1.6

13. What is the concentration in mole per liter of $CO_3^{=}$ ion in solution?

    (A) 8×10^{-9}

    (B) 8×10^{-6}

    (C) 9×10^{-6}

    (D) 9×10^{-5}

Questions 14, 15, and 16 are based on the following:

Automobile exhaust at 760 mm Hg and 120°C is found to contain 3 percent by volume of CO. A catalytic converter utilizes the CO in this exhaust to convert some of the NO_x to N_2 according to a series of complex reactions which can be represented by:

$$2NO + 2CO \rightarrow 2CO_2 + N_2$$

$$NO_2 + 2CO \rightarrow 2CO_2 + \frac{1}{2}N_2$$

14. What is the concentration of CO in gm/m^3 in the automobile exhaust assuming ideal gas behavior?

(A) 0.84   (C) 37.40

(B) 1.21   (D) 1,250.00

15. If the exhaust gas contains 1 percent by volume of NO_x in equal portions of NO and NO_2, and the catalytic converter was 100% efficient, what would the volume percent of CO be?

(A) zero percent   (C) two percent

(B) one percent   (D) three percent

16. If the exhaust gas contains one percent by volume of NO_x in equal portions of NO and NO_2, what is the concentration of NO_2 in gm/m^3 in the automobile exhaust assuming ideal gas behavior?

(A) 6.7   (C) 13.4

(B) 10.3   (D) 20.5

Questions 17, 18, and 19 are based on the following situation.

A 1,000 kg/hr stream of oil having a C_p = 0.6 cal/gm-°C must be cooled from 60°C to 30°C. This oil has a thermal conductivity of k_{oil} = 8 cal/hr-cm-°C and a heat transfer film coefficient of h_{oil} = 300 cal/hr-cm²-°C. Water at 15°C is available as a cooling medium. The properties of this water are: heat capacity of C_p = cal/gm-°C, thermal conductivity of 1.0 k_{wat} = 5 cal/hr-cm-°C, and heat transfer film coefficient of h_{wat} = 600 cal/hr-cm²-°C. Design a counter-current heat exchanger from carbon steel having tubes of 1.5 cm inside diameter and a wall thickness of 5 mm. The thermal conductivity of the carbon steel is k_{stl} = 400 cal/hr-cm-°C. In order to prevent scale formation on the outside of the tubes, the exit temperature of the water must not exceed 25°C.

17. How much cooling water in kg/hr is required to reduce the oil temperature as specified?

(A) 400   (C) 1,800

(B) 1,200   (D) 3,000

18. What is the overall heat transfer coefficient for this exchanger?

(A) 7.63   (C) 14.82

(B) 14.57   (D) 163.90

19. What is the overall heat transfer area in m² for the heat exchanger?

(A) 2.39   (C) 8.86

(B) 5.24   (D) 10.00

Questions 20 and 21 are based on the following:

Air is compressed in a non-flow process along a polytropic path for which $n = 1.4$. The initial pressure and temperature are $T_i = 25°C$ and $p_i = 1$ atm, and the final pressure is $p_f = 10$ atm.

20. What is the final temperature in °C?

(A) 48   (C) 302

(B) 250   (D) 575

21. How much reversible work in Joules/gram can this process perform?

(A) 47.4   (C) 199.6

(B) 162.1   (D) 5,757.0

Questions 22 and 23 are based on the following:

One kilogram of ice at a temperature of −10°C is immersed in 1 kilogram of water whose temperature is +20°C. The heat capacities of the ice and the water are respectively $C_{pice} = 2.11$ kJ/kg-K and C_{pwat} 4.18 kJ/kg-K, and the heat of fusion of ice is $\Delta H_{fus} = 334$ kJ/kg. There is no heat lost to the surroundings.

22. How many grams of ice will be melted?

(A) 187   (C) 437

(B) 250   (D) 1,000

23. Assume the water is 10 kg and at 25°C, using the same constants, what will the final temperature of the water be in °C?

   (A) 0   (C) 17

   (B) 15   (D) 22

Questions 24 and 25 are based on the following situation:

Waste acid from a nitrating process has the following composition by weight: H_2SO_4 = 60 percent, and H_2O = 40 percent. This acid solution is to be strengthened to contain 80 percent H_2SO_4 by adding a concentrated solution of H_2O-H_2SO_4 containing 90 percent by weight H_2SO_4.

24. What is the weight of H_2O-H_2SO_4 solution that must be added to 10 kgs of the original solution to increase its concentration to 80 percent by weight?

   (A) 11   (C) 15

   (B) 13   (D) 20

25. What is the molarity of the original solution (Molarity, M, is the moles of solute per mole of solution)?

   (A) 3   (C) 6

   (B) 4   (D) 10

26. For the reaction below:

$$2A \rightarrow B$$
$$r_A = -k \times (C_A)^2$$

where C_A is in moles/liter,

$$r_A = \left[\frac{1}{V}\right] \times \left[\frac{dN_A}{dt}\right],$$

and the equilibrium constant k = 0.09 liter/mole-sec. A 100 liter batch reactor is charged with 75 liters of solution containing 25 moles of A. For isothermal conditions, how many seconds does it take for 20 moles of A to react?

(A) 42   (C) 178

(B) 133   (D) 1,340

Questions of 27, 28, and 29 are based on the following:

Energy can be supplied to a process by oil or coal. The oil has a higher heating value (HHV) of 5.6 MJ/liter while coal has a HHV of 5 MJ/kg. The oil is delivered to the plant at $0.20 per liter, while the coal is delivered at $0.20 per kg. The plant currently burns coal and it would require an investment of $100,000 to convert the boilers to burn oil. The plant has an annual energy load of 1,000,000 MJ.

27. In terms of the annual energy load, what would the difference in fuel costs be between the coal and the oil?

    (A) $0   (C) Coal $4,286 cheaper

    (B) Coal $600 cheaper   (D) Oil $4,286 cheaper

28. Given the cost differential found in Question 27, and assuming cost of money at 5 percent, what is the payback in years for converting to oil-fired operation?

    (A) 23   (C) 75

    (B) 24   (D) never

29. The choice for the plant is really between converting oil at a cost of $100,000 or adding pollution prevention equipment to the coal-fired boiler at a cost of $75,000. Given this situation and taking into account the fuel cost savings, what is the payback in years for converting to oil?

    (A) 5.8   (C) 9.0

    (B) 6.1   (D) 10.0

30. Water at 20°C with a density of 1 gm/cm^3 and a viscosity of 1.075 centipoise is flowing through 500 m of horizontal cast iron pipe having an internal diameter of 5 cm. For a flow rate of 4,000 liters/hr, approximately what is the pressure drop in mm Hg?

    (A) 7.4   (C) 421.0

    (B) 301.0   (D) 842.0

Questions 31 and 32 are based on the following:

Material containing 50 percent water is fed to a dryer. After drying, it is found that 75 percent of the original water has been removed.

31. For 1,000 kg of material, what is the weight of water removed?

    (A) 125   (C) 450

    (B) 375   (D) 500

32. What is the percent final moisture content of the material after drying?

    (A) 0 percent   (C) 25 percent

    (B) 20 percent   (D) 38 percent

Questions 33 and 34 are based on the following situation:

A stack with a diameter of 200 cm has flue gas flowing through it at a rate of 5,000 liters/min at a temperature of 300°C and a pressure of 800 mm Hg. The concentration of CO is 800 ppm_v. Assume ideal gas behavior.

33. What is the flow rate of CO in kg/hr?

    (A) 0.16   (C) 0.32

    (B) 0.30   (D) 1.61

34. What is the velocity of the stack gas in cm/sec for the conditions given?

    (A) 0.003   (C) 0.270

    (B) 0.265   (D) 2.650

Questions 35 and 36 are based on the following:

A heat engine absorbs 250 kcal at 250°C, produces work, and discards heat at 50°C.

35. Approximately what is the work performed in kcal by the heat engine?

    (A) 0   (C) 154

    (B) 96   (D) 199

36. What is the change in entropy in kcal/K of the heat source?

    (A) +0.5   (C) −1.0

    (B) +1.0   (D) −0.5

Questions 37, 38 and 39 are based on the following information:

A hydrocarbon fuel with a generic formula C_xH_y is burned with excess air at 25°C and atmospheric pressure. The volumetric analysis of the flue gas is:

Gas	Vol %
N_2	63.5 %
H_2O	19.0 %
CO_2	12.5 %
CO	3.0 %
O_2	2.0 %
	100.0 %

37. Approximately how much excess air in percent is being fed?

    (A) 2 percent   (C) 12 percent

    (B) 9 percent   (D) 13 percent

38. The formula for the hydrocarbon is C_xH_y. Of the compounds listed below, what is the likely fuel?

    (A) CH_4 (C) C_3H_8

    (B) C_2H_6 (D) C_4H_{10}

39. How many m^3 of air are being fed per kg of flue gas produced?

    (A) 0.56   (C) 18.00

    (B) 0.64   (D) 310.00

Questions 40 and 41 are based on the following:

Air has the following heat capacities:

$$C_p = 7.0 \text{ cal/gm-mole-°C and}$$
$$C_v = 5.0 \text{ cal/gm-mole-°C.}$$

40. What is the approximate speed of sound in air at 20°C in m/sec?

    (A) 34   (C) 344

    (B) 290   (D) 34,350

41. If the composition of the air changes to 90 percent N_2 and 10 percent O_2 and its temperature increases to 200°C, what is the velocity of sound?

    (A) 286   (C) 440

    (B) 372   (D) 1,369

42. A thin-walled pipe with an inside diameter of 5 cm is covered with a 2 cm thick layer of insulation which has a thermal conductivity of $k = 0.56$ cal/cm-hr-°C. The inner surface of the pipe is at 200°C and the outer surface of the insulation is at 30°C. What is the heat loss in kcal/hr from a 10 m length? (The wall thickness of the pipe is negligible.)

    (A) 1,778   (C) 4,271

    (B) 2,829   (D) 17,780

43. For the reaction below to form ammonia (NH_3):

$$1.5H_2 + 0.5N_2 \rightarrow NH_3$$

One gram mole of H_2 is reacted with a stoichiometric quantity of N_2 at 300 bar pressure. At final equilibrium 0.2 gm-mole of NH_3 is formed. Assuming ideal gas behavior, what is the equilibrium constant K_{eq} for this reaction?

    (A) 8.28×10^{-3} (C) 0.310

    (B) 0.083   (D) 1.330

Questions 44 and 45 are based on the following:

The following data for a catalyst and its displacement by an inert gas and mercury in a test chamber are given:

Mass of catalyst in chamber	=	100 gm
Volume of gas displaced	=	40 cm^3
Volume of mercury displaced	=	85 cm^3

44. What is the pore volume of the catalyst in cm³/gm?

(A) 0.40

(C) 0.85

(B) 0.45

(D) 45.00

45. What is the porosity of this catalyst?

(A) 0.53

(C) 1.89

(B) 1.13

(D) 9.00

46. A pipe with a diameter of 5 cm and having a surface temperature of 200°C radiates heat to the still air in a room with a temperature of 20°C. Assume the emissivity of the pipe is $\varepsilon = 0.8$, what is the approximate net interchange of radiant energy in watts per meter length of pipe (W/m)?

(A) 0.09

(C) 3.80

(B) 0.14

(D) 4.80

47. Methane is flowing through a pipeline where the pressure is 3.5 MPa at a velocity of 10 m/sec. Further down the pipeline the pressure is 1.5 MPa. The density of methane at 3.5 MPa is 25 kg/m³, and at 1.5 MPa is 10 kg/m³. What is the velocity of methane in m/sec in the second section of the pipeline?

(A) 8.96

(C) 10.00

(B) 9.88

(D) 12.75

48. Two parallel rectangular plates with dimensions of 2 m × 4 m are separated by a distance of 3 m. If the temperature of the plates are respectively 1,000°C and 20°C and both behave as black bodies, what is the radiant energy exchange between the plates in kcal/hr assuming a shape factor of $F_{1 \to 2} = 0.165$?

(A) 177,840

(C) 504,900

(B) 192,600

(D) 587,645

49. The primary factor when selecting a device to monitor viscosity continuously in a typical process is

(A) environmental stability.

(C) measurable viscosity range.

(B) cost.

(D) ease of use.

50. Microprocessors and computers are the most versatile and most complicated type of automatic controllers. If electronic, self-operated, and pneumatic controllers are considered (examples, respectively: PID, solenoid, and air actuated controllers), which of the following correctly orders them from least versatile and least complicated to most versatile and most complicated?

    (A) Electronic, pneumatic, self-operated

    (B) Electronic, self-operated, pneumatic

    (C) Self-operated, electronic, pneumatic

    (D) Self-operated, pneumatic, electronic

Questions 51, 52, and 53 are based on the following situation:

A falling film evaporator is used to concentrate a solution from 15 weight percent solids to 40 weight percent solids with a boiling point rise. Liquid enthalpies can be considered those of pure water. The evaporator operates at 50°C with feed entering at 25°C. Saturated steam at 100°C is used as the evaporating medium. The overall heat transfer coefficient is 3 cal/min-cm²-°C.

51. What is the feed flow rate in kg/hr required to produce 1,000 kg/hr of the 40 weight percent solution?

    (A) 1,000   (C) 2,875

    (B) 2,667   (D) 6,667

52. What is the flow rate of steam in kg/hr required to produce 1000 kg/hr of 40 percent concentrated solution?

    (A) 1,100   (C) 1,879

    (B) 1,801   (D) 2,810

53. Approximately what is the heat transfer area of evaporator in m²?

    (A) 7.5   (C) 22.5

    (B) 11.3   (D) 47.1

54. In the following diagram, a material with a property that is outside the desired range is put through a process resulting in a product within the desired property range. At point *A* the property in question is measured and this information is used to alter an adjustable control mechanism which varies the effect of the process on the material's property. This system is known as a(n)

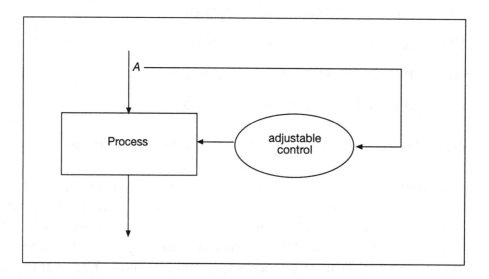

(A) feedback loop.

(C) feed forward loop.

(B) open loop.

(D) None of the above.

55. H_2 gas is transported from one vessel to another through a plastic tube which has an inner diameter of 2 cm and an outer diameter of 2.5 cm. The concentration of H_2 at the inner surface is 0.005 gm-mole/liter and the concentration at the outer surface is negligible due to diffusion. If the diffusion coefficient for H_2 through plastic is 6.5×10^{-3} cm²/hr, approximately how many liters per hour of H_2 will be diffused through a one-meter length of this tube?

(A) 0.002

(C) 0.014

(B) 0.005

(D) 0.092

Questions 56 and 57 are based on the following:

A sphere with a diameter of 10μm and a density of 2 gm/cm³ is settling in air at 20°C. Air has a density of 0.002 gm/cm³ and a viscosity of 0.0182 centipoise.

56. What is the terminal settling velocity in cm/sec of this spherical particle?

(A) 5.98×10^{-6}

(C) 5.75×10^{-3}

(B) 5.87×10^{-3}

(D) 5.75×10^{-2}

57. What is the Reynolds number of this particle at settling velocity?

(A) $68,287 \times 10^{-4}$

(C) 6.9

(B) 68.3×10^{-2}

(D) $6,968$

58. A certain petroleum company developed a Fortran subroutine named SUM to calculate the total flow rate (FF) and average composition (XF) obtained by mixing k streams of certain petroleum fraction. The flow rate and composition of the kth fraction is $F(k)$ and $X(k)$ respectively. For N such streams they used:

$$FF = \sum_{k=1}^{N} F(k)$$

and

$$XF = \frac{\left(\sum_{k=1}^{N} F(k) \times X(k) \right)}{FF}$$

Find the logical mistake in their subroutine:

```
1*        SUBROUTINE SUM(N,FF,XF)
2*        COMMON/DATA/F(50), X(50)
3*        FF = 0.0
4*        XF = 0.0
5*        DO 5 K = 1, N
6*            FF = FF + F(K)
7*            XF = XF + (F(K) × X(K))/FF
8*    5 CONTINUE
9*        RETURN
10*       END
```

(A) On line 1, FF and XF should not be included in the argument list.

(B) On lines 3 and 4, FF and XF should not be initialized to 0.0.

(C) On line 7, the procedure for calculating *XF* is not correct.

(D) On line 10, the END statement should not be included in the subroutine.

59. The effectiveness factor (η) of a particular catalyst is known to be 0.95. The following is a flowchart to calculate the Thiele Modulus (ϕ) using the relation tanh ϕ/ϕ and employs the Newton Raphson method. What would be the output of running such a program? Start with initial guess of $\phi = 0.5$ and proceed till $|\phi_{new} - \phi_{old}| \leq 0.01$.

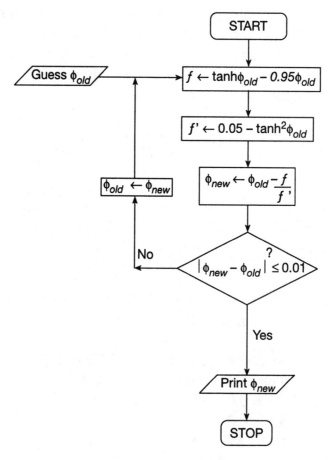

(A) 0.422

(B) 0.400

(C) -0.399

(D) 0.404

60. At constant temperature, the $\dfrac{dV}{dP}$ data for a particular gas is known.

The Taylor series expansion of *V(P)* is:

$$V(P_1 + \Delta P) = V(P_1) + \Delta P \frac{dV}{dP}(P_1) + \frac{(\Delta P)^2}{2!} \frac{d^2V}{dP^2}(P_1) + \ldots$$

The simple Euler's First Order Method considers only the first two terms of this series, i.e.,

$$V(P_1 + \Delta P) \approx V(P_1) + \Delta P \frac{dV}{dP}(P_1)$$

The error involved in this approximation is hence proportional to

(A) 1, i.e., independent of ΔP.

(B) ΔP.

(C) ΔP^2.

(D) $\Delta P^{1.5}$.

TEST 2

ANSWER KEY

1.	(B)	16.	(B)	31.	(B)	46.	(C)
2.	(A)	17.	(C)	32.	(B)	47.	(B)
3.	(B)	18.	(B)	33.	(A)	48.	(C)
4.	(C)	19.	(B)	34.	(D)	49.	(C)
5.	(B)	20.	(C)	35.	(B)	50.	(D)
6.	(A)	21.	(C)	36.	(D)	51.	(B)
7.	(D)	22.	(A)	37.	(D)	52.	(C)
8.	(D)	23.	(B)	38.	(D)	53.	(B)
9.	(B)	24.	(D)	39.	(B)	54.	(C)
10.	(B)	25.	(C)	40.	(C)	55.	(A)
11.	(A)	26.	(B)	41.	(C)	56.	(D)
12.	(C)	27.	(D)	42.	(D)	57.	(B)
13.	(D)	28.	(D)	43.	(A)	58.	(C)
14.	(C)	29.	(C)	44.	(B)	59.	(B)
15.	(A)	30.	(C)	45.	(A)	60.	(B)

DETAILED EXPLANATIONS
OF ANSWERS

TEST 2

1. **(B)**

    MW of $Fe_3O_4 \Rightarrow$ Fe = 56 and O = 16,

    $3 \times 56 + 4 \times 16 = 232$ gm/gm-mole

    $$H_2 = \frac{1,000 \text{ liters}}{22.4 \text{ l/gm-mole}} = 44.6 \text{ gm-moles}$$

    Every four moles of H_2 produced requires three moles of Fe, therefore:

    $$0.75 \times 44.6 \text{ gm-moles } H_2 = 33.5 \text{ gm-moles Fe}$$

    $$Fe = \frac{33.5 \text{ gm-moles} \times 56 \text{ gm/gm-mole}}{1,000 \text{ gm/kg}} = 1.88 \text{ kg}$$

    Answer choice (A) is the amount of H_2 produced, choice (C) is the amount of Fe_3O_4 produced, and choice (D) uses 1,000 liters of H_2 divided by eight gm/gm-mole (for four gm-mole H_2) to calculate the gm-moles of Fe.

2. **(A)**

    Here one mole of steam is required to produce one mole of H_2; therefore, since we found that 1,000 liters of H_2 is 44.6 gm-moles:

    $$H_2O = \frac{44.6 \text{ gm-moles} \times 18 \text{ gm/gm-mole}}{1,000 \text{ gm/kg}} = 0.8 \text{ kg}$$

    Answer choice (B) is the amount of Fe required, choice (C) is the amount of Fe_3O_4 produced, and choice (D) is four times the correct answer gotten by multiplying the molecular weight of water by four.

3. **(B)**

The mass of air in the room = $0.0013 \text{ gm/cm}^3 \times 30 \text{ m}^3 \times 10^6 \text{ cm}^3/\text{m}^3 = 39,000 \text{ gm}$.

$$m = 39 \text{ kg},$$

$$C_p = 1.0 \text{ kJ / kg-K},$$

$$\Delta T = 5K$$

and

$$Q = m \times C_p \times \Delta T = 39 \text{ kg} \times 1.0 \text{ kJ/kg-K} \times 5K = 195 \text{ kJ}$$

$$Q = 195 \text{ kJ} \times 0.239 \text{ kcal/kJ} = 46.6 \text{ kcal} \approx 47 \text{ kcal}$$

Answer choice (A) is the mass of air in the room, choice (C) was calculated using the conversion for J to BTUs, and choice (D) is in kJ not kcal.

4. **(C)**

Convert $p = 3.5$ MPa to bar $\Rightarrow$ 3.5 MPa $\times$ 10 bar/MPa = 35 bar = 35,000 mbar

$$p_{atm} = 1 \text{ bar} \times 1,000 \text{ mbar/bar} = 1,000 \text{ mbar}$$

$$Q = 5.1 \times 10^{-2} \times 0.6 \times 1,000 \times \frac{(35,000 - 1,000)^{\frac{1}{2}}}{25} = 1.224 \times (34,000)^{\frac{1}{2}}$$

$$Q = 225.69 \text{ m}^3/\text{hr} \times \frac{1 \text{ hr}}{60 \text{ min}} \times 10^3 \text{ l/m}^3 = 3,762 \text{ l/min}$$

Answer choice (A) did not convert MPa to bar, choice (B) did not convert m^3 to liters or hr to min, and choice (D) did not convert hr to min.

5. **(B)**

From Question 4 we found the gas leak flow rate as 225.69 m³/hr, thus.

Heat Rate = 225.69 m³/hr $\times$ 30 kJ/m³ $\times$ 1 hr/60 min = 112.85 kJ/min

Answer choice (A) used 7.14 m³/hr as the flow rate, choice (C) used 3,762 l/hr as the flow rate, and choice (D) did not convert hr to min.

6. **(A)**

Rearranging terms for the heat flux equation:

$$r = 0.5 \times \sqrt{\frac{(H_{rad})}{\pi \times q_T}}$$

$H_{rad} = 0.4 \times 20{,}000 \text{ cal/min } 1 \text{ min/60 sec} = 133.33 \text{ cal/sec}$

$q_T = 0.1 \text{ cal/cm}^2\text{-sec}$

$$r = 0.5 \times \sqrt{\frac{(133.33 \text{ cal/sec})}{3.14 \times 0.1 \text{cal/cm}^2\text{-sec}}}$$

$$r = 0.5 \times \sqrt{424.4 \text{ cm}^2} = 10.3 \text{ cm} \approx 10 \text{ cm}$$

Answer choice (B) did not divide by π, choice (C) did not multiply by 0.5, and choice (D) did not take the square root.

7. **(D)**

For incompressible flow $A_1 u_1 = A_2 u_2$:

$$A_1 = \frac{\pi \times (10 \text{ cm})^2}{4} = 78.54 \text{cm}^2$$

$$A_2 = \frac{\pi \times (3 \text{cm})^2}{4} = 7.07 \text{cm}^2$$

$$u_2 = u_1 \times \frac{A_1}{A_2} = 1 \text{ cm/sec} \times \frac{78.54 \text{ cm}^2}{7.07 \text{cm}^2} = 11.11 \text{ cm/sec}$$

Answer choice (A) reverses the areas A_1/A_2, choice (B) assumes no change, and choice (C) is $u_1 \times D_2/D_1$.

8. **(D)**

Bernoulli's Equation:

$$\frac{p_1}{\rho} + \frac{u_1^{\,2}}{2g_c} = \frac{p_2}{\rho} + \frac{u_2^{\,2}}{2g_c}$$

Solving for p_2:

$$p_2 = p_1 - \rho \times \frac{(u_2^{\,2} - u_1^{\,2})}{2g_c}$$

$$= 200 \text{ kPa} - 1 \text{ gm/cm}^3 \times \frac{[(11.11)^2 - (1)^2] \text{ cm}^2/\text{sec}^2}{2 \times 980 \text{ gm-cm/gm}_f\text{-sec}^2}$$

$$p_2 = 200 \text{ kPa} - 0.0625 \text{ gm}_f/\text{cm}^2$$

$$0.0625 \text{ gm}_f/\text{cm}^2 \times 10^{-3} \text{kg}_f/\text{gm}_f \times 98.07 \text{ kPa-cm}^2/\text{kg}_f = 0.0061 \text{ kPa}$$

$$p_2 = 200 \text{ kPa} - 0.0061 \text{ kPa}$$
$$p_2 = 199.98 \text{ kPa} \approx 200$$

Answer choice (A) assumes $p_2 = 0$, choice (B) did not divide by $2g_c$, and choice (C) did not use 10^{-3} kg_f/gm_f.

9. **(B)**

For every gm-mole of HCl reacted at 100% completion, there is $1/4$ gm-mole of O_2 required.

Therefore: HCl at 22.4 l/gm-mole:

$$\frac{1,000 \text{ l/hr}}{22.4 \text{ l/gm-mole}} \times \frac{(25+273)\text{K}}{(250+273)\text{K}} = 25 \text{ gm-mole/hr}$$

O_2 required $= 0.25 \times 25$ gm-mole/hr $= 6.25$ gm-mole/hr

However 20 percent excess is fed:

$$1.2 \times 6.25 \text{ gm-mole/hr} = 7.5 \text{ gm-mole/hr}$$

$$O_2 = 7.5 \text{ gm-mole/hr} \times 22.4 \text{ l/gm-mole} = 168 \text{ l/hr}$$

Answer choice (A) did not take 20 percent excess fed, choice (C) did not take into account the temperature effect, and choice (D) assumes $1/2$ mole of O_2 fed per mole of HCl.

10. **(B)**

The feed rate of pure O_2 as 168 liter/hr and its cost is \$5/liter, thus the cost is:

$$168 \text{ liter/hr} \times \$5/\text{liter} = \$840/\text{hr}$$

Now we need to find out how many l/hr of 98% O_2 is required realizing that this must be fed at 30 percent in excess stoichiometric.

98% O_2 required $= 0.25 \times 25$ gm-mole/hr $\times 1.3 = 8.125$ gm-mole/hr

98% O_2 required $= 8.125$ gm-mole/hr $\times 22.4$ l/gm-mole $= 182$ l/hr

$$\text{Cost} = 182 \text{ l/hr} \times \$4/\text{l} = \$728/\text{hr}$$

Thus, the cost differential is:

$$\text{Pure O}_2 = \$840/\text{hr}$$
$$98\% \text{ O}_2 = \underline{\$728/\text{hr}}$$
$$\$112/\text{hr}$$

Answer choice (A) assumes there is no cost differential, choice (C) used 140 l/hr for both pure and 98% O_2, and choice (D) did not take the 30% vs. 20% excess into consideration.

11. (A)

The amount of steam produced is dependent only upon the HCl fed, thus from the solution to Question 9, we found that:

HCl fed = 25 gm-mole/hr and this produces 12.5 gm-mole/hr of H_2O.

$$\text{Steam} = 12.5 \text{ gm-mole/hr} \times 22.4 \text{ l/gm-mole} = 280 \text{ l/hr}$$

$$\text{Cost} = 280 \text{ l/hr} \times \$0.15 = \$42/\text{hr}$$

Answer choice (B) multiplied the correct answer by 1.3 assuming the excess O_2 was a factor, choice (C) used 500 l/hr of steam which did not take temperature into account, and choice (D) is twice the correct answer and would assume that the moles of HCl reacted equal moles of H_2O produced.

12. (C)

$$8 \times 10^{-9} \text{ mole/liter} \times 197.35 \text{ gm/mole} = 1.598 \times 10^{-8} \text{ gm/liter}$$

$$1.598 \times 10^{-8} \text{ gm/liter} \times 1,000 \text{ mg/gm} \times 1 \text{ liter} = 0.0016 \text{ mg}$$

Answer choice (A) assumes there is nothing dissolved, choice (B) is simply the $K_{sp} \times 1,000$, and choice (D) is $1,000 \times$ the correct answer.

13. (D)

The concentration of Ba^{++} is equivalent to the concentration of $CO_3^=$, and the solubility product K_{sp} is the product of their concentration, therefore:

$$K_{sp} = (Ba^{++}) \times (CO_3^=) = 8 \times 10^{-9} \text{ mole/liter}$$

$$(CO_3^=) = \sqrt{8 \times 10^{-9}} \text{ mole/liter}$$

$$(CO_3^=) = 9 \times 10^{-5} \text{ mole/liter}$$

Answer choice (A) is K_{sp}, choice (B) is $K_{sp} \times 1,000$, and choice (C) is off by 0.1.

14. **(C)**

Basis one gm-mole of exhaust gas at atmospheric pressure (760 mm Hg). This has a volume of 22.4 liters at 760 mm Hg and 60°C.

$$pV = nRT$$

$R = 82.06$ atm-cm^3/gm-mole- K

$p = 760$ mm Hg $= 1$ atm

$$V_{exh} = \frac{n \times R \times T}{p}$$

$$= \frac{1 \text{ gm-mole} \times 82.06 \text{ atm-cm}^3/\text{gm-mole-K} \times (120 + 273)\text{K}}{1 \text{ atm}}$$

$V_{exh} = 32,250 \text{ cm}^3 \times 10^{-6} \text{m}^3/\text{cm}^3 = 0.0323 \text{ m}^3$

CO volume $= 0.03 \times 0.0323 \text{ m}^3 = 9.675 \times 10^{-4} \text{m}^3$

$$\text{CO mass} = \frac{28 \text{ gm/gm-mole} \times 10^3 \text{l/m}^3 \times 9.675 \times 10^{-4} \text{m}^3}{22.4 \text{l/gm-mole}} = 1.21 \text{ gm}$$

$$\text{CO conc.} = \frac{1.21 \text{ gm CO}}{0.0323 \text{ m}^3 \text{ exhaust}} = 37.4 \text{ gm/m}^3$$

Answer choice (A) is 0.03/MW of CO, choice (B) is mass of CO present, and choice (D) did not calculate the volume of CO but used exhaust gas volume to determine the mass of CO.

15. **(A)**

This is a simple problem if you understand that volume % = mole %. For every mole of NO removed, you convert one mole of CO to CO_2, and for every mole of NO_2 removed, you convert 2 moles of CO to CO_2. Thus, you effectively remove all of the CO.

Answer choice (B) assumes a one for one conversion of CO and the two NO_x constituents, choice (C) is a guess, and choice (D) assumes that none of the CO is removed.

16. **(B)**

From Question 14 we determined the volume of exhaust gas:

$$V_{exh} = 32{,}250 \text{ cm}^3 \times 10^{-6} \text{ m}^3/\text{cm}^3 = 0.0323 \text{ m}^3$$

$$NO_2 \text{ volume} = 0.005 \times 0.0323 \text{ m}^3 = 1.615 \times 10^{-4} \text{ m}^3$$

$$NO_2 \text{ mass} = \frac{46 \text{ gm/gm-mole} \times 10^3 \text{l/m}^3 \times 1.615 \times 10^{-4} \text{m}^3}{22.4 \text{ l/gm-mole}}$$

$$= 0.0033 \text{ gm}$$

$$NO_2 \text{ conc.} = \frac{0.0033 \text{ gm } NO_2}{0.0323 \text{ m}^3 \text{ exhaust}}$$

$$= 10.3 \text{ gm/m}^3$$

Answer choice (A) is the concentration of NO, choice (C) uses 1% for the volume of NO_2 and MW for NO, and choice (D) uses 1% for the volume of NO_2.

17. **(C)**

Calculate the heat transferred in cooling the oil from 60°C to 30°C.

$$q_{oil} = 1{,}000 \text{ kg/hr} \times 0.6 \text{ cal/gm-°C} \times (60 - 30)\text{°C} \times 1{,}000 \text{ gm/kg}$$

$$= 18 \times 10^6 \text{ cal/hr}$$

The cooling water required is:

$$\frac{dm_{wat}}{dt} = \frac{q_{oil}}{C_p \times \Delta T} = \frac{18 \times 10^6 \text{ cal/hr}}{1.0 \text{ cal/gm-°C} \times (25 - 15)\text{°C}}$$

$$= 1.8 \times 10^6 \text{ gm/hr} = 1{,}800 \text{ kg/hr}$$

Answer choice (A) used $\Delta T = (60 - 15)$°C, choice (B) used $\Delta T = (60 - 30)$°C, and choice (D) used C_p for oil.

18. **(B)**

$$r_i = \frac{1.5 \text{ cm}}{2} = 0.75 \text{ cm}$$

$$r_o = r_i + x = 0.75 + 0.5 = 1.25 \text{ cm}$$

$$x = 0.5 \text{ cm}$$

$$U = \cfrac{1}{\cfrac{r_o}{h_{wat} \times r_i} + \cfrac{x}{k_{oil}} + \cfrac{1}{h_{oil}}} = \cfrac{1}{\cfrac{1.25}{600 \times 0.75} + \cfrac{0.5}{8} + \cfrac{1}{300}}$$

$$U = \frac{1}{0.0028 + 0.0625 + 0.0033} = \frac{1}{0.0686} = 14.57 \text{ cal/hr-cm}^2\text{-}°\text{C}$$

Answer choice (A) did not use x/k, but $1/k$, choice (C) did not factor r_o/r_i, and choice (D) did not use x/k in the calculation at all.

19. **(B)**

First, calculate the log-mean temperature difference.

$$\Delta T_{lm} = \frac{\Delta T_{max} - \Delta T_{min}}{\ln \dfrac{\Delta T_{max}}{\Delta T_{min}}} = \frac{(30-15)-(60-25)}{\ln \dfrac{(30-15)}{(60-25)}} = \frac{15-35}{\ln \dfrac{15}{35}}$$

$$\Delta T_{lm} = \frac{-20}{\ln(0.429)} = \frac{-20}{-0.847} = 23.6°\text{C}$$

$$q = U \times A \times \Delta T_{lm}$$

We found $q = 18 \times 10^6$ cal/hr in Question 17, and $U = 14.57$ in Question 18.

$$A = \frac{q}{U \times \Delta T_{lm}} = \frac{18 \times 10^6 \text{cal/hr}}{14.57 \text{ cal/hr-cm}^2\text{-}°\text{C} \times 23.6°\text{C}} = 52,348 \text{ cm}^2$$

$$A = 52,348 \text{ cm}^2 \times 10^{-4} \text{m}^2/\text{cm}^2 = 5.24 \text{ m}^2$$

Answer choice (A) used $\Delta T_{max} = (60-15)$ and $T_{min} = (30-25)$ to calculate ΔT_{lm}, choice (C) used $q = 30 \times 10^6$ cal/hr, and choice (D) used $U = 7.63$.

20. **(C)**

$$T_f = T_i \times \left[\frac{p_f}{p_i}\right]^{(n-1/n)} = (25+273) \times \left[\frac{10}{1}\right]^{(1.4-1/1.4)} = 298 \times (10)^{0.286}$$

$$T_f = 298 \times 1.93 = 575°\text{K} = 575 - 273 = 302°\text{C}$$

Answer choice (A) results from not using °K, choice (B) also did not use °K and took the simple pressure ratio of 10, and choice (D) failed to convert K to °C.

21. **(C)**

$$\Delta W_{rev} = \frac{p_f \times V_f - p_i \times V_i}{1-n}$$

However,

$$p \times V = \frac{R \times T}{M},$$

where $M = 28.84$ gm/gm-mole for air

and $R = 1.987$ cal/gm-mole-K

Thus,

$$p_f \times V_f = \frac{R \times T_f}{M}$$

and

$$p_i \times V_i = \frac{R \times T_i}{M} \Rightarrow p_f \times V_f - p_i \times V_i = \frac{R \times (T_f - T_i)}{M}$$

$$\Delta W_{rev} = \frac{R \times (T_f - T_i)}{(1-n) \times M} = \frac{1.987 \text{ cal/gm-mole-K} \times (302 - 25)\text{K}}{(1-1.4) \times 28.84 \text{ gm/gm-mole}}$$

$$= -47.7 \text{ cal/gm}$$

$$\Delta W_{rev} = -47.7 \text{ cal/gm} \times 4.184 \text{ J/cal} = 199.6 \text{ J/gm}$$

Answer choice (A) is in cal/gm, choice (B) uses a temperature difference of 225 K, and choice (D) does not divide RT/M (molecular weight).

22. **(A)**
Heat absorbed by the ice + heat to melt the ice = heat given up by the water.

Let X = kg of ice melted, and assume the equilibrium temperature is 0°C.

Heat absorbed by the ice =

$$1 \text{ kg} \times 2.11 \text{ kJ/kg-K} \times (0 - (-10))\text{K} = 21.1 \text{ kJ}$$

Heat to melt the ice =

$$X \times 334 \text{ kJ/kg} = 334 \times \text{kJ/kg} \times X$$

Heat given up by the water =

$$1 \text{ kg} \times 4.18 \text{ kJ/kg-K} \times (20 - 0)\text{K} = 83.6 \text{ kJ}$$

The overall heat balance is:

$$21.1 + 334X = 83.6$$

Solving for X:

$$X = \frac{83.6 - 21.1 \text{ kJ}}{334 \text{ kJ/kg}} = 0.187 \text{ kg} = 187 \text{ grams}$$

Answer choice (B) neglects the heat required to raise the ice to its melting point, choice (C) uses 2 kg to calculate the heat given up by the water, and choice (D) assumes all of the ice is melted.

23. **(B)**

The solution is similar to Question 22 except here we assume that all the ice melts and the final temperature is greater than 0°C.

Let T_x = equilibrium temperature

Heat gained by the block of ice and subsequent melted water:

$$1 \text{ kg} \times [2.11 \text{ kJ/kg-}^\circ\text{C} \times (0 - (-10))^\circ\text{C} + 334 \text{ kJ/kg} + 4.18 \text{ kJ/kg-}^\circ\text{C} \times (T_x - 0)^\circ\text{C}]$$
$$Q_{gain} = 355.1 + 4.18T_x$$

Heat given up by the water:

$$Q_{loss} = 10 \text{ kg} \times 4.18 \text{ kJ/kg-}^\circ\text{C} \times (25 - T_x)^\circ\text{C} = 1,045 - 41.8T_x$$

Overall heat balance:

$$355.1 + 4.18T_x = 1,045 - 41.8T_x$$
$$T_x = \frac{(1,045 - 355.1)}{45.98} = 15^\circ\text{C}$$

Answer choice (A) assumes the temperature remains at the freezing point, choice (C) does not take into consideration the temperature rise of the melted ice, and choice (D) does not use ΔH_{fus}.

24. **(D)**

Let X = weight of concentrated solution of $H_2O - H_2SO_4$ added.

H_2SO_4 Balance:

Original + Added = Final

$$0.6 \times 10 \text{ kg} + 0.9 \times X = 0.8 \times (10 + X)$$

Rearranging terms:

$$X = \frac{8 - 6 \text{ kg}}{0.1} = 20 \text{ kg}$$

This is a straight forward mass balance problem. If one correctly sets up either a H_2SO_4 balance or a water balance, then the solution follows. Of the incorrect answer choices, (A) divides 90%/80% and multiplies by 10 kg, choice (B) divides the concentrations 80%/60%, and choice (C) divides 90%/60%.

25. **(C)**

The density of water = 1 gm/ml = 1,000 gm/liter

For 1,000 gms of the original solution, there are $0.4 \times 1,000$ gm of water and $0.6 \times 1,000$ gm of H_2SO_4. H_2SO_4 has a molecular weight of 98 gm/gm-mole. Thus,

$$\text{Molarity} = \frac{0.6 \times 1,000 \text{ gm/l}}{98 \text{ gm/gm-mole}} = 6.12 \approx 6$$

Answer choice (A) is half the correct value, choice (B) results from using the weight of water instead of the acid, and (D) divides 1,000 gms by the molecular weight.

26. **(B)**

$$r_A \times V \times dt = -k \times \left[\frac{N_A}{V}\right] \times V \times dt$$

Rearranging terms and solving the differential equation for dt:

$$dt = \frac{V}{k} \times \frac{dN_A}{(NA)^2}$$

Boundary conditions – when $t = 0$, $N_A = 25$ and when $t = t_x$; $N_A = 5$

$$\int_0^{tx} dt = \frac{-V}{k} \times \int_{25}^{5} \frac{dN_A}{(N_A)^2}$$

$$t = \frac{-75\,\text{liter}}{0.09\,\text{liter/mole-sec}} \times (0.04 - 0.2)$$

$$t = 133\text{ sec}$$

Answer choice (A) uses $[1/(25 - 5)]$ in the calculation, choice (C) uses $V = 100$, and choice (D) uses $\ln(1/5) - \ln(1/25)$.

27. **(D)**

Energy load: 1,000,000 MJ/yr

Source	HHV	Required	Price	Cost
Coal	5 MJ/kg	200,000 kg/yr	$0.20/kg	$40,000
Oil	5.6 MJ/l	178,570 l/yr	$0.20/l	$35,714
			Cost differential	$ 4,286

Answer choice (A) assumes there is no cost difference, choice (B) multiplies the HHV difference by 1,000, and choice (C) reverses the order.

28. **(D)**

Cost of conversion = $100,000, annual cost savings was found in Question 27 to be $4,286.

Basic payback equation with n = years payback and i = interest:

$$\$100,000 \times (1 + i)^n = \$4,286 \times n$$
$$\$100,000 \times (1.05)^n = \$4,286 \times n$$
$$\$100,000 \times 0.05 = \$5,000 > \$4,286$$

Looking at this equation you will note that the first year's simple interest on the $100,000 exceeds the annual savings therefore, you cannot pay back the cost of conversion.

Answer choice (A) simply divided the conversion cost by annual savings, choice (B) did the same, but multiplied the conversion by 1.05, and choice (C) is a guess.

29. **(C)**

Here the actual cost of converting is $100,000 − $75,000 = $25,000. Therefore,

$$\$25,000 \times (1 + i)^n = \$4,286 \times n$$
$$\$25,000 \times (1.05)^n = \$4,286 \times n$$

Trial and error:

Let $n = 5$

$$\$25,000 \times (1.05)^5 = \$4,286 \times 5 \Rightarrow \$31,907 \neq \$21,430$$

Let $n = 10$

$$\$25,000 \times (1.05)^{10} = \$4,286 \times 10 \Rightarrow \$40,722 \neq \$42,860$$

Let $n = 9$

$$\$25,000 \times (1.05)^9 = \$4,286 \times 9 \Rightarrow \$38,783 \approx \$38,574$$

Answer choice (A) simply divided the corrected conversion cost by the annual savings, choice (B) did the same, but multiplied the conversion by 1.05, and choice (D) is off by one year.

30. **(C)**

$$\mu = 1.075 \text{ centipoise} \times 0.01 \text{ gm/cm-sec-cp} = 1.075 \times 10^{-2} \text{ gm/cm-sec}$$

$$A = \frac{\pi \times D^2}{4} = \frac{3.14 \times (5 \text{ cm})^2}{4} = 19.635 \text{ cm}^2$$

$$u = \frac{Q}{A} = \frac{4,000 \text{ l/hr} \times 10^3 \text{ cm}^3/\text{l}}{19.635 \text{ cm}^2 \times 3,600 \text{ sec/hr}} = 56.6 \text{ cm/sec}$$

$$N_{Re} = \frac{D \times u \times \rho}{\mu} = \frac{5 \text{ cm} \times 56.6 \text{ cm/sec} \times 1 \text{ gm/cm}^3}{1.075 \times 10^{-2} \text{ gm/cm-sec}} = 26,320$$

Use the Moody Diagram. Cast iron has a roughness $e = 0.25$ mm; therefore,

$$\frac{e}{D} = \frac{0.25 \text{ mm} \times 0.1 \text{ cm/mm}}{5 \text{ cm}} = 0.005$$

For $N_{Re} = 26,320$ and $e/D = 0.005$, the friction factor $f = 0.035$.

The D'Arcy Equation is applied:

$$\Delta p = \frac{L \times \rho \times u^2 \times f}{2 \times D \times g_c} = \frac{50{,}000 \text{ cm} \times 1 \text{ gm/cm}^3 \times (56.6 \text{ cm/sec})^2 \times 0.035}{2 \times 5 \text{ cm} \times 980 \text{ gm-cm/gm}_f\text{-sec}^2}$$

$$\Delta p = \frac{5.606 \times 10^6 \text{ gm/sec}^2}{9{,}800 \text{ gm-cm}^2/\text{gm}_f\text{-sec}^2} = 572.04 \text{ gm}_f/\text{cm}^2 \times 10^{-3} \text{ kg}_f/\text{gm}_f$$

$$\Delta p = 572.04 \text{ gm}_f/\text{cm}^2 \times 10^{-3} \text{ kg}_f/\text{gm}_f \times 7.3556 \times 10^2 \text{ mm Hg-cm}^2/\text{kg}_f$$

$$= 420.77 \text{ mm Hg} \approx 421$$

Answer choice (A) did not square u, choice (B) used smooth pipe for which $f = 0.025$, and choice (D) did not use 2 in the denominator.

31. **(B)**

This question is very straight forward. Water removed % × water in = weight removed.

$$0.75 \times (0.5 \times 1{,}000 \text{ kg}) = 375 \text{ kg}$$

Answer choice (A) is the total water remaining in the material exiting the dryer, choice (C) is a guess, and choice (D) is the water present in the material before drying.

32. **(B)**

$$\text{Water in} - \text{water removed} = \text{water remaining}$$

$$0.5 \times 1{,}000 \text{ kg} - 375 \text{ kg} = 125 \text{ kg}$$

The remaining solution has the same amount of non-water material as the original.

$$\text{Material} = 0.5 \times 1{,}000 \text{ kg} = 500 \text{ kg}$$

$$\text{Moisture \%} = \frac{125 \text{ kg}}{500 + 125 \text{ kg}} \times 100\% = 20\%$$

Answer choice (A) assumes no water remains, choice (C) is 100% − 75% removed, and choice (D) was derived by 375/1,000.

33. **(A)**

$$\text{CO flow} = 800 \times 10^{-6} \times 5{,}000 \text{ l/min} \times 60 \text{ min/hr} = 240 \text{ l/hr}$$

$$\text{CO flow} = \frac{240 \text{ l/hr} \times 28 \text{ gm CO/gm-mole}}{22.4 \text{ l/gm-mole} \times 1{,}000 \text{ gm/kg}} = 0.3 \text{ kg/hr}$$

Correcting for temperature and pressure:

$$\text{CO flow} = 0.3 \text{ kg/hr} \times \frac{293 \text{K}}{573 \text{K}} \times \frac{800 \text{ mm Hg}}{760 \text{ mm Hg}} = 0.16 \text{ kg/hr}$$

Answer choice (B) did not correct for temperature and pressure, choice (C) did not correct for temperature, and choice (D) is off by a factor of 10.

34. **(D)**

$$\text{Volume flow} = u \times A = 5{,}000 \text{ l/min}$$

$$A = \frac{\pi \times D^2}{4} = \frac{3.14 \times (200 \text{ cm})^2}{4} = 31{,}416 \text{ cm}^2$$

$$u = \frac{5{,}000 \text{ l/min} \times 10^3 \text{ cm}^2/\text{l}}{31{,}416 \text{ cm}^2 \times 60 \text{ sec/min}} = 2.65 \text{ cm/sec}$$

Answer choice (A) did not convert liters to cm^3, choice (B) is off by a factor of 10, and choice (C) divided by D^2 rather than A.

35. **(B)**

$$W = Q \times \frac{T_{in} - T_{out}}{T_{in}} = 250 \text{ kcal} \times \frac{(250 - 50) \text{K}}{(250 + 273) \text{K}} = 95.6 \text{ kcal} \approx 96$$

Answer choice (A) states that no work is performed, choice (C) divided by T_{out}, and choice (D) does not use K.

36. **(D)**

Note: Q_{in} is represented as a negative quantity since it is heat added.

$$\Delta S = \frac{Q_{in}}{T_{in}} = \frac{-250 \text{ kcal}}{(250 + 273) \text{K}} = \frac{-250 \text{ kcal}}{523 \text{K}} = -0.48 \text{ kcal/K} \approx -0.5$$

Answer choices (A) and (B) have the incorrect sign. Answer choices (B) and (C) were calculated without converting temperature to K.

37. **(D)**

Basis 1 gm-mole of flue gas (mole % = volume %)

N_2 fed = 0.635 moles, thus the air fed

$$= \frac{0.635 \text{ gm-mole}}{0.79 \text{ mole } N_2/\text{mole air}} = 0.804 \text{ gm-mole}$$

O_2 fed = 0.804 gm-mole × 0.21 = 0.169 gm-mole

O_2 required = O_2 fed – O_2 excess = 0.169 – 0.02 = 0.149 gm-mole

$$\text{air required} = \frac{0.149 \text{ gm-mole}}{0.21 \text{ gm-mole}} = 0.71 \text{ gm-mole}$$

Excess air = air fed – air required = 0.804 – 0.71 = 0.094 gm-mole

$$\% \text{ excess air} = \frac{0.094 \text{ gm-mole}}{0.71 \text{ gm-mole}} \times 100\% = 13.2\% \approx 13\%$$

Answer choice (A) is the oxygen in the flue gas, choice (B) is the moles of excess air not percent, and choice (C) is the excess air divided by the total air fed.

38. **(D)**

The basic combustion reactions are:

$$C + O_2 \rightarrow CO_2$$
$$C + 1/2 O_2 \rightarrow CO$$
$$H_2 + 1/2 O_2 \rightarrow H_2O$$

Moles of C in flue gas = 0.125 + 0.03 = 0.155

Moles of H_2 in flue gas = 0.19

Thus, C = 0.155 atoms of C, and H = 0.19 × 2 atoms of H = 0.38

Multiplying by 100: C = 15.5 and H = 38

$$\frac{C}{H} = \frac{15.5}{38} = 0.408 \approx 0.4 \text{ and } 0.4 = \frac{2}{5}$$

The closest approximation is C_2H_5, however, butane (C_4H_{10}) has the same ratio of C to H and is likely to be the fuel in question.

39. (B)

From the solution to Question 37, we found 0.804 moles of air fed per mole of flue gas produced. We need to calculate the weight of the flue gas.

Gas	Mole %	×	M.W.	=	Weight
N_2	63.5%		28		17.78 gm
H_2O	19.0%		18		3.42 gm
CO_2	12.5%		44		5.50 gm
CO	3.0%		28		0.84 gm
O_2	2.0%		32		0.64 gm
	100.0%				28.18 gm

The flue gas has a molecular weight of 28.18 kg/kg-mole.

0.804 kg-mole air/kg-mole flue gas × 22.4 l/gm-mole × 1,000 gm/kg

=18,009 l air/kg-mole flue gas

$$\frac{18{,}009 \text{ l air/kg-mole flue gas}}{28.18 \text{ kg/kg-mole}} = 639 \text{ l/kg flue gas}$$

$$\frac{639 \text{ l/kg flue gas}}{1{,}000 \text{ l/m}^3} = 0.64 \text{ m}^3/\text{kg}$$

Answer choice (A) is the m^3 of air required, choice (C) is in l/gm, and choice (D) is l/kg of flue gas based on a molecular weight of 58 (C_4H_{10}).

40. (C)

$$u_s = \sqrt{\frac{k \times g_c \times R \times T}{M}}, \text{ where } k = \frac{C_p}{C_v} = \frac{7}{5} = 1.4$$

$R = 82.06$ atm-cm^3/gm-mole-K

$g_c = 980$ gm-cm/gm$_f$-sec^2

$M = 0.79 \times 28 + 0.21 \times 32 = 28.84$ gm/gm-mole for air

$T = (20 + 273)$K

1 atm $= 1.0332$ kg$_f$/cm$^2 = 1{,}033.2$ gm$_f$/cm^2-atm

$R = 82.06$ atm-cm^3/gm-mole-K $\times 1{,}033.2$ gm$_f$/cm^2-atm

$R = 8.478 \times 10^4$ cm-gm$_f$/gm-mole-K

$$g_c \times R \times T = 980 \text{ gm-cm/gm}_f\text{-sec}^2 \times 8.478$$

$$\times 10^4 \text{cm-gm}_f/\text{gm-mole-K} \times 293\text{K}$$

$$g_c \times R \times T = 2.43 \times 10^{10} \text{gm-cm}^2/\text{gm-mole-sec}^2$$

$$u_s = \sqrt{\frac{1.4 \times 2.43 \times 10^{10} \text{gm-cm}^2/\text{gm-mole-sec}^2}{28.84 \text{ gm/gm-mole}}}$$

$$= \sqrt{11.8 \times 10^8 \text{cm}^2/\text{sec}^2}$$

$$u_s = 3.43 \times 10^4 \text{cm/sec} = 343.5 \text{ m/sec} \approx 344 \text{ m/sec}$$

Answer choice (A) did not use g_c and did not convert to meters, choice (B) did not use $k = 1.4$, and choice (D) did not convert to meters.

41. **(C)**

M is calculated as follows: $0.9 \times 28 + 0.1 \times 32 = 28.4$ gm/gm-mole

The same constants apply with $T = (200 + 273)\text{K}$.

$$g_c \times R \times T = 980 \text{ gm-cm/gm}_f\text{-sec}^2 \times 8.478 \times 10^4 \text{cm-gm}_f/\text{gm-mole-K}$$

$$\times 473\text{K}$$

$$g_c \times R \times T = 3.93 \times 10^{10} \text{gm-cm}^2/\text{gm-mole-sec}^2$$

$$u_s = \sqrt{\frac{1.4 \times 3.93 \times 10^{10} \text{gm-cm}^2/\text{gm-mole-sec}^2}{28.4 \text{ gm/gm-mole}}}$$

$$= \sqrt{19.37 \times 10^8 \text{cm}^2/\text{sec}^2}$$

$$u_s = 4.4 \times 10^4 \text{cm/sec} = 440 \text{ m/sec}$$

Answer choice (A) used 200°C instead of 473K, choice (B) did not factor 1.4, and choice (D) did not convert R to gm_f/cm^2-atm and also did not convert the answer to meters.

42. **(D)**

The following equation applies:

$$Q = \frac{2 \times \pi \times k \times L \times (T_1 - T_2)}{\ln(r_2/r_1)}$$

where

$$T_1 = 200°C,$$

$$T_2 = 30°C,$$

and $r_2 = \dfrac{5+2}{2} = 3.5,$

$$r_1 = \dfrac{5}{2} = 2.5$$

$$Q = \frac{2 \times 3.14 \times 0.56 \text{ cal/cm-hr-°C} \times 10,000 \text{ cm} \times (200-30)°C}{\ln \dfrac{3.5}{2.5}}$$

$$= \frac{5.98 \times 10^6 \text{ cal/hr}}{0.3365}$$

$$Q = 17.78 \times 10^7 \text{ cal/hr} \times 10^{-3} \text{ kcal/cal} = 17,780 \text{ kcal/hr}$$

Answer choice (A) did not use the 10 m length and then failed to convert to kcal, choice (B) did not multiply the numerator by $2 \times \pi$, and choice (C) did not take the natural log of the radii in the denominator.

43. **(A)**

N_2 fed = 1/3 of H_2 fed, therefore, N_2 = 0.333 gm-mole. At equilibrium NH_3 formed is 0.2 gm-mole, therefore:

Balance	**gm-mole present**
$H_2 = 1 - (0.667 \times 0.2)$	= 0.867
$N_2 = 0.333 - (0.5 \times 0.2)$	= 0.233
$NH_3 = 0.2$	= 0.200
Total moles	= 1.300

$$p_{H_2} = \frac{0.867}{1.3} \times 300 \text{ bar} = 200.07 \text{ bar}$$

$$p_{N_2} = \frac{0.233}{1.3} \times 300 \text{ bar} = 53.77 \text{ bar}$$

$$p_{NH_3} = \frac{0.2}{1.3} \times 300 \text{ bar} = 46.16 \text{ bar}$$

$$K_{eq} = \frac{p_{NH_3}}{(p_{H_2})^{0.5} \times (p_{N_2})^{1.5}} = \frac{46.16}{(200.07)^{0.5} \times (53.77)^{1.5}} = \frac{46.16}{14.14 \times 394.3}$$

$$K_{eq} = 8.28 \times 10^{-3}$$

Answer choice (B) is off by a factor of 10, choice (C) was derived from $0.2/(0.8)^2$, and choice (D) is derived from $1/[(1.5) \times (0.5)]$.

44. **(B)**

$$\text{Pore Volume} = \frac{\text{Volume of mercury displaced} - \text{Volume of gas displaced}}{\text{Mass of catalyst in chamber}}$$

$$V_{pore} = \frac{85 \text{ cm}^3 - 40 \text{ cm}^3}{100 \text{ gm}} = 0.45 \text{ cm}^3/\text{gm}$$

Answer choice (A) is volume of gas displaced divided by the mass of catalyst in chamber, choice (C) is volume of mercury displaced divided by the mass of catalyst in chamber, and choice (D) is volume of mercury displaced – volume of gas displaced.

45. **(A)**

Determine catalyst density first,

$$\rho = \frac{100 \text{ gm}}{40 \text{ cm}^3} = 2.5 \text{ gm/cm}^3$$

porosity of the catalyst (ε) =

$$\varepsilon = \frac{V_{pore} \times \rho}{(V_{pore} \times \rho) + 1} = \frac{0.45 \text{ cm}^3/\text{gm} \times 2.5 \text{ gm/cm}^3}{(0.45 \text{ cm}^3/\text{gm} \times 2.5 \text{ gm/cm}^3) + 1}$$

$$\varepsilon = \frac{1.125}{0.125} = 0.53$$

Answer choice (B) is 0.45/0.4, choice (C) is the reciprocal of choice (A), and choice (D) subtracted 1 in the denominator of the equation.

46. **(C)**

$$T_1 = 200 + 273 = 473\text{K} \text{ and } T_2 = 20 + 273 = 293\text{K}$$

Boltzmann's constant: $\sigma = 5.67 \times 10^{-8}$ W/m³-K⁴

$$A = \frac{\pi \times D^2}{4} = \frac{3.14 \times (0.05 \text{ m})^2}{4} = 1.96 \times 10^{-3} \text{ m}^2$$

$$Q_{1 \to 2} = \varepsilon \times \sigma \times A \times \Delta(T^4)$$

$$= 0.8 \times 5.67 \times 10^{-8} \text{ W/m}^3 \text{-K}^4 \times 1.96 \times 10^{-3} \text{ m}^2 \times (473^4 - 293^4) \text{K}^4$$

$$Q_{1 \to 2} = 8.89 \times 10^{-11} \text{ W/K}^4 \times (180 \text{K})^4$$

$$= 8.89 \times 10^{-11} \text{ W/m-K}^4 \times (4.268 \times 10^{10}) \text{K}^4$$

$$Q_{1 \to 2} = 3.84 \text{ W/m} \approx 3.8 \text{ W/m}$$

Answer choice (A) took $\Delta(T)^4$ instead of $\Delta(T^4)$, choice (B) used °C instead of K, and choice (D) did not use ε.

47. **(B)**

This is a compressible flow where the densities vary with pressure. However, Bernoulli's Equation can still be used.

Bernoulli's Equation:

$$\frac{p_1}{\rho_1} + \frac{u_1^2}{2g_c} = \frac{p_2}{\rho_2} + \frac{u_2^2}{2g_c}$$

Note: $1\text{Pa} = 1.097 \times 10^{-5} \text{ kg}_f/\text{cm}^2 \to 10.97 \text{ kg}_f/\text{m}^2\text{-MPa}$

Thus, $p_1 = 3.5 \text{ MPa} \times 10.97 \text{ kg}_f/\text{m}^2\text{-MPa} = 38.4 \text{ kg}_f/\text{m}^2$,

and $p_2 = 1.5 \text{ MPa} \times 10.97 \text{ kg}_f/\text{m}^2\text{-MPa} = 16.5 \text{ kg}_f/\text{m}^2$.

Rearranging terms:

$$u_2^2 = u_1^2 + 2g_c \times \left[\frac{p_1}{\rho_1} - \frac{p_2}{\rho_2} \right] \times \left(\frac{38.4 \text{kg}_f/\text{m}^2}{25 \text{ kg}/\text{m}^3} - \frac{16.5 \text{ kg}_f/\text{m}^2}{10 \text{ kg}/\text{m}^3} \right)$$

$$u_2^2 = (10 \text{ m/sec})^2 + 2 \times 980 \text{ kg-cm/kg}_f\text{-sec}^2$$

$$u_2^2 = 100 \text{ m}^2/\text{sec}^2 + 1{,}960 \text{ kg-cm/kg}_f\text{-sec}^2 \times (1.536 - 1.65) \text{ kg}_f\text{-m/kg} \times 10^{-2} \text{ m/cm}$$

$$u_2^2 = 100 \text{ m}^2/\text{sec}^2 - 2.234 \text{ m}^2/\text{sec}^2 = 97.766 \text{ m}^2/\text{sec}^2$$

$$u_2 = \sqrt{97.766 \text{ m}^2/\text{sec}^2} = 9.88 \text{ m/sec}$$

Answer choice (A) did not convert MPa in calculating the velocity, choice (C) assumes no change in velocity, and choice (D) added the p/ρ terms in the equation.

48. (C)

$$Q = A \times \sigma \times F_{1\rightarrow 2} \times \Delta(T^4) \times X$$

$$Q = (2\,\text{m} \times 4\,\text{m}) \times 5.67 \times 10^{-8}\,\text{W/m}^3\text{-K}^4 \times 0.165 \times (1{,}273^4 - 293^4)\text{K}^4 \times 3\,\text{m}$$

$$Q = 7.48 \times 10^{-8}\,\text{W/m-K}^4 \times 2.618 \times 10\text{K}^4 \times 3\,\text{m}$$

$$Q = 587{,}646\,\text{W} \times 1.432 \times 10^{-2}\,\text{kcal/W-min} \times 60\,\text{min/hr} = 504{,}900\,\text{kcal/hr}$$

Answer choice (A) took $\Delta(T)^4$ instead of $\Delta(T^4)$, choice (B) calculated using °C instead of K, and choice (D) did not convert W to kcal/hr.

49. (C)

Environmental stability (A) is not critical because detection of viscosity is done mechanically, not chemically, so the device could be made of or protected by inert materials. Cost of viscosity measuring devices (B) is not high. Viscometers have the ability to measure values within only a few orders of magnitude, so it is important that the selected viscometer can measure the values in the proper range (C). Viscometers are not complicated, so ease of use (D) is not critical.

50. (D)

Self-operated controllers are simple on/off devices or have output that varies linearly with input. Pneumatic controllers can be either of these, or can be configured for derivative or integral output. Electronic controllers can be made even more complex. They are generally smaller and can be integrated to the equipment more easily, but are more difficult to design and are not as easily adapted to different environmental conditions. The answer is therefore self-operated, pneumatic, electronic (D).

51. (B)

Perform a solids balance with X = feed in kg/hr:

$$\text{Solids in} = \text{Solids out}$$

$$0.15 \times X = 0.4 \times 1{,}000$$

$$X = \frac{400 \text{ kg/hr}}{0.15} = 2{,}667 \text{ kg/hr}$$

Answer choice (A) is the total weight of the final product, choice (C) is $1{,}000/0.4 \times 1.15$, and choice (D) is $1{,}000/0.15$.

52. **(C)**

From the steam tables provided:

Feed: Water at 25°C- $h_{feed} = 104.88 \text{ kJ/kg}$

Vapor: Evap at 30°C- $h_{evap} = 2{,}377.4 \text{ kJ/kg}$

Product: Water at 50°C- $h_{prod} = 209.33 \text{ kJ/kg}$

           Steam at 100°C- $h_{stm} = 2{,}257.0 \text{ kJ/kg}$

Steam must heat feed from 25°C to 50°C and evaporate 1,666.7 kg/hr of water.

$$Q_{feed} = 2{,}666.7 \text{ kg/hr} \times (209.33{-}104.88) \text{ kJ/kg}$$

$$Q_{feed} = 278{,}537 \text{ kJ/hr}$$

$$Q_{evap} = 1{,}666.7 \text{ kg/hr} \times 2{,}377.4 \text{ kJ/kg}$$

$$Q_{evap} = 3{,}962{,}413 \text{ kJ/hr}$$

$$Q_{scm} - Q_{feed} + Q_{evap} = 4{,}240{,}950 \text{ kJ/hr}$$

Steam @ 100°C used

$$\text{steam} = \frac{4{,}240{,}950 \text{ kJ/hr}}{2{,}257 \text{ kJ/kg}}$$

$$\text{steam} = 1{,}879 \text{ kg/hr}$$

Answer (A) used 1000 kg for calculating heats required, (B) used 1000 kg/hr for heat from 25° to 50 but used correct evaporation quantity, and (D) used 2,666.7 kg for calculating heats required.

53. **(B)**

$$Q = U \times A \times \Delta T$$

From Question 52 we found $Q = 4{,}240{,}950$ kJ/hr.

$$Q = 3 \text{ cal/min-cm}^2\text{-}^\circ C \times A \times (100 - 50)^\circ C = 4,809,263 \text{ kJ/hr}$$

$$A = \frac{4,240,950 \text{ kJ/hr} \times 0.239 \text{ cal/J} \times 1,000 \text{ J/kJ}}{3 \text{ cal/min-cm}^2\text{-}^\circ C \times 50^\circ C \times 60 \text{ min/hr}} = 112,620 \text{ cm}^2$$

$$A = 112,620 \text{ cm}^2 \times 10^{-4} \text{m}^2/\text{cm}^2 = 11.26 \text{ m}^2 \approx 11.3 \text{ m}^2$$

Answer choice (A) used $\Delta T = 75^\circ C$ and choice (C) used $\Delta T = 25^\circ C$. Answer choice (D) did not convert cal/J.

54. (C)

A feedback loop (A) is one in which the information is collected after the material has undergone the process and the adjustments are then made to improve the process. An open loop system (B) is one in which the property is not measured for the purpose of adjusting the process. The correct answer (C) is a feed forward loop in which the changes necessary to the control are anticipated and adjusted before the material enters the process.

55. (A)

$$N_{H_2} = D_{H_2} \times (C_{in} - C_{out}) \times \frac{2 \times \pi \times L}{\ln(r_o/r_i)}$$

$$C_{in} = 0.005 \text{ gm-mole/liter}$$
$$C_{out} = 0$$

$$N_{H_2} = 6.5 \times 10^{-3} \text{ cm}^2/\text{hr} \times 0.005 \text{ gm-mole/liter} \times \frac{2 \times 3.14 \times 100 \text{cm}}{\ln(2.5/2)}$$

$$N_{H_2} = 3.25 \times 10^{-5} \text{ cm}^2\text{-gm-mole/liter-hr} \times \frac{628.3 \text{ cm}}{0.2231}$$

$$= 0.092 \text{ cm}^3\text{-gm-mole/liter-hr}$$

$$N_{H_2} = 0.092 \text{ cm}^3\text{-gm-mole/liter-hr} \times 10^{-3} \text{liter/cm}^3 \times 22.4 \text{ liter/gm-mole}$$

$$= 0.00205 \text{ l/hr} \approx 0.002 \text{ l/hr}$$

Answer choice (B) used $\log_{10}(2.5/2)$ instead of $\ln(2.5/2)$, choice (C) did not use $2 \times \pi$ and did not convert from cm³-gm-mole/liter-hr, and choice (D) is the concentration in cm³-gm-mole/liter-hr.

56. **(D)**

According to Stokes Law:

$$u_{set} = g \times D^2 \times \frac{(\rho_{part} - \rho_{air})}{18 \times \mu}$$

$$\mu = 0.0182 \, cp \times 100 \text{ poise/cp} \times 1.0197 \times 10^{-5} \text{ kg}_f/\text{cm}^2\text{-sec-poise}$$

$$\mu = 1.86 \times 10^{-5} \text{ kg}_f/\text{cm}^2\text{-sec}$$

$$u_{set} = 980 \text{ cm / sec}^2 \times (10^{-4} \text{ cm})^2 \times \frac{(2 - 0.002) \text{ gm/cm}^3}{18 \times 1.86 \times 10^{-5} \text{ kg}_f/\text{cm}^2\text{-sec}}$$

$$u_{set} = \frac{1.96 \times 10^{-5} \text{ gm/sec}^2}{3.34 \times 10^{-4} \text{ kg}_f/\text{cm}^2\text{-sec}}$$

$$u_{set} = 5.87 \times 10^{-2} \text{ gm-cm}^2/\text{kg}_f\text{-sec} \times 10^{-3} \text{ kg/gm} \times 9.8 \text{ kg}_f\text{-cm/kg-sec}^2$$

$$u_{set} = 5.75 \times 10^{-2} \text{ cm/sec}$$

Answer choice (A) did not convert 0.0182 poise, choice (B) did not use 9.8 kg_f-sec^2/kg-cm conversion factor, and choice (C) is off by a factor of 10.

57. **(B)**

This answer is based on the answer from Question 56.

$$N_{Re} = \frac{D \times u \times \rho}{\mu}$$

$$= \frac{10^{-4} \text{ cm} \times 5.75 \times 10^{-2} \text{ cm/sec} \times 2 \text{ gm/cm}^3}{1.86 \times 10^{-5} \text{ kg}_f/\text{cm}^2\text{-sec}} \times 9.8 \text{ kg}_f\text{-sec}^2/\text{kg-cm}$$

$$N_{Re} = \frac{1.27 \text{ gm-sec-kg}_f/\text{kg-cm}^2}{1.86 \times 10^{-5} \text{ kg}_f/\text{cm}^2\text{-sec}} = 68,287 \text{ gm/kg}$$

$$N_{Re} = 68,287 \text{ gm/kg} \times 10^{-3} \text{ kg/gm} = 68.3$$

Answer choice (A) did not use 10^{-3} kg/gm, choice (C) did not use 9.8 kg_f-sec^2/kg-cm, and choice (D) did not use 9.8 kg_f-sec^2/kg-cm nor 10^{-3} kg/gm.

58. **(C)**

The formula used for calculating *XF* is:

$$XF = \frac{\sum_{k=1}^{N} F(k) \times X(k)}{FF} = \frac{F(1) \times X(1)}{FF} + \ldots + \frac{F(N) \times X(N)}{FF}$$

XF can only be calculated after computing the value of *FF*. As written, the program would be using different values of *FF* depending on the point in iteration to which it has progressed. Subsequent to computing FF, another loop for calculating XF needs to be added to the subroutine.

Therefore, choice (C) is correct. Choice (A) is incorrect since *FF* and *XF* need to be included in the argument list to transfer these values back to the main program, especially since they are not shown to be common parameters between the subroutine and the main program. Choice (B) is incorrect because it is preferable to initialize *FF* and *XF* to 0.0 since computed values would constantly be added to them over the range $k = 1,N$. Choice (D) is incorrect since an END statement is required at the end of a subroutine.

The corrected subroutine is thus:

```
 1*        SUBROUTINE SUM (N,FF,XF)
 2*        COMMON/DATA/F(50),X(50)
 3*        FF = 0.0
 4*        XF = 0.0
 5*        DO 5 K = 1,N
 6*            FF = FF + F(K)
 7*      5 CONTINUE
 8*        DO 10 K = 1, N
 9*            XF = XF + (F(K) × X(K))/FF
10*     10 CONTINUE
11*        RETURN
12*        END
```

59. **(B)**

Following the iteration procedure we get:

ϕ_{old}	f	f'	ϕ_{new}	$|\phi_{new} - \phi_{old}|$
0.500	−0.013	−0.164	0.421	0.079
0.421	−0.002	−0.108	0.401	0.020
0.401	−0.000	−0.095	0.400	0.001 (< 0.01)

Therefore, choice (B) is correct.

Choice (C) is incorrect because it is obtained if we use $\phi_{new} \leftarrow \phi_{old} - f'/f$. Choice (D) is incorrect because it is obtained by using $\tan\phi$ in all the calculations instead of $\tanh\phi$. Choice (A) is a guess and is incorrect.

60. **(B)**

The truncation error involved in the approximation will be the sum of the remaining terms of the series. Since a Taylor series converges fairly rapidly, the first term of the neglected series of terms can be considered to represent the bulk of the error, that is:

$$\text{Error} \approx \frac{(\Delta P)^2}{2!} \frac{d^2 V(P_1)}{dP^2}$$

$$= \frac{(\Delta P)^2}{2!} \left(\frac{\frac{dV}{dP}(P_1 + \Delta P) - \frac{dV}{dP}(P_1)}{\Delta P} \right)$$

$$= \frac{(\Delta P)}{2!} \left(\frac{dV}{dP}(P_1 + \Delta P) - \frac{dV}{dP}(P_1) \right)$$

$$\propto \Delta P$$

Therefore, choice (B) is correct.

Choices (A), (C), and (D) are incorrect since they involve ΔP raised to powers other than one.

FE/EIT

FE: PM Chemical Engineering Exam

Answer Sheets

FE: PM CHEMICAL ENGINEERING
Test 1
ANSWER SHEET

1. Ⓐ Ⓑ Ⓒ Ⓓ Ⓔ
2. Ⓐ Ⓑ Ⓒ Ⓓ Ⓔ
3. Ⓐ Ⓑ Ⓒ Ⓓ Ⓔ
4. Ⓐ Ⓑ Ⓒ Ⓓ Ⓔ
5. Ⓐ Ⓑ Ⓒ Ⓓ Ⓔ
6. Ⓐ Ⓑ Ⓒ Ⓓ Ⓔ
7. Ⓐ Ⓑ Ⓒ Ⓓ Ⓔ
8. Ⓐ Ⓑ Ⓒ Ⓓ Ⓔ
9. Ⓐ Ⓑ Ⓒ Ⓓ Ⓔ
10. Ⓐ Ⓑ Ⓒ Ⓓ Ⓔ
11. Ⓐ Ⓑ Ⓒ Ⓓ Ⓔ
12. Ⓐ Ⓑ Ⓒ Ⓓ Ⓔ
13. Ⓐ Ⓑ Ⓒ Ⓓ Ⓔ
14. Ⓐ Ⓑ Ⓒ Ⓓ Ⓔ
15. Ⓐ Ⓑ Ⓒ Ⓓ Ⓔ
16. Ⓐ Ⓑ Ⓒ Ⓓ Ⓔ
17. Ⓐ Ⓑ Ⓒ Ⓓ Ⓔ
18. Ⓐ Ⓑ Ⓒ Ⓓ Ⓔ
19. Ⓐ Ⓑ Ⓒ Ⓓ Ⓔ
20. Ⓐ Ⓑ Ⓒ Ⓓ Ⓔ
21. Ⓐ Ⓑ Ⓒ Ⓓ Ⓔ
22. Ⓐ Ⓑ Ⓒ Ⓓ Ⓔ
23. Ⓐ Ⓑ Ⓒ Ⓓ Ⓔ
24. Ⓐ Ⓑ Ⓒ Ⓓ Ⓔ
25. Ⓐ Ⓑ Ⓒ Ⓓ Ⓔ
26. Ⓐ Ⓑ Ⓒ Ⓓ Ⓔ
27. Ⓐ Ⓑ Ⓒ Ⓓ Ⓔ
28. Ⓐ Ⓑ Ⓒ Ⓓ Ⓔ
29. Ⓐ Ⓑ Ⓒ Ⓓ Ⓔ
30. Ⓐ Ⓑ Ⓒ Ⓓ Ⓔ

31. Ⓐ Ⓑ Ⓒ Ⓓ Ⓔ
32. Ⓐ Ⓑ Ⓒ Ⓓ Ⓔ
33. Ⓐ Ⓑ Ⓒ Ⓓ Ⓔ
34. Ⓐ Ⓑ Ⓒ Ⓓ Ⓔ
35. Ⓐ Ⓑ Ⓒ Ⓓ Ⓔ
36. Ⓐ Ⓑ Ⓒ Ⓓ Ⓔ
37. Ⓐ Ⓑ Ⓒ Ⓓ Ⓔ
38. Ⓐ Ⓑ Ⓒ Ⓓ Ⓔ
39. Ⓐ Ⓑ Ⓒ Ⓓ Ⓔ
40. Ⓐ Ⓑ Ⓒ Ⓓ Ⓔ
41. Ⓐ Ⓑ Ⓒ Ⓓ Ⓔ
42. Ⓐ Ⓑ Ⓒ Ⓓ Ⓔ
43. Ⓐ Ⓑ Ⓒ Ⓓ Ⓔ
44. Ⓐ Ⓑ Ⓒ Ⓓ Ⓔ
45. Ⓐ Ⓑ Ⓒ Ⓓ Ⓔ
46. Ⓐ Ⓑ Ⓒ Ⓓ Ⓔ
47. Ⓐ Ⓑ Ⓒ Ⓓ Ⓔ
48. Ⓐ Ⓑ Ⓒ Ⓓ Ⓔ
49. Ⓐ Ⓑ Ⓒ Ⓓ Ⓔ
50. Ⓐ Ⓑ Ⓒ Ⓓ Ⓔ
51. Ⓐ Ⓑ Ⓒ Ⓓ Ⓔ
52. Ⓐ Ⓑ Ⓒ Ⓓ Ⓔ
53. Ⓐ Ⓑ Ⓒ Ⓓ Ⓔ
54. Ⓐ Ⓑ Ⓒ Ⓓ Ⓔ
55. Ⓐ Ⓑ Ⓒ Ⓓ Ⓔ
56. Ⓐ Ⓑ Ⓒ Ⓓ Ⓔ
57. Ⓐ Ⓑ Ⓒ Ⓓ Ⓔ
58. Ⓐ Ⓑ Ⓒ Ⓓ Ⓔ
59. Ⓐ Ⓑ Ⓒ Ⓓ Ⓔ
60. Ⓐ Ⓑ Ⓒ Ⓓ Ⓔ

FE: PM CHEMICAL ENGINEERING
Test 2
ANSWER SHEET

1. Ⓐ Ⓑ Ⓒ Ⓓ Ⓔ
2. Ⓐ Ⓑ Ⓒ Ⓓ Ⓔ
3. Ⓐ Ⓑ Ⓒ Ⓓ Ⓔ
4. Ⓐ Ⓑ Ⓒ Ⓓ Ⓔ
5. Ⓐ Ⓑ Ⓒ Ⓓ Ⓔ
6. Ⓐ Ⓑ Ⓒ Ⓓ Ⓔ
7. Ⓐ Ⓑ Ⓒ Ⓓ Ⓔ
8. Ⓐ Ⓑ Ⓒ Ⓓ Ⓔ
9. Ⓐ Ⓑ Ⓒ Ⓓ Ⓔ
10. Ⓐ Ⓑ Ⓒ Ⓓ Ⓔ
11. Ⓐ Ⓑ Ⓒ Ⓓ Ⓔ
12. Ⓐ Ⓑ Ⓒ Ⓓ Ⓔ
13. Ⓐ Ⓑ Ⓒ Ⓓ Ⓔ
14. Ⓐ Ⓑ Ⓒ Ⓓ Ⓔ
15. Ⓐ Ⓑ Ⓒ Ⓓ Ⓔ
16. Ⓐ Ⓑ Ⓒ Ⓓ Ⓔ
17. Ⓐ Ⓑ Ⓒ Ⓓ Ⓔ
18. Ⓐ Ⓑ Ⓒ Ⓓ Ⓔ
19. Ⓐ Ⓑ Ⓒ Ⓓ Ⓔ
20. Ⓐ Ⓑ Ⓒ Ⓓ Ⓔ
21. Ⓐ Ⓑ Ⓒ Ⓓ Ⓔ
22. Ⓐ Ⓑ Ⓒ Ⓓ Ⓔ
23. Ⓐ Ⓑ Ⓒ Ⓓ Ⓔ
24. Ⓐ Ⓑ Ⓒ Ⓓ Ⓔ
25. Ⓐ Ⓑ Ⓒ Ⓓ Ⓔ
26. Ⓐ Ⓑ Ⓒ Ⓓ Ⓔ
27. Ⓐ Ⓑ Ⓒ Ⓓ Ⓔ
28. Ⓐ Ⓑ Ⓒ Ⓓ Ⓔ
29. Ⓐ Ⓑ Ⓒ Ⓓ Ⓔ
30. Ⓐ Ⓑ Ⓒ Ⓓ Ⓔ

31. Ⓐ Ⓑ Ⓒ Ⓓ Ⓔ
32. Ⓐ Ⓑ Ⓒ Ⓓ Ⓔ
33. Ⓐ Ⓑ Ⓒ Ⓓ Ⓔ
34. Ⓐ Ⓑ Ⓒ Ⓓ Ⓔ
35. Ⓐ Ⓑ Ⓒ Ⓓ Ⓔ
36. Ⓐ Ⓑ Ⓒ Ⓓ Ⓔ
37. Ⓐ Ⓑ Ⓒ Ⓓ Ⓔ
38. Ⓐ Ⓑ Ⓒ Ⓓ Ⓔ
39. Ⓐ Ⓑ Ⓒ Ⓓ Ⓔ
40. Ⓐ Ⓑ Ⓒ Ⓓ Ⓔ
41. Ⓐ Ⓑ Ⓒ Ⓓ Ⓔ
42. Ⓐ Ⓑ Ⓒ Ⓓ Ⓔ
43. Ⓐ Ⓑ Ⓒ Ⓓ Ⓔ
44. Ⓐ Ⓑ Ⓒ Ⓓ Ⓔ
45. Ⓐ Ⓑ Ⓒ Ⓓ Ⓔ
46. Ⓐ Ⓑ Ⓒ Ⓓ Ⓔ
47. Ⓐ Ⓑ Ⓒ Ⓓ Ⓔ
48. Ⓐ Ⓑ Ⓒ Ⓓ Ⓔ
49. Ⓐ Ⓑ Ⓒ Ⓓ Ⓔ
50. Ⓐ Ⓑ Ⓒ Ⓓ Ⓔ
51. Ⓐ Ⓑ Ⓒ Ⓓ Ⓔ
52. Ⓐ Ⓑ Ⓒ Ⓓ Ⓔ
53. Ⓐ Ⓑ Ⓒ Ⓓ Ⓔ
54. Ⓐ Ⓑ Ⓒ Ⓓ Ⓔ
55. Ⓐ Ⓑ Ⓒ Ⓓ Ⓔ
56. Ⓐ Ⓑ Ⓒ Ⓓ Ⓔ
57. Ⓐ Ⓑ Ⓒ Ⓓ Ⓔ
58. Ⓐ Ⓑ Ⓒ Ⓓ Ⓔ
59. Ⓐ Ⓑ Ⓒ Ⓓ Ⓔ
60. Ⓐ Ⓑ Ⓒ Ⓓ Ⓔ

FE/EIT

FE: PM Chemical Engineering Exam

Appendix

VARIABLES

a	$=$	acceleration
a_t	$=$	tangential acceleration
a_r	$=$	radial acceleration
d	$=$	distance
e	$=$	coefficient of restitution
f	$=$	frequency
F	$=$	force
g	$=$	gravity = 32.2 ft/sec^2 or 9.81 m/sec^2
h	$=$	height
I	$=$	mass inertia
k	$=$	spring constant, radius of gyration
KE	$=$	kinetic energy
m	$=$	mass
M	$=$	moment
PE	$=$	potential energy
r	$=$	radius
s	$=$	position
t	$=$	time
T	$=$	tension, torsion, period
v	$=$	velocity
w	$=$	weight
x	$=$	horizontal position
y	$=$	vertical position
α	$=$	angular acceleration
ω	$=$	angular velocity
θ	$=$	angle
μ	$=$	coefficient of friction

EQUATIONS

Kinematics

Linear Particle Motion

Constant velocity

$$s = s_o + vt$$

Constant acceleration

$$v = v_o + at$$

$$s = s_o + v_o t + \left(\frac{1}{2}\right)at^2$$

$$v^2 = v_o^2 + 2a(s - s_o)$$

Projectile Motion

$$x = x_o + v_x t$$

$$v_y = v_{yo} - gt$$

$$y = y_o + v_{yo}t - \left(\frac{1}{2}\right)gt^2$$

$$v_y^2 = v_{yo}^2 - 2g\,(y - y_o)$$

Rotational Motion

Constant rotational velocity

$$\theta = \theta_o + \omega t$$

Constant angular acceleration

$$\omega = \omega_o + \alpha t$$

$$\theta = \theta_o + \omega_o t + \left(\frac{1}{2}\right)\alpha t^2$$

$$\omega^2 = \omega_o^2 + 2\alpha\,(\theta - \theta_o)$$

Tangential velocity

$$v_t = r\omega$$

Tangential acceleration

$$a_t = r\alpha$$

Radial acceleration

$$a_r = r\omega^2 = \frac{v_t^2}{r}$$

Polar coordinates

$$a_r = \frac{d^2r}{dt^2} - r\left(\frac{d\theta}{dt}\right)^2 = \frac{d^2r}{dt^2} - r\omega^2$$

$$a_\theta = r\left(\frac{d^2\theta}{dt^2}\right) + 2\left(\frac{dr}{dt}\right)\left(\frac{d\theta}{dt}\right) = r\alpha + 2\left(\frac{dr}{dt}\right)\omega$$

$$v_r = \frac{dr}{dt}$$

$$v_\theta = r\left(\frac{d\theta}{dt}\right) = r\omega$$

Relative and Related Motion

Acceleration

$$a_A = a_B + a_{A/B}$$

Velocity

$$v_A = v_B + v_{A/B}$$

Position

$$x_A = x_B + x_{A/B}$$

Kinetics

$$w = mg$$
$$F = ma$$

$$F_c = ma_n = \frac{mv_t^2}{r}$$

$$F_f = \mu N$$

Kinetic Energy

$$KE = \left(\frac{1}{2}\right)mv^2$$

Work of a force $= \int F ds$

$$KE_1 + \text{Work}_{1-2} = KE_2$$

Potential Energy

Spring $PE = \left(\frac{1}{2}\right)kx^2$

Weight $PE = wy$

$$KE_1 + PE_1 = KE_2 + PE_2$$

Power

Linear power $P = Fv$

Torsional or rotational power $P = T\omega$

Impulse-Momentum

$$mv_1 + \int F dt = mv_2$$

Impact

$$m_A v_{A1} + m_B v_{B1} = m_A v_{A2} + m_B v_{B2}$$

$$e = \frac{v_{B2} - v_{A2}}{v_{A1} - v_{B1}}$$

Perfectly plastic impact ($e = 0$)

$$m_A v_{A1} + m_B v_{B1} = (m_A + m_B) v'$$

One mass is infinite

$$v_2 = e v_1$$

Inertia

Beam $\quad I_A = \left(\frac{1}{12}\right) m l^2 + m \left(\frac{1}{2}\right)^2 = \left(\frac{1}{3}\right) m l^2$

Plate

$$I_A = \left(\frac{1}{12}\right) m (a^2 + b^2) + m \left[\left(\frac{a}{b}\right)^2 + \left(\frac{b}{2}\right)^2 \right] = \left(\frac{1}{3}\right) m (a^2 + b^2)$$

Wheel $\quad I_A = m k^2 + m r^2$

Two-Dimensional Rigid Body Motion

$$F_x = m a_x$$
$$F_y = m a_y$$
$$M_A = I_A \alpha = I_{cg} \alpha + m(a) d$$

Rolling Resistance

$$F_r = \frac{mga}{r}$$

Energy Methods for Rigid Body Motion

$$KE_1 + \text{Work}_{1-2} = KE_2$$

$$\text{Work} = \int F ds + \int M d\theta$$

Mechanical Vibration

Differential equation

$$\frac{m d^2 x}{dt^2} + kx = 0$$

Position

$$x = x_m \sin\left[\sqrt{\frac{k}{m}} t + \theta \right]$$

Velocity

$$v = \frac{dx}{dt} = x_m \sqrt{\frac{k}{m}} \cos\left[\sqrt{\frac{k}{m}} t + \theta \right]$$

Acceleration

$$a = \frac{d^2 x}{dt^2} = -x_m \left(\frac{k}{m}\right) \sin\left[\sqrt{\frac{k}{m}}\, t + \theta\right]$$

Maximum values

$$x = x_m, v = x_m \sqrt{\frac{k}{m}}, a = -x_m \left(\frac{k}{m}\right)$$

Period

$$T = \frac{2\pi}{\left(\sqrt{\frac{k}{m}}\right)}$$

Frequency

$$f = \frac{1}{T} = \frac{\sqrt{\frac{k}{m}}}{2\pi}$$

Springs in parallel

$$k = k_1 + k_2$$

Springs in series

$$\frac{1}{k} = \frac{1}{k_1} + \frac{1}{k_2}$$

AREA UNDER NORMAL CURVE

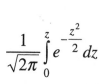

$$\frac{1}{\sqrt{2\pi}}\int_0^z e^{-\frac{z^2}{2}}\,dz$$

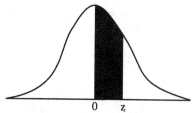

Z	0	1	2	3	4	5	6	7	8	9
0.0	.0000	.0040	.0080	.0120	.0160	.0199	0239	.0279	.0319	.0359
0.1	.0398	.0438	.0478	.0517	.0557	.0596	.0636	.0675	.0714	.0754
0.2	.0793	.0832	.0871	.0910	.0948	.0987	.1026	.1064	.1103	.1141
0.3	.1179	.1217	.1255	.1293	.1331	.1368	.1406	.1443	.1480	.1517
0.4	.1554	.1591	.1628	.1664	.1700	.1736	.1772	.1808	.1844	.1879
0.5	.1915	.1950	.1985	.2019	.2054	.2088	.2123	.2157	.2190	.2224
0.6	.2258	.2291	.2324	.2357	.2389	.2422	.2454	.2486	.2518	.2549
0.7	.2580	.2612	.2642	.2673	.2704	.2734	.2764	.2794	.2823	.2852
0.8	.2881	.2910	.2939	.2967	.2996	.3023	.3051	.3078	.3106	.3133
0.9	.3159	.3186	.3212	.3238	.3264	.3289	.3315	.3340	.3365	.3389
1.0	.3413	.3438	.3461	.3485	.3508	.3531	.3554	.3577	.3599	.3621
1.1	.3643	.3665	.3686	.3708	.3729	.3749	.3770	.3790	.3810	.3830
1.2	.3849	.3869	.3888	.3907	.3925	.3944	.3962	.3980	.3997	.4015
1.3	.4032	.4049	.4066	.4082	.4099	.4115	.4131	.4147	.4162	.4177
1.4	.4192	.4207	.4222	.4236	.4251	.4265	.4279	.4292	.4306	.4319
1.5	.4332	.4345	.4357	.4370	.4382	.4394	.4406	.4418	.4429	.4441
1.6	.4452	.4463	.4474	.4484	.4495	.4505	.4515	.4525	.4535	.4545
1.7	.4554	.4564	.4573	.4582	.4591	.4599	.4608	.4616	.4625	.4633
1.8	.4641	.4649	.4656	.4664	.4671	.4678	.4686	.4693	.4699	.4706
1.9	.4713	.4719	.4726	.4732	.4738	.4744	.4750	.4756	.4761	.4767
2.0	.4772	.4778	.4783	.4788	.4793	.4798	.4803	.4808	.4812	.4817
2.1	.4821	.4826	.4830	.4834	.4838	.4842	.4846	.4850	.4854	.4857
2.2	.4861	.4864	.4868	.4871	.4875	.4878	.4881	.4884	.4887	.4890
2.3	.4893	.4896	.4898	.4901	.4904	.4906	.4909	.4911	.4913	.4916
2.4	.4918	.4920	.4922	.4925	.4927	.4929	.4931	.4932	.4934	.4936
2.5	.4938	.4940	.4941	.4943	.4945	.4946	.4948	.4949	.4951	.4952
2.6	.4953	.4955	.4956	.4957	.4959	.4960	.4961	.4962	.4963	.4964
2.7	.4965	.4966	.4967	.4968	.4969	.4970	.4971	.4972	.4973	.4974
2.8	.4974	.4975	.4976	.4977	.4977	.4978	.4979	.4979	.4980	.4981
2.9	.4981	.4982	.4982	.4983	.4984	.4984	.4985	.4985	.4986	.4986
3.0	.4987	.4987	.4987	.4988	.4988	.4989	.4989	.4989	.4990	.4990
3.1	.4990	.4991	.4991	.4991	.4992	.4992	.4992	.4992	.4993	.4993
3.2	.4993	.4993	.4994	.4994	.4994	.4994	.4994	.4995	.4995	.4995
3.3	.4995	.4995	.4995	.4996	.4996	.4996	.4996	.4996	.4996	.4997
3.4	.4997	.4997	.4997	.4997	.4997	.4997	.4997	.4997	.4997	.4998
3.5	.4998	.4998	.4998	.4998	.4998	.4998	.4998	.4998	.4998	.4998
3.6	.4998	.4998	.4999	.4999	.4999	.4999	.4999	.4999	.4999	.4999
3.7	.4999	.4999	.4999	.4999	.4999	.4999	.4999	.4999	.4999	.4999
3.8	.4999	.4999	.4999	.4999	.4999	.4999	.4999	.4999	.4999	.4999
3.9	.5000	.5000	.5000	.5000	.5000	.5000	.5000	.5000	.5000	.5000

POWER SERIES FOR ELEMENTARY FUNCTIONS

$$\frac{1}{x} = 1 - (x-1) + (x-1)^2 - (x-1)^3 + (x-1)^4 - \ldots + (-1)^n (x-1)^n + \ldots,$$
$$0 < x < 2$$

$$\frac{1}{1+x} = 1 - x + x^2 - x^3 + x^4 - x^5 + \ldots + (-1)^n x^n + \ldots, \qquad -1 < x < 1$$

$$\ln x = (x-1) - \frac{(x-1)^2}{2} + \frac{(x-1)^3}{3} - \frac{(x-1)^4}{4} + \ldots + \frac{(-1)^{n-1}(x-1)^n}{n} + \ldots,$$
$$0 < x \leq 2$$

$$e^x = 1 + x + \frac{x^2}{2!} + \frac{x^3}{3!} + \frac{x^4}{4!} + \frac{x^5}{5!} + \ldots + \frac{x^n}{n!} + \ldots, \qquad -\infty < x < \infty$$

$$\sin x = x - \frac{x^3}{3!} + \frac{x^5}{5!} - \frac{x^7}{7!} + \frac{x^9}{9!} - \ldots + \frac{(-1)^n x^{2n+1}}{(2n+1)!} + \ldots, \qquad -\infty < x < \infty$$

$$\cos x = x - \frac{x^2}{2!} + \frac{x^4}{4!} - \frac{x^6}{6!} + \frac{x^8}{8!} - \ldots + \frac{(-1)^n x^{2n}}{(2n)!} + \ldots, \qquad -\infty < x < \infty$$

$$\arctan x = x - \frac{x^3}{3} + \frac{x^5}{5} - \frac{x^7}{7} + \frac{x^9}{9} - \ldots + \frac{(-1)^n x^{2n+1}}{2n+1} + \ldots, \qquad -1 \leq x \leq 1$$

$$\arctan x = x - \frac{x^3}{3} + \frac{x^5}{5} - \frac{x^7}{7} + \frac{x^9}{9} - \ldots + \frac{(-1)^n x^{2n+1}}{2n+1} + \ldots, \qquad -1 \leq x \leq 1$$

$$(1+x)^k = 1 + kx + \frac{k(k-1)x^2}{2!} + \frac{k(k-1)(k-2)x^3}{3!}$$
$$+ \frac{k(k-1)(k-2)(k-3)x^4}{4!} + \ldots, \qquad -1 < x < 1$$

$$(1+x)^{-k} = 1 - kx + \frac{k(k+1)x^2}{2!} - \frac{k(k+1)(k+2)x^3}{3!}$$
$$+ \frac{k(k+1)(k+2)(k+3)x^4}{4!} - \ldots, \qquad -1 < x < 1$$

TABLE OF MORE COMMON LAPLACE TRANSFORMS

$f(t) = L^{-1}\{F(s)\}$	$F(s) = L\{f(t)\}$
1	$\dfrac{1}{s}$
t	$\dfrac{1}{s^2}$
$\dfrac{t^{n-1}}{(n-1)!}; n = 1, 2, \ldots$	$\dfrac{1}{s^n}$
e^{at}	$\dfrac{1}{s-a}$
$t\,e^{at}$	$\dfrac{1}{(s-a)^2}$
$\dfrac{t^{n-1}e^{-at}}{(n-1)!}$	$\dfrac{1}{(s+a)^n}; n = 1, 2, \ldots$
$\dfrac{e^{-at} - e^{-bt}}{b-a}; a \neq b$	$\dfrac{1}{(s+a)(s+b)}$
$\dfrac{a\,e^{-at} - b\,e^{-bt}}{a-b}; a \neq b$	$\dfrac{s}{(s+a)(s+b)}$
$\sin st$	$\dfrac{a}{s^2 + a^2}$
$\cos at$	$\dfrac{s}{s^2 + a^2}$
$\sinh at$	$\dfrac{a}{s^2 - a^2}$

$f(t) = L^{-1}\{F(s)\}$	$F(s) = L\{f(t)\}$
$\cosh at$	$\dfrac{s}{s^2 - a^2}$
$\dfrac{1}{a^2}(1 - \cos at)$	$\dfrac{1}{s(s^2 + a^2)}$
$\dfrac{1}{a^3}(at - \sin at)$	$\dfrac{1}{s(s^2 + a^2)}$
$\dfrac{t}{2a}\sin at$	$\dfrac{s}{(s^2 + a^2)^2}$
$\dfrac{1}{b}e^{-at}\sin bt$	$\dfrac{1}{(s + a)^2 + b^2}$
$e^{-at}\cos bt$	$\dfrac{s + a}{(s + a)^2 + b^2}$
$h_1(t - a)$	$\dfrac{1}{s}e^{-as}$
$h_1(t) - h_1(t - a)$	$\dfrac{1 - e^{-as}}{s}$
$\dfrac{1}{t}\sin kt$	$\arctan\dfrac{k}{s}$

REA's Test Prep Books Are The Best!
(a sample of the <u>hundreds of letters</u> REA receives each year)

" I am writing to congratulate you on preparing an exceptional study guide. In five years of teaching this course I have never encountered a more thorough, comprehensive, concise and realistic preparation for this examination. "
Teacher, Davie, FL

" I have found your publications, *The Best Test Preparation...*, to be exactly that. "
Teacher, Aptos, CA

" I used your *CLEP Introductory Sociology* book and rank it 99% – thank you! "
Student, Jerusalem, Israel

" Your GMAT book greatly helped me on the test. Thank you. "
Student, Oxford, OH

" I recently got the French SAT II Exam book from REA. I congratulate you on first-rate French practice tests."
Instructor, Los Angeles, CA

" Your AP English Literature and Composition book is most impressive."
Student, Montgomery, AL

" The REA LSAT Test Preparation guide is a winner! "
Instructor, Spartanburg, SC

(more on front page)